READINGS IN THE BIOLOGICAL BASES OF HUMAN BEHAVIOR

FOURTH EDITION

PAUL A. GARBER   STEVE LEIGH

PEARSON CUSTOM PUBLISHING

ISBN 0–536–02406–5
BA 990147

PEARSON CUSTOM PUBLISHING
160 Gould Street/Needham Heights, MA 02494
A Pearson Education Company

COPYRIGHT ACKNOWLEDGMENTS

TABLE OF CONTENTS

1

THE PANDA'S THUMB

STEPHEN JAY GOULD

Few heroes lower their sights in the prime of their lives; triumph leads inexorably on, often to destruction. Alexander wept because he had no new worlds to conquer; Napoleon, overextended, sealed his doom in the depth of a Russian winter. But Charles Darwin did not follow the *Origin of Species* (1859) with a general defense of natural selection or with its evident extension to human evolution (he waited until 1871 to publish *The Descent of Man*). Instead, he wrote his most obscure work, a book entitled: *On the Various Contrivances by Which British and Foreign Orchids Are Fertilized by Insects* (1862).

Darwin's many excursions into the minutiae of natural history—he wrote a taxonomy of barnacles, a book on climbing plants and a treatise on the formation of vegetable mold by earthworms—won him an undeserving reputation as an old-fashioned, somewhat doddering describer of curious plants and animals, a man who had one lucky insight at the right time. A rash of Darwinian scholarship had laid this myth firmly to rest during the past twenty years. Before then, one prominent scholar spoke for many ill-informed colleagues when he judged Darwin as a "poor joiner of ideas . . . a man who does not belong with the great thinkers."

In fact, each of Darwin's books played its part in the grand and coherent scheme of his life's work—demonstrating the fact of evolution and defending natural selection as its primary mechanism. Darwin did not study orchids solely for their own sake. Michael Ghiselin, a California biologist who finally took the trouble to read all of Darwin's books (see his *Triumph of the Darwinian Method*), has correctly identified the treatise on orchids as an important episode in Darwin's campaign for evolution.

Darwin begins his orchid book with an important evolutionary premise: continued self-fertilization is a poor strategy for long-term survival, since offspring carry only the genes of their single parent, and populations do not maintain enough variation for evolutionary flexibility in the face of environmental change. Thus, plants bearing flowers with both male and female parts usually evolve mechanisms to ensure cross-pollination. Orchids have formed an alliance with insects. They have evolved an astonishing variety of "contrivances" to attract insects, guarantee that sticky pollen adheres to their visitor, and ensure that the attached pollen comes in contact with female parts of the next orchid visited by the insect.

Darwin's book is a compendium of these contrivances, the botanical equivalent of a bestiary. And, like the medieval bestiaries, it is designed to instruct. The message is paradoxical but profound. Orchids manufacture their intricate devices from the common components of ordinary flowers, parts usually fitted for very different functions. If God had designed a beautiful machine to reflect his wisdom and power, surely he would not have used a collection of parts generally fashioned for other purposes. Orchids were not made by an ideal engineer; they are jury-rigged from a limited set of available components. Thus, they must have evolved from ordinary flowers.

Thus, the paradox, and the common theme of this trilogy of essays: Our textbooks like to illustrate evolution with examples of optimal design— nearly perfect mimicry of a dead leaf by a butterfly or of a poisonous species by a palatable relative. But ideal design is a lousy argument for evolution, for it mimics the postulated action of an omnipotent creator. Odd arrangements and funny solutions are the proof of evolution—paths that a sensible God would never tread but that a natural process, constrained by history, follows perforce. No one understood this better than Darwin. Ernst Mayr has shown how Darwin, in defending evolution, consistently turned to organic parts and geographic distributions that make the least sense. Which brings me to the giant panda and its "thumb."

Giant pandas are peculiar bears, members of the order Carnivora. Conventional bears are the most omnivorous representatives of their order, but pandas have restricted this catholicity of taste in the other direction— they belie the name of their order by subsisting almost entirely on bamboo. They live in dense forests of bamboo at high elevations in the mountains of western China. There they sit, largely unthreatened by predators, munching bamboo ten to twelve hours each day.

As a childhood fan of Andy Panda, and former owner of a stuffed toy won by some fluke when all the milk bottles actually tumbled at the county fair, I was delighted when the first fruits of our thaw with China went beyond ping pong to the shipment of two pandas to the Washington zoo. I went and watched in appropriate awe. They yawned, stretched, and ambled a bit, but they spent nearly all their time feeding on their beloved bamboo. They sat upright and manipulated the stalks with their forepaws, shedding the leaves and consuming only the shoots.

I was amazed by their dexterity and wondered how the scion of a stock adapted for running could use its hands so adroitly. They held the stalks of bamboo in their paws and stripped off the leaves by passing the stalks between an apparently flexible thumb and the remaining fingers. This puzzled me. I had learned that a dexterous, opposable thumb stood among the hallmarks of human success. We had maintained, even exaggerated, this important flexibility of our primate forebears, while most mammals had sacrificed it in specializing their digits. Carnivores run, stab, and scratch. My cat may manipulate me psychologically, but he'll never type or play the piano.

So I counted the panda's other digits and received an even greater surprise: there were five, not four. Was the "thumb" a separately evolved sixth finger? Fortunately, the giant panda has its bible, a monograph by D. Dwight Davis, late curator of vertebrate anatomy at Chicago's Field Museum of Natural History. It is probably the greatest work of modern evolutionary comparative anatomy, and it contains more than anyone would ever want to know about pandas. Davis had the answer, of course.

The panda's "thumb" is not, anatomically, a finger at all. It is constructed from a bone called the radial sesamoid, normally a small component of the wrist. In pandas, the radial sesamoid is greatly enlarged and elongated until it almost equals the metapodial bones of the true digits in length. The radial sesamoid underlies a pad on the panda's forepaw; the five digits form the framework of another pad, the palmar. A shallow furrow separates the two pads and serves as a channelway for bamboo stalks.

The panda's thumb comes equipped not only with a bone to give it strength but also with muscles to sustain its agility. These muscles, like the radial sesamoid bone itself, did not arise *de novo*. Like the parts of Darwin's orchids, they are familiar bits of anatomy remodeled for a new function. The abductor of the radial sesamoid (the muscle that pulls it away from the true digits) bears the formidable name *abductor pollicis longus* ("the long abductor of the thumb"—*pollicis* is the genitive of *pollex,* Latin for "thumb"). Its name is a giveaway. In other carnivores, this muscle attaches to the first digit, or true thumb. Two shorter muscles run between the radial sesamoid and the pollex. They pull the sesamoid "thumb" towards the true digits.

Does the anatomy of other carnivores give us any clue to the origin of this odd arrangement in pandas? Davis points out that ordinary bears and raccoons, the closest relatives of giant pandas, far surpass all other carnivores in using their forelegs for manipulating objects in feeding. Pardon the backward metaphor, but pandas, thanks to their ancestry, began with a leg up for evolving greater dexterity in feeding. Moreover, ordinary bears already have a slightly enlarged radial sesamoid.

In most carnivores, the same muscles that move the radial sesamoid in pandas attach exclusively to the base of the pollex, or true thumb. But in ordinary bears, the long abductor muscle ends in two tendons: one inserts into the base of the thumb as in most carnivores, but the other attaches to the radial sesamoid. The two shorter muscles also attach, in part, to the radial sesamoid in bears. "Thus," Davis concludes, "the musculature for operating this remarkable new mechanism—functionally a new digit— required no intrinsic change from conditions already present in the panda's closest relatives, the bears. Furthermore, it appears that the whole sequence of events in the musculature follows automatically from simple hypertrophy of the sesamoid bone."

The sesamoid thumb of pandas is a complex structure formed by marked enlargement of a bone and an extensive rearrangement of musculature. Yet Davis argues that the entire apparatus arose as a mechanical response to growth of the radial sesamoid itself. Muscles shifted because the enlarged bone blocked them short of their original sites. Moreover, Davis postulates that the enlarged radial sesamoid may have been fashioned by a simple genetic change, perhaps a single mutation affecting the timing and rate of growth.

In a panda's foot, the counterpart of the radial sesamoid, called the tibial sesamoid, is also enlarged, although not so much as the radial sesamoid. Yet the tibial sesamoid supports no new digit, and its increased size confers no advantage, so far as we know. Davis argues that the coordinated increase of both bones, in response to natural selection upon one alone, probably reflects a simple kind of genetic change. Repeated parts of the body are not fashioned by the action of individual genes—there is no gene "for" your thumb, another for your big toe, or a third for your pinky. Repeated parts are coordinated in development; selection for a change in one element causes a corresponding modification in others. It may be genetically more complex to enlarge a thumb and *not* to modify a big toe, than to increase both together. (In the first case, a general coordination must be broken, the thumb favored separately, and correlated increase of related structures suppressed. In the second, a single gene may increase the rate of growth in a field regulating the development of corresponding digits.)

The panda's thumb provides an elegant zoological counterpart to Darwin's orchids. An engineer's best solution is debarred by history. The panda's true thumb is committed to another role, too specialized for a different function to become an opposable, manipulating digit. So the panda must use parts on hand and settle for an enlarged wrist bone and a somewhat clumsy, but quite workable solution. The sesamoid thumb wins no prize in an engineer's derby. It is, to use Michael Ghiselin's phrase, a contraption, not a lovely contrivance. But it does its job and excites our imagination all the more because it builds on such improbable foundations.

Darwin's orchid book is filled with similar illustrations. The marsh Epipactus, for example, uses its labellum—an enlarged petal—as a trap. The labellum is divided into two parts. One, near the flower's base, forms a large cup filled with nectar—the object of an insect's visit. The other, near the flower's edge, forms a sort of landing stage. An insect alighting on this runway depresses it and thus gains entrance to the nectar cup beyond. It enters the cup, but the runway is so elastic that it instantly springs up, trapping the insect within the nectar cup. The insect must then back out through the only available exit—a path that forces it to brush against the pollen masses. A remarkable machine but all developed from a conventional petal, a part readily available in an orchid's ancestor.

Darwin then shows how the same labellum in other orchids evolves into a series of ingenious devices to ensure cross-fertilization. It may develop a complex fold that forces an insect to detour its proboscis around and past the pollen masses in order to reach nectar. It may contain deep channels or guiding ridges that lead insects both to nectar and pollen. The channels sometimes form a tunnel, producing a tubular flower. All these adaptations have been built from a part that began as a conventional petal in some ancestral form. Yet nature can do so much with so little that it displays, in Darwin's words, "a prodigality of resources for gaining the very same end, namely, the fertilization of one flower by pollen from another plant."

Darwin's metaphor for organic form reflects his sense of wonder that evolution can fashion such a world of diversity and adequate design with such limited raw material:

> Although an organ may not have been originally formed for some special purpose, if it now serves for this end we are justified in saying that it is specially contrived for it. On the same principle, if a man were to make a machine for some special purpose, but were to use old wheels, springs, and pulleys, only slightly altered, the whole machine, with all its parts, might be said to be specially contrived for that purpose. Thus throughout nature almost every part of each living being has probably served, in a slightly modified condition, for diverse purposes, and has acted in the living machinery of many ancient and distinct specific forms.

We may not be flattered by the metaphor of refurbished wheels and pulleys, but consider how well we work. Nature is, in biologist François Jacob's words, an excellent tinkerer, not a divine artificer. And who shall sit in judgment between these exemplary skills?

2

RETHINKING GENES

JONATHAN MARKS AND R. BRENT LYLES

The gene is the central construct of twentieth-century biology and evolution. It is a construct because, like "culture" in anthropology, "gene" is widely used and is central to the discipline's discourse, but eludes rigorous definition. Although the gene is acknowledged as a material entity, its membership criteria are unclear and its boundaries are fuzzy—indeed, more than one can occupy the same space at the same time. The purpose of this essay is to bring to light recent refinements in our conception of the gene and their implications for its use in biological anthropology.

> The gene has been considered to be an undefined unit, a unit-character, a unit factor, a factor, an abstract point on a recombination map, a three-dimensional segment of an anaphase chromosome, a sac of genomeres, a series of linear subgenes, a spherical unit defined by target theory, a dynamic functional quantity of one specific unit, a pseudoallele. A specific chromosome segment subject to position effect, a rearrangement within a continuous chromosome molecule, a cistron within which fine structure can be demonstrated, and a linear segment of nucleic acid specifying a structural or regulatory product.[1]
>
> —E. A. Carlson, p. 259

In biology, the word "gene" now refers, not to a single kind of corpuscular unit, but to a variety of hereditary determinants, for which various names are available for those who need them. By the same token, we realize that the corpuscularity of genes was a mere assumption, and that we must not presuppose that they are "atomic," or that each of them controls a single "character." That

> these matters are important is clear from the fact that we keep falling
> into the same old mistakes.[2]
>
> —M. T. Ghiselin, p. 174

The word "gene" is derived from the terminology of Johannsen who, in 1909, used it to refer to the link between the inherent potential for a physical trait and the trait itself. Although the subject of the gene has been periodically reviewed,[3-5] only recently has it come under historical scrutiny.[1,6-8] We will follow Portin's[9] tripartite analysis of the concept.

The early mendelians focused on the gene as the source of the discrete unit-character. Running parallel to this was the recognition that genes are associated with chromosomes, which are transmitted across generations as visible structures. It was the work of Thomas Hunt Morgan's group on the fruitfly that ultimately reconciled the chromosome and unit-character theories of inheritance. Accordingly, genes came to be recognized as occupying specific locations on a chromosome and the chromosome itself was likened to a "string of beads."[10]

The "classical" era of the gene reflected a consensus that had emerged by the early 1940s. The "one gene-one enzyme" hypothesis of Beadle and Tatum articulated a one-to-one relationship between enzymes and genes.[11]

A few years later, Beadle concluded that the primary function of genes is the production of specific proteins that guide biochemical reactions. The gene was seen as a discrete physical entity, an indivisible unit of inheritance and function.

The power of this classical view of the gene was sufficient to relegate alternative hypotheses to marginal status. Richard Goldschmidt,[12] for example, denied the activity of genes in isolation, instead seeing the entire chromosome as an interacting functional unit. Barbara McClintock[13] challenged the view that the position of a gene is fixed on a chromosome. Neither idea received much credence.

The "neoclassical" view of the gene was launched by the DNA revolution led by Watson and Crick, whose physical model was now applicable to the discrete units of heredity. This mode, however, shattered the view that the units of function, mutation, and recombination are identical. In 1961, Benzer[14] proposed names for these units: "cistron," "muton," and "recon," respectively. Inherent in the molecular view of the gene that emerged from "cracking the genetic code" was the colinearity hypothesis, which stated that the linear configuration of the genetic material determines the linear arrangement of the resulting gene product, a protein or polypeptide.[15]

The "modern" view of the gene, derived from the detailed study of DNA sequence and genome structure, suggests that to some extent the gene has been reified. For example, if the genome is to be seen as a string of beads,

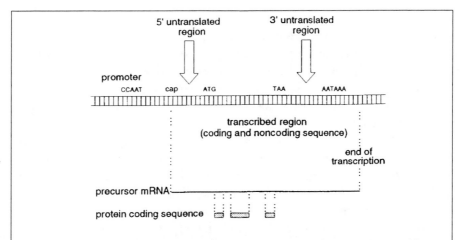

FIGURE 1. A stylized functional gene as a specialized DNA segment, with some major sequence landmarks given. "Cap" designates the origin of transcription. The first translated codon is ATG; one of three possible termination codons is TAA—these bound the protein-coding sequence, which is itself interrupted by noncording regions. AATAAA is a recognition sequence, within the transcript but outside the coding region, involved in processing the mRNA prior to translation.

then not only are there few beads relative to a great deal of string, but the beads themselves are composed of string.[16] The nature of the gene therefore becomes a question of how to distinguish the DNA of a gene from the DNA of a non-gene.

GENES AS FUNCTIONAL UNITS

Contemporary theory in molecular biology undermines several assumptions of the classical view of genes inherited from Morgan. If, as has generally been the case since the 1960s, a gene is regarded as a stretch of DNA encoding a protein, the precise nature of its boundaries has become very unclear.

The major landmarks of a protein-coding DNA sequence are shown in Figure 1. The DNA regions transcribed to RNA spans a length ranging from the "cap" site (transcription initiation) to a still-uncharacterized site far beyond the end of the sequence of protein-coding base triplets. The protein-coding regions actually represent a small minority of the transcribed DNA. If our concept of "gene" is limited to simply the protein-coding (i.e., phenotypically expressed) regions, we define it as small and discontinuous DNA segments. Defining the gene as the entire transcribed region makes it contiguous, but largely untranslated. Most significantly, however, defining the gene in terms of a translated protein product ignores the fact that in some cases the functional product of a gene is not a protein, but an RNA molecule. Consequently, if the gene is to be defined as a functional entity, it must be taken as a transcribed unit, rather than as a translated unit.

Nevertheless, even if we choose to broaden the definition of the gene to include not just the translated regions but the entire transcript, we still ignore DNA sequences before and after the transcript, which even though they are not transcribed into RNA, are no less a part of the functional unit. These DNA sequences include the promoter regions upstream (i.e., left of the transcript), and the poorly characterized but functionally significant regions downstream (i.e., right of the transcript).

More important, however, is the fact that DNA can have a function without even being transcriptionally active. For example, some degree of genetic regulation is effected by the ability of the product of one gene to bind to another specific DNA segment. These recognition sites must be considered genes if "gene" is to be used in a functional sense. That, however, removes the criterion of transcription from the definition of the word. The solution would be to use the word to refer to a structural unit rather than to a narrowly defined functional unit.

QUASI-GENES

The molecular evolutionary processes that create tandemly duplicated regions of DNA often yield clusters of genes, localized regions in which several structurally similar genes are separated from one another by small stretches of non-genic DNA. Not all members of these clusters are functional. Three fates can befall a duplicate gene, as shown in Figure 2: it can continue to carry on the same function, acquire mutations that alter its functions, or it can acquire mutations that shut it down. In the first two cases, the duplicate gene is unambiguously a gene; in the last case, it is

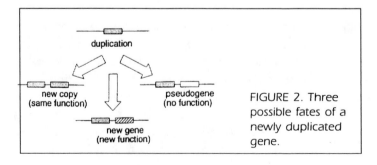

FIGURE 2. Three possible fates of a newly duplicated gene.

structurally very similar to a gene, but is not identifiably functional. These genomic structures are commonly called pseudogenes.

A pseudogene, then, bears some or all of the structure of a gene, but lacks function. Is this genetic *Doppelgänger* a gene or not? It certainly appears to sit on the boundary between gene-ness and nongene-ness. Pseudogenes are routinely incorporated into genetic maps. They are certainly loci—they occupy discrete positions on chromosomes. Further, there is a continuum of dysfunction for pseudogenes including, for example, weak transition, and transcription without efficient translation. Also, a pseudogene in one species may be homologous to a functional gene in another.[17,18]

Repetitive elements distributed throughout the genome are more difficult to classify as "genes or not." The first class of repetitive DNA discovered was found to be highly localized on chromosomes and to have little structural complexity; these regions posed no challenge to the concept of the gene.[19] The subsequent discovery of interspersed repetitive elements provides another significant example of genetic structures without discernible functions.[20] In primate genomes, the most numerous of these repetitive elements are *Alu* repeats (Fig. 3).

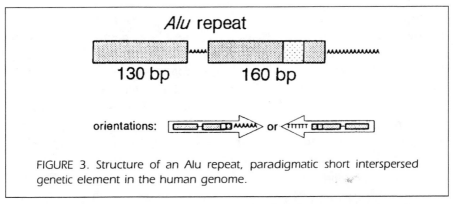

FIGURE 3. Structure of an Alu repeat, paradigmatic short interspersed genetic element in the human genome.

Each *Alu* repeat is about 300 base-pairs (bp) long, consisting of a 130-bp element, a 160-bp element, and a tail of adenines. These repeats are produced by retrotransposition: somewhere in the genome a "master *Alu*" is transcribed, its RNA transcripts are reversed-transcribed to DNA, and the DNA segments are reintegrated into the genome.[21] Each *Alu* repeat is not transcriptionally active in vivo although, obviously, the "master *Alu*" is. On the other hand, the hundreds of thousands of *Alu* repeats distributed throughout the genome can serve as sites of illegitimate recombination— short regions of serial homology where transient meiotic pairing and crossing-over can result in new genetic arrangements.[22]

In *Alu* repeats we once again find genomic structure without function, or at least without traditionally defined function. These elements lie at the boundary between gene and non-gene. Genome sites not translated into phenotypic product. Nevertheless, in *Alus* we retain the traditional appreciation that a gene has geographic stability within the genome, invariably found at a specific locus. The exemption to this is a small class of new *Alus* that have been generated in humans and their close relatives,[23] sometimes resulting in polymorphism for the presence of the sequence.[24] The α-globins on chromosome 16, which are responsible for the 141-amino-acid polypeptide subunit of hemoglobin (Fig. 4), demonstrate the ambiguity in equating gene with locus. A pseudogene, approximately 70% identical base-or-base with the functional gene, is, known as ψα1. The two-functional α-globin genes differ from one another only in their non-coding regions.[25] Furthest downstream, θ1 is structurally intact and transcriptionally active, but no corresponding protein has yet been detected.[26] Interpersed among these are six *Alu* repeats in both orientations. Compared to the homologous region in the gibbon, the "genes" lie in the same orientation, but several additional *Alus* have been integrated.[27] (Insertion is considered to be far more common than site-specific deletion, for which mechanisms are largely unknown.)

Other insertional elements, however, are not so positionally stable. The identification of a gene with a stable locus was a fundamental aspect of the paradigm that emerged from the *Drosophila* research of Thomas Hunt Morgan in this century. In the 1950s, Barbara McClintock[13] presented evidence of transposable genetic elements—genetically active hereditary units producing phenotypic consequences but lacking a stable position in the genome. McClintock's work,[13] incomprehensible within the established paradigm, was respected but, in large measure, ignored until the 1970s. Today, however, transposable elements are well known in eukaryotic genomes, although poorly understood.[28]

THE LOCUS IN SPACE

One broader implication of the new genetics with regard to the equation of gene and locus is the recognition that more than one identifiable locus can occupy the same space. The integration of repetitive elements into the non-coding, or even into the coding sequences of genes is the most obvious example of a locus-within-a-locus. However, even transcribed functional sequences are known to be nested within larger such sequences in the human genome.[29] Additionally, genes are known whose DNA sequences overlap, thus precluding a discrete manner of spatially delimiting them.

Further, the same RNA transcript can be spliced different ways, thus producing different polypeptides with different functions from the same DNA segment.

The implication, then, is that the spatial integrity of the gene is not as secure as an earlier generation had assumed. Genes can not only move, but two or more can share the same structure, and some can yield multifarious products. The conception of a gene as a DNA segment having a discrete, fixed position and being responsible for the production of a single active biomolecule is thus merely a special case of what genes really are and what they really do.

GENES: WHAT THEY DO

We are constantly bombarded by words and images of gene function in our hereditarian society: genes "for" homosexuality, aggression, and other behavioral attributes. It is consequently useful to question the colloquial sense of the gene and its function in light of contemporary molecular data.

A paradigm for understanding how genetics and behavior intersect is Lesch-Nyhan Syndrome, the result of a rare X-linked mutation. The gene is a protein-coding locus for an enzyme involved in purine metabolism, hypoanthine-guanine phosphoribosyl transferase (HPRT or HGPRT). Its major phenotype is a terrible and uncontrollable urge toward violent self-mutilation. Affected individuals, unless forcibly restrained, bite off their lips and fingertips. Does this gene affect behavior? Most assuredly.

Is it a gene "for" behavior? Not clearly. The fact that altered behavior is a phenotypic consequence of the altered gene does not mean that normal variation in the structure of the gene maps on to normal variation in behavior. The bizarre behavioral phenotype of Lesch-Nyhan is simply a pleiotropic situation derived from the complex physiology of development.

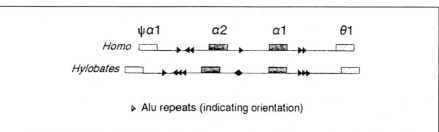

▷ Alu repeats (indicating orientation)

FIGURE 4. Part of the alpha-globin gene cluster in humans and gibbons. Another pseudogene, a functional embryonic gene, and an embryonic pseudogene, are just to the left, or upstream, or those shown, Total length shown is about 12 kilobases.

Suppose our interest is in understanding human behavior, particularly the nature of any genetic basis it might have. How enlightening is a genetic disease like Lesch-Nyha syndrome for the general issues of human behavioral biology?

The Pathology Paradigm

Morgan's influence established the dominant paradigm in genetic research: the search for stable inherited variation, and identification of the mutated gene responsible. This has been especially productive in two major areas, fruitfly genetics and human medical genetics.

The study of the human genome, dominated by medical concerns, focuses almost exclusively on disease—on genes that have gone awry in the ordinary course of development and functioning of the human body. As a consequence, two classes of genes have been mapped in the human genome. The first encompasses biochemical minutiae, specifically those genes encoding features that are understood only at the most fundamental levels. These genes, including, for example, enzymes and other proteins, generally produce little or no observable organism variation. The second category, those that produce disease, encompasses virtually all known human organismal variation attributable directly to mapped genes. (Traits like eye color and earlobe shape, renowned for their pedagogical value, are not actually mapped genes, but phenotypes that segregate in a Mendelian fashion.)

These two categories overlap to the extent that some disease genes are understood in terms of the dysfunction of the primary gene product; for example, phenylketonuria is the result of a corrupted form of the enzyme phenylalanine hydroxylase. The distinction between the two categories of genes is crucial, however, the genes encoding biochemical minutiae are diverse in structure, but maintain an identifiably normal range of function. Hence the classic findings of Lewontin and Hubby and of Harris in 1966 on the extensive biochemical genetic variation in natural populations of flies and humans, respectively.[33] The genes observed to result in altered organismal phenotypes, on the other hand, are the cause of pathologies in humans. They are consequently attributed a narrow range of normal function. Detectable deviations from their normal function are the result of a large range of abnormal variations in structure.

The epistemological problem faced when studying gene function in terms of disease is that we are not presented with knowledge about the range of abnormal variations in structure.

The epistemological problem faced when studying gene function in terms of disease is that we are not presented with knowledge about the range of *normal* function and variation, but only with the range of *pathological* function and variation. We cannot legitimately extract an understanding of a former from a knowledge of the latter.

An analogy may be helpful. Imagine trying to learn the function of the carburetor in your car if the only means available was to open the hood, randomly smash the carburetor with a hammer, and then observe how the car would run after a few hits. You might well observe a change in the color of the exhaust fumes as the dominant phenotypic change. But it would be too simple, or simply wrong, to conclude that the function of the carburetor is to regulate the color of the exhaust. The carburetor's function in an internal combustion engine is to regulate the mixture of fuel and air. Although damaging the carburetor can affect the color of the exhaust, it would not be legitimate to infer that any detectable variation in the color of exhaust fumes can be attributed to a malfunctioning carburetor. Many other factors can vary to produce the "natural range" of the color of auto exhaust fumes.

By the same token, we would not wish to infer that the Lesch-Nyhan allele represents a "gene for behavior," even though one result of compromising its function is to produce a strange behavioral phenotype. It is not at all clear that understanding pathological variation in the gene bears a significant relation to understanding normal variation in human behavior (or rather, the range of behaviors expressed by normal people). Aggression and self-injury are far more common than is the Lesch-Nyhan allele. Because such behaviors generally occur independently of any variation in the HPRT/Lesch-Nyhan gene, it follows that one does not need to consider the HPRT/Lesch-Nyhan gene in order to understand the general manifestations of these behaviors.

There is, consequently, a large jump from the study of disease genes to comprehending the normal function of genes and the basis for the range of normal phenotypic variation. The failure to appreciate this is the cause of some of the confusion about the Human Genome Project. In medical genetics, one can conceive of a single normal gene and a spectrum of dysfunctional variants. It is easy to conceive of human genetic variation as being generally structured in just this manner. Consequently, according to the theory behind the Human Genome Project, sequencing a single human genome should reveal the "normal" or "non-disease" allele at nearly every locus. The principal objection raised by evolutionary geneticists involves the consideration of genes for non-disease phenotypes, such as blood groups, in which A, B, and O all represent "normal" alleles. The same objection applies to the phenotypes we know to be genetically flawed, such as faces, which are all individual, all normal, and obviously subsume considerable genetic variation within and between groups.[34-35] It is under-appreciated that a medical paradigm derived from the study of pathological variation fails to tell us what we as anthropologists are generally interested in: what genes do, how variation in our species is structured, and the etiology of phenotypic variation.

A gene "for" cystic fibrosis,[36-38] therefore, and a gene "for" aggression[39-41] are exceedingly different. In both cases, the gene stands for a structure with a primary function that is not well known, but ostensibly is the production of a protein involved in certain biochemical, and ultimately physiological, pathways. The "cystic fibrosis gene," however, reflects the basis of a clinical condition with a reasonably straight forward diagnosis. All instances of this condition are linked diverse pathological genotypes, and are different from the normal genotype. The "aggression gene" represents a non-clinical condition that is difficult to diagnose, most expressions of which turn up in genotypically normal individuals. Moreover, any expression of this condition is dependent on the context, value system, and experience of the individual. The equivalence of the genetic unit represented by these two loci is a reification: although we call both of them genes "for" traits, they are quite different in concept and nature.

The gene is thus often conceived as doing a job, but that job is operationally defined by what happens to the organism when the gene is compromised. Although the "cystic fibrosis gene" represents an extrapolation of genetic function from observing its malfunction, it is nevertheless situated within contemporary genetic discourse. The "aggression gene," on the other hand, in using genetic pathology to explain a range of situation-dependent behaviors by otherwise genetically normal people, expresses a theory of folk heredity—a pre-Mendelian, pre-molecular genetics—to which a veneer of molecular terminology has been applied.

A significant consequence of this ambiguity about the gene involves our conception of genes in evolution. Even though the relative frequencies of variant alleles for biochemical minutiae have been successfully traced across generations, the adaptive changes in organismal phenotypes constitute evolution's "major features." The relationship between the biochemical variants and the morphologies has never been well established.

Obviously, morphological evolution is under genetic control, but what—and where—are the genes "for" morphology? Drosophila genetics has yielded the homeobox, a string of 180 nucleotides which are translated into a protein domain that binds DNA. Homeoboxes are highly conserved across higher taxa, and are involved in laying out the fundamental body plan of the fly.[42-44] However, homeoboxes do not bridge the epistemological gap between biochemical and organismal evolution.[45,46] Their extreme degree of conservation alone makes them insufficiently variable to have explanatory value: one can hardly invoke a constant to explain a variable. Homeoboxes certainly may help explain how an organism develops, but not why organisms from two species develop differently. The answer could lie in differences in the larger genes within which homeoboxes are embedded or in different patterns of expression of homeobox genes, but not in the homeoboxes themselves. The homeoboxes would serve merely to identify some of the genes of interest.

A related example of the problem of reifying a gene's function from its pathological absence can be seen in a paper that follows the recent trend of using a declarative sentence as a title: "*Hox11* controls the genesis of the spleen."[47] Without this homeobox gene, a mouse develops without a spleen. But this is control only in a very narrow and unconventional sense: a necessary but not sufficient condition for the development of the organ. Most likely, *Hox11* is not "the spleen gene;" most likely, there is no "spleen gene." Rather, it is likely that the function of this gene, like that of others, is required for the normal development of that organ and of that organism.

Evolutionary Consequences of the Pathology Paradigm

The pathology paradigm is partly responsible for a renaissance of macro-mutational models of evolution, in which minor genetic changes have major, direct phenotypic consequences, resulting in a "hopeful monster."[48-50] The hopeful monster, however, is a consequence of thinking of gene function in terms of the largely destructive nature of a mutation that results in a genetic disease. Accordingly, regardless of the nature of the mutation, genetic changes are linked to organismal change in a one-to-one correspondence. This is true, for example, in the classic paper by King and Wilson,[57] in which they distinguish the biochemical similarity from the anatomical differences between humans and chimpanzees. The mutations held responsible for organismal change have included repetitive DNA mutations,[52] chromosomal mutations,[53] and "regulatory" mutations.[54] These are all variations on a common macromutational theme: particular anatomies being directly attributable to particular genetic changes. What they share is a lack of appreciation for two key features. One is the genetic variation translated into normal morphological variation in nature. The other is that different morphologies can be produced by the same genes (plasticity),[55,56] and that the same morphologies can be produced by different genes (canalization).[57]

The first feature, the relationship between genetic and morphological variation in nature, is the largest unexplored terrain in physical anthropol-

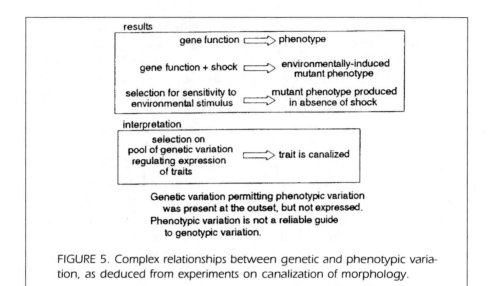

FIGURE 5. Complex relationships between genetic and phenotypic variation, as deduced from experiments on canalization of morphology.

ogy. Although differences in blood-group allele frequencies across human populations are widely known, as are differences in morphology across human populations, nothing is known about the genetic basis of the classic variable human features such as body build, nasal shape, and hair form. These features are variable, clinically distributed in human populations, and genetically based, although the genes in question and their functions are unknown. Further, in seeing the human gene map as a map of diseases, it is unlikely that these genes can be found, for their variants are not diseases, but alternative normal states.

The second feature, the combination of plasticity and canalization, reflects the higher-order structure of information in the genome. Although in some way genetic changes are responsible for major morphological transformations, it is unlikely that we accurately reflect the genetic situation when we speak of genes "for" bipedalism or "for" cranial expansion in human evolution.[58] The misleading implication of such phraseology is that, as with cystic fibrosis, there is a simple deterministic relationship between the allele and anatomy.

Yet, as Waddington argued decades ago, there is a broad range of genetic diversity in normal populations that can produce variant morphologies under variant conditions, due to either an environmental disturbance (as in crossveinless-wings flies)[59] or a genetic disturbance (as in vibrissa number in mice).[60] Selection can then operate to alter the threshold required to elicit the variant morphology (Fig. 5). The genes that establish this threshold (and whose alleles can be selected) are not so much genes for specific individual morphologies, but genes governing the "reaction norm," the breadth of developmental possibilities for an organism given a specific genotype and environment. They would be genes in a physiological hierarchy, in which the relationship of alleles to morphologies is not one-to-one, but many-to-many.[61] More importantly, these genes would be variable in natural populations, rather than essentially monomorphic, with rare pathological variants. In other words, these genes would be governed by different microevolutionary forces than those we infer for the disease genes with which we are so familiar.

The population genetics governing genes that are understood principally by reference to the diseases they cause when corrupted may be familiar as the "classical" theory established by T. H. Morgan and H. B. J. Muller. There is considered to be a single "normal" allele for each locus, for which most individuals are homozygous, and mutation represents rare degeneration or deterioration. It was against this view that Dobzhansky cast the "balance" theory in 1955. Here, genetic variation at each locus is common (maintained by balancing selection) and the range of genetic normalcy is far broader.[62]

The epistemological conflict between these theories, and the failure of molecular genetics to resolve it, are well known.[63] It is important, however, to appreciate the compatibility of the classical theory with the eugenics program of the 1920s. To the eugenicists (i.e., the genetics mainstream of that era) a narrow range of the genetic normalcy, representing the genotypes of the majority of people, contrasts with a broad range of genetic abnormalities (thought to cause pauperism and crime) whose bearers were best dealt with by extirpation or sterilization.[64,65] Ultimately, these views are the result of seeing the world through the lens of what we have called the pathology paradigm.

We are now in a position to call into questions the basic assumptions of the pathology paradigm, which are that: the human genome is essentially composed of genes for diseases; the human gene pool is composed of a simple juxtaposition of normalcy against pathology; and medical genetics adequately represents the information of interest to evolutionary genetics or anthropology. If these assumptions do not hold, then both the classical model and the eugenics program are undermined. The paradigm from medical genetics obviously is useful within that realm; contemporary "eugenics" focuses on genetic screening. But the issue is whether it is appropriate to extend these ideas about human genes beyond strictly medical applications.

It probably is not. Our thinking about genes has been shaped by the ideas that they occupy a discrete space and code for a protein, and that when altered they produce gross clinical symptoms which reciprocally describe their normal function. Both of these ideas can now be appreciated as special cases of a more general paradigm: the composition of the genome, on the one hand, and the composition of the gene pool, on the other.

The implication, possibly pernicious, of this narrow frame of thought about genes can be seen in considering the widely publicized presumptive "homosexuality gene" on the X-chromosome.[66-68] Independently of the valid criticisms of the work,[69,70] the implications of mapping a homosexuality gene to the X-chromosome involve acknowledging the other functional genes that are presently known on the X-chromosome. Those genes as we noted, are for biochemical minutiae and diseases, the latter composing the class of genes that are identified by their organismal phenotypes. Although the homosexual community has generally lauded the suggestions of a mapped gene governing homosexuality, the consequences of associating it with hemophilia A, red-green colorblindness, Lesch-Nyhan syndrome, and Duchenne muscular dystrophy apparently have not been widely considered. The implication would be that homosexuality is a genetic disease. Indeed, a recent review of human behavioral genetics lists the following "reported linkages and associations with complex behaviors": mental retardation, Alzheimer's disease, violence, hyperactivity, paranoid schizophrenia, alcoholism and drug abuse, reading disability, and sexual orientation.[71]

This list carries an implicit judgment about the homosexual "phenotype" that is reinforced by the underlying view of the gene. If the "homosexuality gene" were considered to be a normal phenotypic variant mapped to the X-chromosome, like pug nose at the organismal level or the ABO blood group at the biochemical level, it would be the first genetically detectable variant organismal phenotype to be considered nonpathological.

CONCLUSIONS

To consider problems of behavioral genetics under a paradigm of medical genetics is to invite inappropriate consequences. The viewpoints of contemporary evolutionary genetics and molecular genetics provide ways of thinking about genes that are different from traditionally familiar medical and folk views.

From the standpoint of evolutionary genetics, we can acknowledge the non-pathological nature of most phenotypes and try to distinguish analytically between the genetic causes of normal and of pathological phenotypic variation. Genetic diseases imply the need for cures, but it is not clear that the variation segregating in the human gene pool is, for the most part, disease.

From the standpoint of molecular genetics, we can acknowledge that genes are simply a special case of the genome; that is, they are restricted regions of DNA with identifiable structure or function. The cellular unit that mutates, segregates, and determines phenotypic possibilities is the genome. As the genome evolves, the genes are carried along with it.

Popular conceptions of genes as being responsible for producing single unit-characters of the phenotype probably owe more to folk conceptions of heredity than to contemporary research in genetics. Further, the attribution of properties such as "selfishness" to genes[72] has little meaning in the context of molecular genetics, except as it represents an extreme reification of the actual functional,[73,74] structural, and inter-generationally transmitted entities[75] discernible in the genome.

None of this is means to suggest that genes "aren't real" or "don't exist," but simply that we continue to take for granted a great deal about them. To the extent that biological anthropology sits on the boundary between the natural and social sciences, it may well be appropriate to take stock of the theoretical apparatus in common use and to acknowledge the tensions within it.

ACKNOWLEDGMENTS

We thank David Daegling, Ken Weiss, Amos Deinard, and the anonymous reviewers for their comments and advice.

REFERENCES

1. Carlson EA (1966). *The Gene: A Critical History*. Philadelphia: W. B. Saunders.

2. Ghiselin MT (1989). *Intellectual Compromise: The Bottom Line*. New York: Paragon House.

3. Demerec M (1933). What is a gene? J Hered *24*:368–378.

4. Stadler L (1954). The gene. Science *120*:811–819.

5. Demerec M (1953). What is a gene:—Twenty years later. Am Nat *89*:5–20.

6. Kitcher P (1982). Genes. Br J Phil Sci *33*:337–359.

7. Falk R (1986). What is a gene? Studies Hist Phil Sci *17*:133–173.

8. Maienschein J (1992). Gene: Historical perspectives. In Keller EF, Lloyd EA (eds) *Key-words in Evolutionary Biology*, pp. 122–127. New York: Cambridge University Press.

9. Portin P (1993). The concept of the gene: Short history and present status. Q Rev Biol 68:173–223.

10. Castle WE (1924). *Heredity and Eugenics, 4th ed.* Cambridge: Harvard University Press.

11. Beadle GW, Tatum EL (1941). Genetic control of biochemical reactions in *Neurospora*. Proc Natl Acad Sci USA 27:499–506.

12. Goldschmidt RB (1937). Spontaneous chromatin rearrangements and the theory of the gene. Proc Natl Acad Sci USA 23:621–623.

13. McClintock B (1951). Chromosome organization and genic expression. Cold Spring Harbor Symp Quant Biol 16:13–47.

14. Benzer S (1961). On the topology of the genetic fine structure. Proc Natl Acad Sci USA 47:403–415.

15. Yanofsky C, Carlton BC, Guest JR, Helinski DR, Henning U (1964). On the colinearity of gene structure and protein structure. Proc Natl Acad Sci USA 51:266–272.

16. Marks J (1992). Beads and string: The genome in evolutionary theory. In: Devor EJ (ed) *Molecular Applications in Biological Anthropology*, pp. 234–255. New York: Cambridge University Press.

17. Martin SL, Vincent KA, Wilson AC (1983). Rise and fall of the delta globin gene. J Mol Biol 164:513–528.

18. Goodman M, Koop BF, Czelusniak J, Weiss ML, Slightom JR (1984). The n-globin gene: Its long evolutionary history in the b-globin gene family of mammals. J Mol Biol 180:803–823.

19. Britten RJ, Kohne DE (1968). Repeated sequences in DNA. Science 161:529–540.

20. Schmid CW, Jelinek WR (1982). The Alu family of dispersed repetitive sequences. Science 216:1065–1070.

21. Weiner AM, Deininger PL, Efstradiatis, A. (1986). Nonviral retroposons: Genes, pseudogenes, and transposable elements generated by the reverse flow of genetic information. Ann Rev Biochem 55:531–561.

22. Stoppa-Lyonnet D, Carter PE, Meo T, Tosi M (199). Clusters of intragenic *Alu* repeats redispose the human C1 inhibitor locus to deleterious rearrangements. Proc Natl Acad Sci USA 87:1551–1555.

23. Leeflang EP, Leu WM, Hashimoto C, Choudary PV, Schmid CW (1992). Phylogenetic evidence for multiple source Alu genes. J Mol Evol 35:7–16.

24. Perna NT, Batzer MA, Deininger PL, Stoneking M (1992). Alue insertion polymorphism: A new type of marker for human population studies. Um Biol 64:641–648.

25. Marks J (1989). Molecular micro- and macro-evolution in the primate alpha-globin gene family. Am J Hum Biol 1:555–566.

26. Hsu S-L, Marks J, Shaw J-P, Tam M, Higgs DR, Shen CC, Shen C-KJ (1988). Structure and expression of the human 0-1 globin gene. Nature 331:94–96.

27. Bailey AD, Shen C-KJ (1993). Sequential insertion of Alu family repeats into specific genomic sites of higher primates. Proc Natl Acad Sci USA 90:7205–7209.

28. Capy P, Anxolabehere D, Langin T (1994). The strange phylogenies of transposable elements: Are horizontal transfers the only explanation? Trends Genet 10:7–12.

29. Levinson B, Denwrick S, Lakich D, Hammonds G, Gitschier J (1990). A transcribed gene in an intron of the human factor VIII gene. Genomics 7: 1–11.

30. Adelman JP, Bond CT, Douglass J, Herbert E (1987). Two mammalian genes transcribed from opposite strands of the same DNA locus. Science 235:1514–1517.

31. Wieczorek DF, Smith CWJ, Nadal-Ginard B (1988). The rat a-tropomosin gene generates a minimum of six different mRNAs coding for striated, smooth, and nonmuscle isoforms by alternative splicing. Mol Cell Biol 8:679–694.

32. Sculley D, Dawson P, Emmerson B, Gordon R (1992). A review of the molecular basis of hypoxanthine-guanine phosphoribosyltransferase (HPRT) deficiency. Hum Genet 90:195–207.

33. Lewontin RC (1991). Electrophoresis in the development of evolutionary genetics: Milestone or millstone? Genetics 128:657–662.

34. Walsh JB, Marks J (1986). Sequencing the human genome. Nature 322:590.

35. Lewontin RC (1992). The dream of the human genome. New York Review of Books, May 28:31–40.

36. Rommers JM, et al. (1989). Identification of the cystic fibrosis gene: Chromosome walking and jumping. Science 245:1059–1065.

37. Riordan JR, et al. (1989). Identification of the cystic fibrosis gene: Cloning and characterization of complementary DNA. Science 245:1066–1073.

38. Kerem B, et al. (1989). Identification of the cystic fibrosis gene: Genetic analysis. Science 245:1073–1080.

39. Brunner HG, Nelen MR, van Zandvoort P, Abeling NGGM, van Gennip, AH, Wolters EC, Kuiper MA, Robers HH, van Oost BA (1993). X-linked

borderline mental retardation with prominent behavioral disturbance: Phenotype, genetic localization, and evidence for disturbed monoamine metabolism. Am J Hum Genet 52:1032–1039.

40. Morrell V (1993). Evidence found for a possible "aggression gene." Science 260:1722–1723.

41. Brunner HG, Nelen M, Breakefield XO, Ropers HH, van Oost BA (1993). Abnormal behavior associated with a point mutation in the structural gene for monoamine oxidase A. Science 262:578–580.

42. Gehring WJ (1987). Homeo boxes in the study of development. Science 236:1245–1252.

43. Pendleton JW, Nagai BK, Murtha MT, Ruddle FH (1993). Expansion of the ox gene family and the evolution of chordates. Proc Natl Acad Sci USA 90:6300–6304.

44. Weiss KM (1994). A tooth, a toe, and a vertebra: The genetic dimensions of complex morphological traits. Evol Anthropol 2:121–134.

45. Nijhout HF (1990). Metaphors and the role of genes in development. Bioessays 12:441–446.

46. Smith K (1992). Neo-rationalism versus neo-Darwinism: Integrating development and evolution. Biol Phil 7:435–454.

47. Roberts CWM, Shutter JR, Korsmeyer SJ (1994). Hox11 controls the genesis of the spleen. Nature 268:747–749.

48. Goldschmidt RB (1933). Some aspects of evolution. Science 78:539–547.

49. Wilson AC, Maxson LR, Sarich VM (1974). Two types of molecular evolution. Evidence from studies of interspecific hybridization. Proc Natl Acad Sci USA 71:2843–2847.

50. Gould SJ (1977). The return of hopeful monsters. Nat Hist 86:22–30.

51. King M-C, Wilson AC (1975). Evolution at two levels in humans and chimpanzees. Science 188:107–116.

52. Britten RJ, Davidson EH (1971). Repetitive and non-repetitive DNA sequences and a speculation on the origins of evolutionary novelty. Q Rev Biol 46:111–138.

53. Wilson AC, Sarich VM, Maxson LR (1974). The importance of gene rearrangement in evolution: Evidence from studies on rates of chromosomal, protein, and anatomical evolution. Proc Natl Acad Sci USA 71:3028–3030.

54. Valentine JW, Campbell CA (1975). Genetic regulation and the fossil record. Am Sci 63:673–680.

55. Boas F (1912). Changes in the bodily form of descendants of immigrants. Am Anthropol 14:530–562.

56. Scheiner SM (1993). Genetics and evolution of phenotypic plasticity. Ann Rev Ecol Syst 24:35–68.

57. Waddington CH (1942). Canalization of development and the inheritance of acquired characters. Nature 150:563–565.

58. Marks J (1989). Genetic assimilation in the evolution of bipedalism. Hum Evol 4:493–499.

59. Waddington CH (1952). Genetic assimilation of an acquired character. Evolution 7:118–126.

60. Dun RB, Fraser AS (1958). Selection for an invariant character—"vibrissa number"—in the house mouse. Nature 181:1018–1019.

61. Waddington CH (1957). *The Strategy of the Genes*. London: George Allen and Unwin.

62. Dobzhansky T (1955). A review of some fundamental concepts and problems of population genetics. Cold Spring Harbor Symp Quant Biol 20: 1–15.

63. Lewontin RC (1974). *The Genetic Basis of Evolutionary Change*. New York: Columbia University Press.

64. Ludmerer K (1972). *Genetics and American Society*. Baltimore: The Johns Hopkins University Press.

65. Kevles D (1985). *In the Name of Eugenics*. Berkeley: University of California Press.

66. Hamer DH, Hu S, Magnuson VL, Hu N, Pattatucci AML (1993). A linkage between DNA markers on the X chromosome and male sexual orientation. Science 261:321–327.

67. Pool R (1993). Evidence for homosexuality gene. Science 261:291–292.

68. LeVay S, Hamer DH (1994). Evidence for a biological influence in male homosexuality. Sci Am 270:44–49.

69. Risch N, Squires-Wheeler E, Keats BJB (1993). Male sexual orientation and genetic evidence. Science 262:2063–2065.

70. Byne W (1994). The biological evidence challenged. Sci Am 270:50–55.

71. Plomin R, Owen MJ, McGuffin P (1994). The genetic basis of complex human behaviors. Science 264:1733–1739.

72. Dawkins R (1976). *The Selfish Gene*. New York: Oxford University Press.

73. Falk R (1990). Between beanbag genetics and natural selection. Biol Phil 5:313–326.

74. Gifford F (1990). Genetic traits. Biol Phil 5:327–348.

75. Fogl T (1990). Are genes units of inheritance? Biol Phil 5:349–372.

Jonathan Marks is Associate Professor of Anthropology at Yale University. His research focus is on molecular anthropology. He is the co-author of a textbook, Evolutionary Anthropology *(Harcourt, Brace, Jovanovic, 1992), and author of* Human Biodiversity: Genes, Race, and History *(Aldine de Gruyter, 1995), from which some parts of this essay are derived. R. Brent Lyles is a graduate student in anthropology at Yale University. His primary research interest is in paleoecology.*

3

THE EVOLUTION OF PRIMATE BEHAVIOR

ALISON JOLLY

*A survey of the primate order traces the
progressive development of intelligence as a way of life*

Primates stand at a turning point in the course of evolution. Primates are to the biologist what viruses are to the biochemist. They can be analyzed and partly understood according to the rules of a simpler discipline, but they also present another level of complexity: viruses are living chemicals, and primates are animals who love and hate and think.

The primates are an order of mammals that is difficult to characterize by any single feature. However, a number of anatomical trends are apparent within the order (Le Gross Clark 1960). Most are directly related to behavioral complexity. Free and precise movement of the hands and forelimbs culminates in our own cleverness with tools. A shift from reliance on smell to reliance on vision leads to the capability for detailed spatial patterning of a world full of objects. The cerebral cortex increases in size and complexity. Finally, the lengthening of prenatal and postnatal life demands prolonged care of our dependent young and allows time for them to learn the resources of their environment and the manners of their tribe. If there is an essence of being a primate, it is the progressive evolution of intelligence as a way of life. Such trends long predate the emergence of humanity and, to a surprising degree, are represented at different levels of development among the species living today.

The modern primates fall into four groups: the strepsirhines (from the Greek for "turned nose"), the new-world monkeys, the old-world monkeys, and the hominoids, or apes together with humans. Twenty-eight of the 185 primate species live on Madagascar, and about 50 each live in South America, Africa, and Asia. Representatives of the four groups are shown in Figure 1.

At least 80% of all primate species live in rain forest. This was probably the original home of the group, and it is not surprising that the most diverse array still live there. A few are specialized to this habitat, but many are able to occupy both moist and dry forest. Half the species on each continent may at times range into dry woodland; only in Africa and Asia do some primates live on the open savannah. Humans, of course, are terrestrial, rather than arboreal; but at what point our ancestors left the forests to take to the open plains is a matter of lively debate, with many interpretations possible because of the lack of analogous species surviving today and the fragmentary nature of the fossil record.

In the last ten years, four developments have challenged long-held assumptions in the study of primate behavior. First, far more data are now available on the ranging patterns, food choice, and population dynamics of wild primates. Ecological principles, as formulated by Hutchinson in *An Introduction to Population Ecology* (1978), have finally penetrated primate studies. This means we have a far clearer idea than before how environmental pressures shaped primate society and intelligence.

Second, Wilson, in his book *Sociobiology* (1975), crystallized the possibility of calculating the evolutionary advantages of social behavior. He was certainly not the only one; he built on work by Hamilton, Trivers, and, chiefly, Darwin. Nonetheless his book provoked outcry at the thought that we might quantify the evolutionary advantages of love. Meanwhile, data on primate kinship and mutual aid began to do just that.

The third development is the recognition of consciousness in animals other than ourselves. Griffin points out, in *The Question of Animal Awareness* (1976) and *Animal Thinking* (1984a, b), that behaviorists cannot have it both ways. They cannot equate the workings of the mind to the workings of the nervous system and then deny conscious mind to creatures with nervous systems very much like our own. By this reasoning, consciousness is a real property of the complex organization of a brain, just as the capacity of a virus to reproduce itself is a property of its complex chemical architecture. Although the issue of whether apes use language as we do is still far from settled, on one point there is a clear consensus; it is no longer possible to doubt conscious awareness in the great apes.

These three currents of thought have clarified some of the links between primate environment, social emotions, and the emergence of mind. The fourth development is the realization that the urgent need in primate studies is conservation.

This realization has been painful. It began for me in Madagascar, where the tragedy of forest felling, erosion, and desertification is a tragedy without villains. Malagasy peasant farmers are only trying to change the wild environment in order to feed their own families, as mankind has done ever since the invention of agriculture.

Thus, the study of primates describes a circle that starts and ends with ecology. We can faintly trace the biological steps that led from the dangerous, lush, complicated environment of the early primates to the first grouping in loose societies for defense, reinforcement, and communication, and then to the fostering of wider-ranging, quicker mental abilities. The development of intelligence leads us back to ecology again, for the future of our environment and that of all other species is now within the scope of the human mind to foresee and, in large part, to determine.

CHALLENGES IN THE PRIMATE DIET

Primates, like other animals, need to eat protein for growth and replacement of tissues, carbohydrates and fat for energy, and various trace elements and vitamins for chemicals which they cannot produce themselves.

Proteins come from leaves, particularly young leaves, and from insect and vertebrate prey. To some extent, leaves and prey are alternates in the diet of a primate. Animals that can digest leaves have less need of protein from prey, particularly as they also harvest the leaf-fermenting microbes of their gut as an additional source of protein.

The energy provided by carbohydrates and fat is used for metabolism, primarily for basal metabolism. This means that body size is the most important single measure of the amount of energy needed. Secondary factors are the amount of activity and whether the animal maintains a constant temperature. Many prosimians, for example, save energy by letting their temperature drop several degrees at night, and basking in the sun to warm themselves as the day begins. Fruit containing sugar, starch, or oil is the most common source of energy; meat and insects are more concentrated sources, but obtaining them requires more skill, more time, and more risk of wasted time and energy. Vitamins and trace elements come mainly from the normal diet of fruit, leaves, and prey.

Fruit is the staple for most species, often accounting for nearly half the total intake of food, at least among diurnal primates. Fruit-eating can be handled in more than one way. Most primates tolerate a high proportion of green or bitter fruits, which means medium-sized sources of food at medium distances. Some primates, such as the spider monkey and the chimpanzee, specialize in ripe fruit. These animals range widely, because there is usually little ripe fruit on a single tree. Their social groups join and split, with members often foraging singly or in small subgroups.

Among the fruits eaten by primates, one holds a special place. The fig tree may have played a distinctive role in primate evolution (MacKinnon 1979). There are some 900 species of *Ficus,* a genus extraordinary in many ways. The fruits are eaten by a large number of vertebrates, mostly seed dispersers rather than seed predators. Flowering and fruiting do not coincide from one fig tree to another, but on any one tree most of the figs tend to ripen at the same time. Many species of fig coexist in a tropical forest, and yet they do not compete for pollinators, for each is fertilized by its own coevolved fig wasp which functions almost like the active gametes of an animal. There is frequently a fig tree in fruit somewhere and each tree puts colossal energy into the bonanza of fruit that attracts seed dispersers (Janzen 1979). In return, primates may expend considerable energy to reach a ripe fig tree.

The vertebrates that eat figs have at least one qualification for social tolerance: a large clump of food to eat all at once. If early primates traveled together from one fig tree to another they had already begun to fulfill a condition of longer-term social bonding. In such forests as the Krau game reserve in Malaysia, fig trees are still major plants that determine the movements of primate groups (MacKinnon and MacKinnon 1980).

Leaves are another important element in the primate diet. The amount of foliage eaten varies widely; in most cases it makes up between about 10% and 30% of the diet, but a few species may take half or three-quarters of the food in this form. Leaf-eating involves specializations of teeth, gut, and behavior, and, like fruit-eating, can be carried out in more than one fashion. There is a gradation from more active, wide-ranging animals that concentrate on new leaves with an ad-mixture of fruit, to those that eat more mature leaves and rely on energy-saving and sedentary habits. The contrast appears consistently in pairs of closely related species: the wide-ranging hanuman langur and the purple-faced langur in Sri Lanka (Hladik 1975), the ringtailed lemur and the brown lemur in western Madagascar (Sussman 1974), and the red colobus and the guereza colobus monkey in East Africa (Clutton-Brock 1975).

Insects, although significant in terms of foraging time and protein supply, make up a minimal proportion of the diet. The chimpanzee, famous for its "fishing" with a stripped twig for termites in a dead log, actually takes in as little as 4% of its diet in the form of insect prey. However, insect-eating is probably very ancient in the primate line, and it is practiced today not only by small-bodied, "primitive" primates but by members of every primate group, including humans.

There are three main techniques for catching insects: the slow stalk, the quick grab, and poking into things. Cartmill (1974) points out that our forward-facing eyes and grasping hands are characteristic of arboreal predators like the potto and the slender loris. Our earlier steps toward binocular vision and fine manipulation may have evolved for stalking cockroaches. Later, emphasis on extracting concealed prey by poking into things favored a longer attention span, manual skill, and the imagination to work for something that is out of sight (Parker and Gibson 1979).

The eating of meat among primates is a matter of considerable interest, because meat-eating, and hunting, are thought by many to have provided an impetus to the course of human evolution. Meat can of course also be obtained by scavenging—eating what is left of an abandoned carcass, or stealing from a less alert predator—but this is far rarer than true hunting in wild primates (Butynski 1982). Most primates are at least adept enough to bite the head and neck off their prey, although without the innate precision of many carnivores (Steklis and King 1978).

Hunting seems not to be a fixed, innate tendency, but it is readily learned. Baboons at Gigil Ranch, in Kenya, gradually developed the tradition. At first only the adult males hunted, but a few females also took to chasing prey, and both females and infants ate prey if they could get a piece; hunting as whole increased in frequency. Infants and juveniles at first associated casually with others around a carcass, but once a young baboon had tasted meat, it actively tried to get a share the next time. Andrew (1962) and others have attributed the long-term increase in mammalian brain size to selection by predators for quicker-thinking prey and by prey for quicker-thinking, more strategically minded predators. The "hunting hypothesis" as one major selective trend in human evolution still stands, even though modified by the recent realization that gathering insects and seeds, with the necessary tool use and multiple-step attention, has filled a parallel role.

Eating gum, the sticky sap exuded from the bark of various trees, is a specialty little considered ten years ago. It now appears that many prosimians and a few new-world monkeys are specialized gumnivores; their mark on a tree, once seen, is unmistakable. Feeding on flowers, another little-known specialization, may be important in helping an animal through a vulnerable stage of life. The soft acacia flower, for example, is an ideal weaning food for young baboons lucky enough to mature in the proper season (Altmann 1980).

Just as some primates have been observed partaking of foods previously unknown, others have been found to draw fine distinctions between the edible and inedible parts of a familiar food, especially in plants. Leaves are not just young or old. Frequently, only the petiole or the leaf tip is consumed. The "fruit" may be merely a particular seed coat, meticulously scraped from pulp and seed, while the monkey discards all the rest.

ADAPTATIONS FOR FEEDING

The challenge of maintaining a sufficient, varied, and digestible diet can be met by physical or behavioral adaptation, or both. For the red colobus monkey, to take an example, nearly half the diet comes from so-called toxic plants (Struhsaker 1978). The combination of physiological resistance and great selectivity in the part of leaf or the age of leaf eaten allows the red colobus to survive. The home of this species, the Kibale forest in Uganda, is one of the richest primate habitats in the world, but even there the monkeys must choose from among the available food.

With the realization that what looks like food can often be poisonous, our view of habitats has changed. No longer an abundant larder, the jungle is a treacherous place demanding great discrimination of taste (Freeland and Janzen 1974).

The primates offer some curious examples of physical adaptations for feeding. Most striking is the toothcomb of lemurs and lorises, which probably evolved as a tool for scraping gum from bark, although it is too fragile actually to bore holes; instead, these prosimians depend on the holes of wood-boring insects for their source of gum (Szalay and Seligsohn 1977). The association between small body size, nocturnality, gum-eating, and the primitive six-tooth comb suggests that it was a feeding adaptation at the start, later modified in the larger and more gregarious animals as a tool for social grooming. In South America the marmosets also have specialized, procumbent lower incisors, permitting them to drill holes for sap (Moynihan 1976).

Many species are anatomically specialized, such as the colobine with its sacculated stomach for fermenting leaves, or the aye-aye, with its long, skeletal third finger for extracting wood-boring grubs from the holes of trees. Like the toothcomb of the lemur, however, these physical structures are made more versatile by the animals' behavior. The aye-aye uses its insect-eating teeth and its specialized hand to chisel open coconuts and flick out the pulp. The colobine not only eats fruit as well as leaves but uses the same digestive apparatus to ferment nature leaves or a more usual diet of new leaves, or even terrestrial herbs.

Perhaps most characteristic of primates are the adaptations that exist entirely in the behavior of the animal. In La Marcarena National Park, in Colombia, the blackcapped cebus monkey obtains food from the black palm nut, or cumare, by one of several approaches, depending on the ripeness of the nut (Izawa and Mizuno 1977). At its earliest stage of ripening, the monkey can bite open the base of the nut and sip the milk inside as from a cup. Later in the season, it finds the soft "eye" and punctures it with a canine tooth to drink the milk; then it taps the soft-shelled nut on a bamboo joint, licking the contents, which resemble yogurt, from the bamboo after every three strokes or so. Still later, when the nuts are hard-shelled, the monkey makes a fulcrum of its hind legs and tail, and bashes the nut on a bamboo joint with all its strength.

This set of alternatives is a local adaptation, absent in other populations of black capped cebus monkeys. It seems to have developed at La Marcarena because the cumare palm grows next to many clumps of the hard bamboo, and because the terrain is hilly, which means that there are trees and vines adjacent to the curmare palms at the right height to permit monkeys to jump past the lethal spines of the trunk and land at the fruit. At Manu National Park, in Peru, the cebus monkey uses a different strategy (Terborgh 1984). It investigates the fallen palm nuts, choosing those that have been bored by a beetle (which weakens the shell), but only those in which the beetle has left some of the meat. These nuts it cracks open on branches or against one another. Even here, it is only the cebus that has developed nutcracking. Woolly and spider monkeys and bearded sakis in the same forest bite open the green fruit but are baffled thereafter, whereas cebus monkeys of many species, in many environments, hit food onto branches or cages (Izawa and Mizuno 1977). It seems that a propensity for bashing things pays off.

Like most mammals, primates in the wild have traditions about which foods to eat in each area and which predators to avoid. Primates also have local habits for the handling of food. Marais (1969) describes troops of baboons that hammered the gourdlike baobab fruit with stones, and a troop that cooled the water from a hot spring by scooping drainage channels in the soft mud beside the spring.

Chimpanzees in some West African populations use large sticks in fishing for insects; unlike their East African counterparts, they peel off the bark (McGrew et al. 1979). Adjacent populations, in East Africa, use different tools and techniques to deal with different species of termite (Nishida and Uehara 1980; Uehara 1982). Apparently only West African chimpanzees use hammerstones and anvils to crack palm nuts (Sugiyama and Koman 1979).

Although local differences may appear random or arbitrary in some cases (for example, why do East African chimpanzees *not* use stones to crack nuts as their western neighbors do?), they clearly have an adaptive value in others. One group of vervet guenons has invaded some artificial clearings in true rain forest, far from its normal habitat in the savannah or forest fringe. In these manmade clearings the vervets forage in unpredictable patterns and communicate with their softest calls. If dogs approach, the monkeys suppress all noise and hide, whereas in the savannah they would give loud alarms. These local habits keep them safe from humans, including the habit of treating dogs as a warning about the presence of humans (Kavanagh 1980). The two specialized strategies of the cebus monkey in La Marcarena, Colombia, and in Manu, Peru, are also evidently adaptive to their specific regions.

Local traditions in foods, in tool-using, and in defense against predators are dependent on the ability of a small, more or less cohesive group of primates to learn from one another. Occasionally tool-using and the growth of knowledge combine in the social group, with dramatic results, as in the chimpanzee group of Boussou, Guinea (Sugiyama and Koman 1979). This group had in its range a huge fig tree whose trunk was too thick to climb. There were no adjacent trees allowing direct access but a thorny kapok tree that extended below. The fig is a favorite fruit of the chimpanzee, as well as of other primates, and this group persistently climbed the kapok and grappled with the problem, for some time without success. One day for fifty minutes, the dominant and the third-ranking male alternated positions on the kapok branch. They broke kapok branches, peeled off the thorny bark, and flailed at the fig branch with a total of nine different stick tools. Whenever a stick caught momentarily, all the watching chimpanzees called and barked. All at once the third-ranking male began quickly to break branches from the limb he was standing on and drop them to the ground without any attempt to use them. This so lightened the limb that it rose slightly, until by bounding and stretching upright the chimpanzee was able to seize a twig of the fig tree. He climbed up, and then the second-ranked male succeeded in hanging a stick on the dangling fig. Taking advantage of one another's weight to pull the fig branch lower, the whole group swarmed upward.

LEARNING IN PRIMATE SOCIETY

A species or a local population may modify its form or behavior by means of evolutionary change, which comes through the selection of advantageous genes, or by historical change, which can be passed along to the offspring directly. There is ample feedback between the two levels of change. A chance mutation may lead to quicker or more practical learning ability, and so be selected for. Learning ability may buffer the rigors of the environment, favoring genes for bodily vigor at later ages, or allowing formerly lethal genetic anomalies to live and make their own contribution to society.

There are many current attempts to quantify and explain these interactions (Lumsden and Wilson 1981; Bonner 1980; Pulliam and Dunford 1980). One of the major themes is that of polymorphism, or variability. Does mammalian social life allow or depend on a diversity of genotype and behavior and on diverse roles within the group? Or is there an "ideal type" toward which all the individuals of a species tend? Other major questions are how knowledge accumulates within the social group and how quickly such knowledge can change with changing circumstances.

One of the dangerous tendencies of humans is that we so often picture ideal types: the Aryan superman, the Hollywood goddess, the high school senior who scores perfectly on a standardized test. The workings of biology, however, do not support this tendency; instead, the great advances seem to involve randomization. We go through all the confusion of sexual reproduction just to mix up our genes.

Hutchinson (1981) suggests that selection has favored some "noise," even in the creation of our proud brain. If the reading of the genetic instruction or the pattern used to record experience contains a random element, this allows polymorphism of intellect within a kin group, which may in turn be adaptive. Differing powers of intelligence from innovative genius to complaisant follower, and differing styles of intelligence from quick-witted hunter to tribal bard have allowed us to mix ideas, not merely genes.

Studies in both the field and the laboratory tend to show that what and how primates learn can vary with their age, their sex, and even their rank within the social group. On the whole, it is semi-independent infants and juveniles who approach and handle new objects most often and for the longest time. They thus perpetrate most of the useful innovations.

The Japanese macaque troop of Koshima Island is famous for its cultural innovations. One infant female called Imo began to wash sweet potatoes to remove the grit when she was eighteen months old. The innovation spread to her playmates and her mother, and from mother to baby sibling. Imo was likewise among the first to swim, and to "placer wash" wheat kernels by throwing a handful of wheat and sand in the water so that the sand would sink and the kernels would float. These discoveries also spread quickly through the troop.

Infants may be most playful, but adolescents are perhaps particularly quick to learn formal tasks. Tsumori (1966, 1967; Tsumori et al. 1965) tested the entire Koshima troop by burying peanuts in the beach sand, patiently arranging the situation so that each troop member in turn had a chance to dig without too much interference from others. Late adolescents, 6 to 7 years old, were quickest and most successful at unearthing the peanuts. This result agrees with laboratory tests that show learning speed to increase until near-adulthood.

Although older adults are slower to solve individual tasks, they have a greater store of knowledge in which to integrate new facts. When Menzel (1969), released a group of chimpanzees in a new enclosure, the adults glanced around and apparently accumulated a great deal of information, whereas the youngsters probably learned little from bouncing several times up and down each tree.

Social rank, as well, appears to affect learning ability. Within two captive troops of rhesus monkeys, the three most dominant males performed worse than other males on several types of learning and reasoning tasks (Bunnell and Perkins 1980; Bunnell et al. 1980). It is not clear what underlay this effect—perhaps a simple circumstance, such as that dominants are not as hungry and therefore not as highly motivated to perform well in experiments. Age may have been a factor as well since the animals ranged from 4 to 16 years old. Their performance shifted as their rank shifted, however, which suggests that the effect is related to dominance, rather than to individual age or intelligence.

Such tests confirm the observation in the wild that dominant males are less likely than others to take up new habits. On Koshima Island the dominants continued to eat their sweet potatoes gritty, and would never dream of going swimming, whereas juveniles splashed into the water all around them. This conservatism may in turn be useful. One dominant Japanese macaque kept his troop away from a novel object, which was, in fact, a trap. In another case, an adult male chacma baboon frustrated seven successive attempts to trap his troop with drugged oranges. Each time he approached, tasted, and discarded an orange first, then chased away the infants and juveniles who tried to eat (Fletemeyer 1978).

In addition, differences between males and females in their feeding patterns may reflect two distinct casts of mind. It is possible that such differences underlay the evolution of food-sharing and division of labor in our own line. Among orangutans, for example, the huge males forage on the ground and are thus more likely than females to find termites nesting in dead logs. In one study lasting eight and a half years, males were seen on three occasions to carry termite-infested logs into the trees and share with their consorts (Galdikas and Teleki 1981). Although very rare, these episodes seem similar to the more frequent sharing of vertebrate prey by hunting male chimpanzees, who commonly give pieces of the carcass to females and young.

If the foraging of our ancestors differed by sex, it may have become increasingly worthwhile for male and female to exchange food. Furthermore, it could have been adaptive to evolve slightly different mentalities, initially for the particular blend of stamina, patience, and attention to detail that would be appropriate either for hunting vertebrates or for gathering insects and fruit. Then, as sharing food became normal, it would have been advantageous to both sexes and to their jointly supported offspring if the *other* sex was good at its tasks. Perhaps we can see the foundation for this long history even today, in the patience of the female chimpanzee who squats for hours fishing at a termite mound, while her baby plays alongside (McGrew 1979, 1981).

COMMUNICATING NEW IDEAS

We know that human babies achieve the use of language in several stages: from acts that are involuntarily repeated, such as crying, to the apparently conscious imitation of acts such as babbling and clapping, to the effortful imitation of novel actions such as the forming of words. Great apes and some monkeys also imitate not only familiar acts, but novel actions as well. For instance, orangutans of the Tanjung Puting Reserve, in Indonesian Borneo, imitated using logs as bridges after observing a workman who was in such a hurry to escape (they had sunk his boat and charged him) that he dragged a log to the river and scrambled over. He pulled the log up after him, but the two most aggressive orangutans, among eight watching, dragged everything they could find toward the river and succeeded in crossing on a vine before the end of the day. In the years before this incident no orangutan had ever been known to make a bridge, but thereafter the scientists were obliged to collect and destroy every usable log, and even then the orangutans sometimes cross the river to the camp using vines they had pulled down from the forest canopy (Galdikas 1982).

Even a relatively simple act may be enough to transmit information particularly if it is about biologically important, easily learned matters, such as predation (Hall 1963). Young vervets apparently learn which predators are worthy of eagle alarms, and baboons must learn whether to fear Landrovers (DeVore and Hall 1965). In wild troops, animals tend to learn from close kin or associates. Subordinates are more likely to copy dominants, possibly because they are keeping a wary eye on the dominants' moves in general (Miyadi 1967).

Although it is clear that animals who are observing are actively learning, it has long been supposed that there is no active teaching. However, it is sometimes difficult to distinguish the two. Many mammals place their young in situations conducive to learning (Ewer 1968).

The active passing of information, if not teaching as such, also occurs among peers and between social ranks in the primate group. Menzel (1971) kept a group of eight young chimpanzees in an observation house with access to a 4-hectare field. He took out one chimpanzee at a time and showed it a hidden pile of fruit, then returned it to the group and let them all into the field. The apes were too young to venture out alone; instead, the guiding ape would lead its companions to the trove. If dominant, it might stride off confidently, sure that the others would follow. If subordinate, it begged and tugged the others' hands and fur. Sometimes when they paid no attention the guide would fling itself on the ground in a tantrum.

Once the group knew what to expect, Menzel made his experiments more elaborate. The chimpanzees learned to distinguish which of two guides had seen a bigger reward. Now they would march past an apple on a stick, following a guide with more to offer. Next, Menzel hid frightening objects such as rubber snakes. Again the group followed the guide, but with bristling fur and tentative approach, unearthing the reptile with sticks and slapping the ground. When Menzel removed his rubber snake before the group arrived, they searched the area around its hiding place, slapping piles of leaves and poking along the boundary fence.

The form of his communication is not mysterious: it consists of bodily cues which are obvious to everyone, unambiguous and at the same time flexible enough to suit changing circumstances. However, as a means of passing messages about facts removed in space and time, this level of communication approaches social control of the environment, for which language was invented and through which the human intellect evolved. We should perhaps not be surprised that the chimpanzee Washoe, taught American Sign Language since her infancy, has shown her own adopted infant a chair and modeled the sign *chair* five times, while looking at him, or that she has signed *food* to him and then molded his hands in hers into the sign for *food* (Chevalier-Skolnikoff 1981). The use of sign language among trained primate subjects is a rich field for inquiry.

A HUMAN RESPONSIBILITY

What conclusions can be drawn from the study of primate behavior? The inferences shed a harsh light on our treatment of other primates. Too often we cage them without regard for their sociability and their manipulative curiosity. We breed them without regard for their own preferences, or their long-evolved incest taboos. We rear their infants in isolation, which was fascinating when we could not imagine the results, but which can now be seen as cruelty, based on a fallacy that primates other than ourselves are bodies without minds.

Far more dangerous is our treatment of primates in the wild. Many species are in danger of losing their habitat altogether. Meanwhile, there have been no bounds set on the human habitat—even in the United States which pioneered the preservation of wilderness land. When we omit to guard a tropical rain forest or a mountain watershed, we are condemning not just individuals but entire species and ecosystems. For every endangered species that breeds in captivity and every park that is protected, far more species and wildlands are lost.

It would be hubris to claim that no organism other than *Homo sapiens* has so transformed the earth's environment. After all, the plants and their offspring created our oxygenated atmosphere. We are, however, approaching the same power. We have tilled land, felled forest, polluted at least the smaller oceans, and developed the potential for nuclear mutual assured destruction. We do not yet know whether our technological venture will succeed or fail, or even whether success would leave room for any species other than our crops, our parasites and ourselves.

The evolutionary ventures of being alive, being cellular, and then being multicelled were all successful. Yet there are intermediate creatures still present in the world today that illustrate other viable modes of existence: viruses, oozing slime molds, and sponge cells, which when sieved and separated creep together to reconstruct their communal form.

The primates living today are such transitional forms, instructing us with their alien and yet familiar minds, their richly complex societies, their rudimentary tools. The primates stand at the hinge of evolution. Whether they will continue to do so depends on us.

REFERENCES

Altmann, J. 1980. *Baboon Mothers and Infants*. Harvard Univ. Press.

Andrew, R.J. 1962. Evolution of intelligence and vocal mimicking. *Science* 137:585–89.

Bonner, J.T. 1980. *The Evolution of Culture in Animals*. Princeton Univ. Press.

Bunnell, B.N., and M.N. Perkins. 1980. Performance correlates of social behavior and organization: Social rank and complex problem solving in crab-eating macaques (*M. fascicularis*). *Primates* 21:515–23.

Bunnell, B.N., W.T. Gore, and M.N. Perkins. 1980. Performance correlates of social behavior and organization: Social rank and reversal learning in crab-eating macaques (*M. fascicularis*), *Primates* 21:376–88.

Butynski, T.M. 1982. Vertebrate predation by primates: A review of hunting patterns and prey. *J. Human Evol.* 11:421–30.

Cartmill, M. 1974. Rethinking primate origins. *Science* 184:436–43.

Chevalier-Skolnikoff, S. 1981. The Clever Hans phenomenon, cueing and ape signing: A Piagetian analysis of methods for instructing animals. In *The Clever Hans Phenomenon,* ed. T.A. Sebeok and R. Rosenthal, pp. 60–94. Annals of New York Acad. of Science, 364.

Clutton-Brock, T.H. 1975. Feeding behavior of red colobus and black-and-white colobus in East Africa. *Folia Primatol.* 23:165–207.

DeVore, I., and K.R.L. Hall. 1965. Baboon ecology. In *Primate Behavior,* ed. I. Devore, pp. 20–52. Holt.

Ewer, R.F. 1968. *The Ethology of Mammals.* London: Logos.

Fletemeyer, J.R. 1978. Communication about potentially harmful foods in free-ranging chacma baboons, *Papio ursinus. Primates* 19:223–26.

Freeland, W.J., and D.H. Janzen. 1974. Strategies in herbivory by mammals: The role of plant secondary compounds. *Am. Nat.* 108:269–89.

Galdikas, B.M.F. Orangutan tool use at Tanjung Puting Reserve, Central Indonesian Borneo (Kalimantan Tengah). *J. Human Evol.* 11:19–33.

Galdikas, B.M.F., and G. Teleki. 1981. Variations in subsistence activities of female and male pongids: New perspectives on the origins of hominid labor division. *Current Anthropol.* 22:241–56.

Griffin, D.R. 1976 (2d ed. 1981). *The Question of Animal Awareness.* The Rockefeller Univ. Press.

_____. 1984a. *Animal Thinking.* Harvard Univ. Press.

_____. 1984b. Animal Thinking. *Am. Sci.* 72:456-64.

Hall, K.R.L. 1963. Tool using performances as indications of behavioral adaptability. *Current Anthropol.* 4:479–94.

Hladik, C.M. 1975. Ecology, diet, and social patterning in Old and New World primates. In *Socioecology and Psychology of Primates,* ed. R.H. Tuttle, pp. 3–35. The Hague: Mouton.

Hutchinson, G.E. 1978. *An Introduction to Population Ecology.* Yale Univ. Press.

_____. 1981. Random adaptation and imitation in human development. *Am. Sci.* 69:161–65.

Izawa, K., and A. Mizuno. 1977. Palm-fruit cracking behavior of wild black-capped capuchin (*Cebus apella*). *Primates* 18:773–92.

Janzen, D.H. 1979. How to be a fig. *Ann. Rev. Ecol. Systemat.* 10:13–52.

Kavanagh, M. 1980. Invasion of the forest by an African savannah monkey: Behavioral adaptations. *Behaviour* 73:238–60.

Le Gros Clark, W.E. 1960. *Antecedents of Man.* Quadrangle Books.

Lumsden, C.J., and E.O. Wilson. 1981. *Genes, Mind, and Culture.* Harvard Univ. Press.

McGrew, W.C. 1979. Evolutionary implications of sex differences in chimpanzee predation and tool use. In *The Great Apes,* ed. D.A. Hamburg and E.R. McCown, pp. 441–64. Benjamin/Cummings.

_____. 1981. The female chimpanzee as a human evolutionary prototype. In *Woman the Gatherer,* ed. F. Dahlberg, p. 35–72. Yale Univ. Press.

McGrew, W.C., E.G. Tutin, and P.J. Baldwin. 1979. New data on meat eating by wild chimpanzees. *Current Anthropol.* 20:238–39.

MacKinnon, J.R. 1979. Reproductive behavior in wild orangutan populations. In *The Great Apes,* ed. D.A. Hamburg and E.R. McCown, pp. 257–74. Benjamin/Cummings.

MacKinnon, J.R., and K.S. MacKinnon. 1980. Niche differentiation in a primate community. In *Malayan Forest Primates,* ed. D.J. Chivers, pp. 167–90. Plenum.

Marais, E. 1969. *The Soul of the Ape.* London: Anthony Blond.

Menzel, E.W. 1969. Responsiveness to food and signs of food in chimpanzee discrimination learning. *J. Comp. Physiol. Psychol.* 56:78–85.

_____. 1971. Communication about the environment in a group of young chimpanzees. *Folia Primatol.* 15:220–32.

Miyadi, D. 1967. Differences in social behavior among Japanese macaque troops. In *Neue Ergebnisse der Primatologie,* ed. D. Stark, R. Schneider, and H.J. Kuhn. Stuttgart: Fischer.

Moynihan, M. 1976. *The New World Primates.* Princeton Univ. Press.

Nishida, T., and S. Uehara. 1980. Chimpanzees, tools, and termites: Another example from Tanzania. *Current Anthropol.* 21:671–72.

Parker, S.T., and K.R. Gibson, 1979. A developmental model of the evolution of language and intelligence in early homonids. *Brain Behav. Sci.* 2:367–408.

Pulliam, H.R., and C. Dunford. 1980. *Programmed to Learn: An Essay on the Evolution of Culture.* Columbia Univ. Press.

Steklish, H.D., and G.E. King. 1978. The craniocervical killing bite: Toward an ethology of primate predatory behavior. *J. Human Evol.* 7:567–81.

Struhsaker, T.T. 1978. Interrelations of red colobus monkeys and rain forest trees in the Kibale Forest, Uganda. In *Ecology of the Arboreal Folivores,* ed. G.G. Montgomery, pp. 397–492. Smithsonian Inst. Press.

Sugiyama, Y., and J. Koman. 1979. Tool-using and -making behavior in wild chimpanzees at Boussou, Guinea. *Primates* 20:513–24.

Sussman, R.W. 1974. Ecological distinctions in sympatric species of *Lemur*. In *Prosimian Biology*, ed. R.D. Martin, G.A. Doyle, and A.C. Walker, pp. 75–108. Duckworth.

Szalay, F.S., and D. Seligsohn. 1977. Why did the strepsirhine tooth comb evolve? *Folia Primatol*. 27:75–82.

Terborgh, J. 1984. *Five New World Primates: A Study in Comparative Ecology*. Princeton Univ. Press.

Tsumori, A. 1966. Delayed response of wild Japanese monkeys by the sand-digging method, II. Cases of the Takasakiyama troops and the Ohiragama troop. *Primates* 7:363–80.

———. 1967. Newly acquired behavior and social interactions of Japanese monkeys. In *Social Communication among Primates*, ed. S.A. Altmann, pp. 207–20. Chicago Univ. Press.

Tsumori, A., M. Kawai, and R. Motoyoshi. 1965. Delayed response of wild Japanese monkeys by the sand-digging method. *Primates* 6:195–212.

Uehara, S. 1982. Seasonal changes in the techniques employed by wild chimpanzees in the Mahale Mountains, Tanzania, to feed on termites (*Pseudacanthus spiniger*). *Folioa Primatol*. 37:44–76.

Wilson, E.O. 1975. *Sociobiology, The New Synthesis*. Harvard Univ. Press.

4

BODIES, BRAINS, AND ENERGY

R. LEWIN

Ideas of human evolution have traditionally been dominated by the supposed intellectual and technological skills displayed by our large-brained ancestors. In fact, as Cambridge University anthropologist Robert Foley has recently stressed, 'Many aspects of human evolution are explicable in terms of the causes and consequences of increased body size.'

This unit will explore the impact of size—of both brains and bodies—on life-history variables and behavioral ecology. We will see why hominids, with their large body size, have many more options open to them in terms of diet, foraging range, sociality, expanded brain capacity, and so on, than, say, the diminutive mouse lemur.

In 1978 Princeton ecologist Henry Horn encapsulated the range of potential ecological options by posing the following set of questions: 'In the game of life an animal stakes its offspring against a more or less capricious environment. The game is won if offspring live to play another round. What is an appropriate tactical strategy for winning this game? How many offspring are needed? At what age should they be born? Should they be born in one large batch or spread out over a long lifespan? Should the offspring in a particular batch be few and tough or many and flimsy? Should parents lavish care on their offspring? Should parents lavish care on themselves to survive and breed again? Should the young grow up as a family, or should they be broadcast over the landscape at an early age to seek their fortunes independently?'

In responding to these challenges the animal kingdom as a whole has come up with a vast spectrum of strategies, ranging from species (oysters, for instance) that produce millions of offspring in a lifetime, upon which no parental care is lavished, to species (such as elephants) that produce just a

43

handful of offspring in a lifetime, each born singly and becoming the object of intense and extensive parental care. In the first case the potential reproductive output on a single individual is enormous, though typically curtailed by environmental attrition; in the second case it is small.

By their nature, mammals are constrained in the range of life-history patterns open to them: mammalian mothers are limited in the number of offspring that can be carried successfully through gestation and suckling. Nevertheless, potential reproductive output can be relatively high if more than one litter is raised each year over a lifetime of several years.

In the order Primates, potential reproductive output is low compared with mammals as a whole, litters being restricted in the vast majority of species to a single offspring. In the parlance of population biology, primates are therefore said to be K-selected. (Species with a high potential reproductive output are said to be r-selected.) And of all the primates, humans are the most extremely K-selected species.

Success in simple Darwinian terms is often measured in the currency of reproductive output, which is determined by a series of interrelated life-history factors. These include age at maturity, length of gestation, litter size, duration of lactation period, interbirth interval, and lifespan.

Some species live 'fast' lives: within a short life-span they mature early, produce large litters after a short gestation period, and wean early. The result is a large potential reproductive output. Other species live 'slow' lives: within a long lifespan they mature late, produce small litters (a single offspring) after a long gestation period, and wean late. Here, the potential reproductive output is small.

As it happens, the best predictor as to whether a species lives fast or slow is its body size: small species live fast lives, large species live slow lives. As potential reproductive output is highest in species that live fast lives, it might be thought that all species would be small. That some species are large implies that there are benefits in a bigger body size that trade off for a reduced potential reproductive output.

Such benefits might include (for a carnivore) a different spectrum of prey species or (for potential prey) better anti-predator defenses. Another potential benefit of increased body size is the ability to subsist on poorer quality food resources. The reason for this is that basal energy demands increase as the 0.75 power of body weight: in other words, as body weight increases, the basal energy requirement *per kilogram of body weight* decreases, a relationship known as the Kleiber curve. This is why mouse lemurs must feed on energy-rich insects and gums, for instance, while gorillas can subsist on energy-poor foliage. A further potential benefit of increased body size is an improved thermoregulatory efficiency. And so on.

The generally close relationship between body size and the value of the various life-history factors is the outcome of certain basic geometric and bioenergetic constraints. The result is that for any particular body size increase there is a more or less predictable change in, say, gestation length, age at maturity, and so on. For each life-history variable, therefore, a log/log plot against body size produces a straight line, with a particular exponent which describes the relationship (0.75 for basal energy needs, 0.37 for interbirth interval (in primates), 0.56 for weaning age, and so on). In effect, such plots *take out* body size in species comparisons.

If basic engineering constraints were all that underpinned life-history factors, then every species would be directly equivalent with every other species *when body weight is taken into account:* all the figures for each life-history variable would fall on the appropriate straight lines. In fact, individual figures often fall above or below the line, indicating a good deal of life-history variation. It is this variation that reveals an individual species' (or, more usually, a group of related species') adaptive strategy.

In recent years researchers have realized that, in addition to body size, brain size is also highly correlated with certain life-history factors, in some cases much more so than is body size.

Among mammals as a whole there is a key dichotomy in developmental strategy that has important implications for life-history measures: this is the altricial/precocial dichotomy. Altricial species produce extremely immature young that are unable to feed or care for themselves. The young of precocial species, on the other hand, are relatively mature and can fend for themselves to a degree.

Life-history factors critically associated with altriciality and precociality include gestation length. In altricial species gestation is short and neonatal brain size is small. Gestation in precocial species is relatively long, and neonatal brain size is large. There is, however, no consistent differences in *adult* brain size between altricial and precocial species. Primates as a group are precocial but *Homo sapiens* is an exception among primates, having developed a secondary altriciality and an unusually large brain.

In addition to the distinction between fast and slow lives according to absolute body size, some species' lives may be fast or slow *for its body size*. Such deviations have traditionally been explained in terms of classic *r*- and *K*-selection theory. According to this theory, environments that are unstable in terms of food supply (that is, are subject to booms and busts) encourage *r*-selection: fast lives, with high potential reproductive output. Alternatively, stable environments (which are close to carrying capacity and in which competition is therefore keen) favor *K*-selection: slow lives with low potential reproductive output.

As mentioned earlier, primates are close to the *K*-selection end of the spectrum among mammals as a whole, but some primates are less *K*-selected than others. For instance, Caroline Ross has recently shown that, when body size is taken into account, primate species that live in unpredictable environments have higher potential reproductive output than species in more stable environments.

A second factor that influences whether a species might live relatively fast or slow for its body size has recently been identified by Paul Harvey and Daniel Promislow. In a survey of 48 mammal species Promislow and Harvey found that 'those species with higher rates of mortality than expected had shorter gestation lengths, smaller neonates, larger litter, as well as earlier ages at weaning and maturity'. In other words, species that suffer high natural rates of mortality live fast. The reason is that species with higher rates of mortality are less likely to survive to the following breeding season and will therefore be selected to pay the higher costs associated with earlier reproduction.

Again, does the very slow life lived by *Homo sapiens* imply evolution from an ancestor that experienced very low levels of mortality?

Given that most mammals measure less than 32 cm in length, hominids—even the early, small species—must be classified as large mammals. The earlier known hominid species, *Australopithecus afarensis,* stood 1 meter (females) to 1.7 meters (males) tall, and weighed some 30 to 65 kilograms. These general proportions persisted until about 1.5 million years ago with the evolution of *Homo erectus,* which stood close to 1.8 meters (with a much reduced difference between males and females).

Knowing these general body proportions and the estimates of brain size it then becomes possible to make estimates of various life-history factors for the early hominid species, given also what is known of the only extant hominid, *Homo sapiens*. Surely, hominids lived slow lives in the terms of life-history variables, with a vastly increased brain capacity eventually distorting some of them.

In addition it is possible to identify several behavioral ecology traits that would also be associated with large body size, as Foley has done recently. For instance, dietary scope could be broad; day and home ranges could be large; mobility could be high, predator-prey relations would be shifted from that of smaller primates; thermoregulatory efficiency would be improved; sociality would be extended; and enhanced encephalization would be possible.

In sum, studies of life-history strategies have identified body size, brain size, environmental variability, and mortality rates as being crucial to the rate at which a species will live. Much of human evolution may therefore be explicable in terms of a large hominoid exploiting a relatively stable food

Characteristics of r- and K-selection		
	r-Selection	**K-Selection**
Climate	Variable and/or unpredictable; uncertain	Fairly constant and/or predicable; more certain
Mortality	Often catastrophic, non-directed, density independent	More direct, density dependent
Survivorship	High juvenile mortality	More constant mortality
Population size	Variable in time, non-equilibrium; usually well below carrying capacity of the environment unsaturated communities or portions thereof; ecological vacuums; recolonization each year	Fairly constant in time, equilibrium, at or near carrying capacity of the environment; saturated communities; no recolonization necessary
Intra- and interspecific competition	Variable, often lax	Usually keen
Selection favors	• Rapid development • High maximal rate of increase, r_{max} • Early reproduction • Small body size • Single reproduction • Many small offspring	• Slower development • Greater competitive ability • Delayed reproduction • Larger body size • Repeated reproduction • Fewer larger progeny
Length of life	Short, usually less than 1 year	Longer, usually more than 1 year
Leads to	Productivity	Efficiency

supply, its stability perhaps being enhanced by virtue of its breadth. Technology may eventually have contributed to this stability by allowing a more efficient exploitation of meat and certain plant foods, thus broadening the diet still further. A reduction in mortality, perhaps through improved anti-predator defense, would further encourage a 'slow' life-history strategy. But the selection pressure leading to increased body size still has to be identified.

KEY QUESTIONS

- What are the limitations of a simple Darwinian measure of reproductive success?

- At any particular body size, which is the riskier strategy, living fast or living slow?

- Primates as a group are twice as brainy as other mammals: how might this have arisen?

- Could the first hominids have originated in tropical rain forests?

KEY REFERENCES

Robert Foley, *Another unique species,* Longman Scientific and Technical, 1987.

Paul Harvey, Robert Martin, and Tim Clutton-Brock, 'Life histories in comparative perspective,' in *Primate societies,* edited by B.B. Smuts, D.L. Cheney, R.M. Seyfarth, R.W. Wrangham, and T.T. Struthsaker, University of Chicago Press, 1986, pp. 181–196.

Robert Martin and Paul Harvey, 'Human bodies of evidence,' *Nature,* vol. 330, pp. 697–698 (1987).

Daniel Promislow and Paul Harvey, 'Living fast and dying young,' *American Naturalist* (in press).

Caroline Ross, 'The intrinsic rate of natural increase and reproductive effort in primates,' *Journal of Zoology,* vol. 214, p. 199 (1988).

5

TAMARINS IN THE AMAZON

DAVID ABRAHAMSON

One thing that countless Hollywood jungle epics can never prepare you for is the palpable quiet of a tropical rain forest. Deep in the stillness of the triple-canopy shadows, the loudest sound is the occasional buzz of a hummingbird—a fluttering, almost bee-like hum.

Paul Garber doesn't hear it, focusing instead on a sporadic motion a hundred feet overhead in the dense Amazonian foliage. Field notebook in one hand, binoculars raised in the other, the 32-year-old University of Illinois primatologist strains to follow the fleeting movements of a group of tamarins, small, squirrel-sized New World monkeys. High above, almost a dozen animals are foraging. But only a few are visible through the overlapping greenery at a given moment, typically when they pause to search arboreal blossoms for insects.

Suddenly Garber and his Peruvian field assistant are in animated conversation, speaking Spanish in urgent whispers. Seconds before, one of the group's males, after extracting an insect from a flower, had offered it to an infant. A seemingly small gesture, but Garber's wide grin underscores its importance. Solicitous parental behavior by male tamarins has long been known; it is the males who usually carry the clinging young as the group makes its acrobatic way through the forest canopy. But as a new element of a larger pattern of male parental care, the "provisioning" incident—and Garber's recording of it—have the status of a first documented "field observation."

Almost 550 air miles to the south, in Peru's Manu National Park, Princeton's John Terborgh and Anne Wilson also have a first documented observation to their credit. Terborgh has long been interested in tamarins, which along with marmosets, make up the 20-species Callitrichidae family. Though virtually all the scientific literature on callitrichids categorically declare them to be monogamous, Terborgh and Wilson have recorded a number of occasions in which two unrelated males copulated with a female in full view of each other without provoking any sign of aggression—a clear example of polyandry.

The field studies of Terborgh, Wilson, and Garber promise practical results. Because tamarins have proven critical to hepatitis vaccine research, scientists need to understand the animals' reproductive strategy, including their mating system and their pattern of parental care. "Tamarins are very difficult to raise in captivity," explains Garber. "After a few generations, they seem to lose their ability to care for their young. Captive infant mortality is over 50 percent. I called one American supplier last year, and they told me they had 200 live animals on hand—and 2,000 dead ones."

In both the popular imagination and much of the scientific literature, mistaken beliefs about members of the order Primates—which along with *Homo sapiens* includes more than 180 species of apes, monkeys, and lemurs—are far from uncommon. Perhaps because of, rather than despite, the fact that they are humans' closest relatives, we seem to have great difficulty understanding them, most particularly in matters of evolution and sexual behavior. Garber playfully proved the point to a visitor over a rice and beans dinner at his primitive research camp in the Amazon. "Many people think they know a fair amount about primates," he said. "Let me ask you a couple of questions. First, on what continent did primates first evolve?"

"Africa, of course," was the reply.

"Sorry," smiled Garber, "but the oldest primate fossil discovered to date, named *Purgatorius*, was found in western North America. How big was the largest primate that ever lived?"

Male gorillas can top 500 pounds, so 600 seemed a safe guess.

"Nope, you've got to increase that by another 50 percent. *Gigantopithecus* fossil remains suggest a weight of over 900 pounds. Who's more closely related: South American monkeys and African monkeys, or African monkeys and humans?"

"The monkeys?"

"Sorry again," replied Garber, "but we and Old World monkeys share a more recent common ancestor. Let's try a reproduction question: What percentage of human cultures would you say are something other than monogamous? Keep in mind we're talking about number of different cultures, not numbers of people."

The visitor hesitated. "Hmmmm, perhaps a third," was the response.

"Cross-cultural anthropological studies of the world's 863 different cultures," Garber said, "suggest that the correct percentage is over 80. But don't feel to bad about all of this. You've got a number of my fellow primatologists for company."

It isn't surprising that much of what primatology claimed to know yesterday—for example, tamarin monogamy—is today being reconsidered. The first credible field study of primate behavior was published only 51 years ago. "We're not just a young science, we're barely born." says Irven DeVore, curator of primatology at Harvard's Peabody Museum. "And in truth, a great deal of primatology has been done that is really not up to the best scientific standards."

Moreover, one of the central themes of primatology is to broaden our understanding of ourselves. Primates stand at the hinge of evolution, says Alison Jolly of Rockefeller University. "They are to the biologist what viruses are to the biochemist. But viruses are living chemicals and primates are animals who love and hate and think." When studying any animal, generalizing from, or to, human behavior is always risky, yet many primatologists do it for a living. Little wonder that the historical record suggests they have occasionally gone astray.

Every scientific field has its fashions, its subject of emphasis at any moment. Primatology is no exception. "After World War II," recalls Harvard's DeVore, "because we were looking for models of human evolution, there was a great interest in baboons—like early man, a ground dwelling primate. But we were convinced that the male was all-important, and we were over-enamored with the idea of male dominance."

"Most of the theories at the time," says Sarah Blaffer Hrdy of the University of California at Davis, "emphasized male-male competition and 'the coy female,' which is only a small part of the way primates really act. It was as if scientists had projected onto primates a mirror image of the political and social views of an American corporation or university."

Nowhere were primatology's youthful biases more explicit than in the realm of reproduction. "The strongest stereotype is that the reproductive strategy of the male determines any species' mating system," says Jane Lancaster at the University of Oklahoma. "It's a projection of our own cultural values: parental care depends on females; social organization on males."

Part of the problem was methodological. "You have to remember," continues Lancaster, "that for many primates, the larger, more demonstrative males are simply easier for scientists to observe." Recalling his early research efforts, DeVore says, "Male baboons are fabulous data-generating machines. In contrast a really exciting day with an orangutan is watching one move a few dozen yards from one tree to another, and then counting the pits that fall a hundred feet to the ground below. I didn't last too long at that."

According to science historian Thomas Kuhn, one of the most interesting moments in the development of any science occurs when an existing, generally agreed-upon interpretation is confronted with new and contradictory knowledge. In light of the recent work of Terborgh and Garber in the wilds of Peru, past assumptions concerning tamarin reproductive strategy are clearly crumbling. The obvious question is, Why were we wrong? Specifically, Why were tamarins so widely believed to be monogamous, especially since most other primates are known to be polygynous?

"There has been a constant bias toward finding monogamous animals to serve as models for humans," says Robert Sussman, a Washington University physical anthropologist. Harvard's DeVore is blunter: "Don't think that scientists are above projecting their values onto their work. A surprising number have what I call the Walt Disney view of animal life."

Perhaps even more central to the past misunderstanding of tamarin social behavior is that as recently as nine years ago, all long-term observations of tamarins were from captive studies. "Most primate species are not well suited to laboratory experimentation such as vaccine research," explains Warren Kinzey at City University of New York. "They're large, difficult to handle, need a lot of space, and have lengthy growth cycles. Tamarins, however, are ideal; they need only small cages, breed frequently, and grow quickly." So in the late 1960s and early 1970s, a number of primate centers turned to callitrichids to meet their experimental requirements. And much of what was published about tamarin behavior was based on observations of those animals.

Typically, tamarins have been caged in male-female pairs. "Otherwise, you might get fights, says Patricia Wright of Duke University. Those fights are often between females. Gisela Epple of the West German Primate Center in Göttingen says that trios of two males and one female have been kept together. "But you can never allow two unrelated adult females in the same cage. We've tried two females together—and lost some animals." So, on the basis of breeding that occurred between animals caged only in male-female pairs, it was assumed that tamarins were monogamous.

"Why did we rely on captive data?" asks Thelma Rowell, a zoologist at the University of California in Berkeley. "Because field studies are very costly and very difficult. With the scarcity of funding, the only ones who do it are the dedicated nuts. Of course, it's the dedicated nuts who do the most important work."

"Up until the 1960s," says CUNY's Kinzey, "the few attempts at studying forest primates were not very successful. About the only behavior many early researchers could record was fleeing."

"But you have to have field data," says DeVore. "It's always very dangerous to make too much book on primates on the basis of anything less than long-term field studies." It is the efforts of field researchers like Terborgh, Garber, and others that have led Alison Jolly to observe, "We've learned more about primate behavior in the last 10 years than in the previous 10 centuries."

"Can you imagine what will happen when polyandry comes out a primate mating system?" asks Duke's Wright. "There'll be surprise, shock," she jests, "maybe even horror."

"You know what's going to be asked," says John Fleagle, a primate biologists at the State University of New York at Stony Brook. "Given that 50 percent of American marriages end in divorce, is there now a cultural bias toward finding 'unstable' primate societies? But you know, monogamy has always been the exception. It's actually quite rare." According to Kinzey, only 12 percent of all primate species are monogamous.

A mating system, however, is only one portion of an animal's reproductive strategy. The ultimate objective is reproductive success—subsequent generations surviving to reproductive maturity themselves. For primates, paternal care is pivotal. And of special interest is the nature of male parental care.

In the wild, different species of tamarins often forage together, but they don't interbreed. The average group contains four to six adults of the same species, typically two or more adult females and two or more adult males. But usually only one female, known as the alpha, is sexually active. Indeed, she seems to effect ovulation suppression of her female cohorts. If high levels of aggression among females are common in the wild, the suppression may be stress related.

The alpha actively mates with a number of the group's males. Given the high incidence of migration of both sexes into and out of groups it isn't likely that the males are related. Copulations occur both during the alpha female's normal estrus and during the "false" estrus—behaviorally indistinguishable from her normal estrus—that occurs midway through her five-month gestation period. Twins are the rule in tamarin births. Afterwards, parental care is essential to infant survival, and a major portion of that effort is provided by the group's males, who carry the young and, as observed by Garber, share choice morsels of food with them.

"There has to be some mechanism to explain the attraction of tamarin males to the offspring, whether they're theirs or not," says Washington

University's Robert Sussman, Garber's former mentor and the Callitrichidae authority who first suggested a reconsideration of the animals' reproductive strategy.

At present, three explanations have been offered that are not mutually exclusive. One is simply that male parental care is a learned behavior. Tamarins are very social animals, and male adolescents have plenty of opportunity to observe, even tentatively emulate, adult male-infant interaction.

But that doesn't explain how the behavior might have originated. According to a sociobiological interpretation, the polyandrous mating system of tamarins confuses the issue of paternity. No male who copulated with the alpha female can be certain that he is not the father of the infant. Sociobiology's tenet of genetic self-interest (that is, the struggle to insure that one's genes are represented in subsequent generations—which, in turn, must survive to sexual maturity) suggests that most of the males have a clear interest in contributing to the welfare of the young. "Their breeding system," says Hrdy, "can be viewed as a way for the female to extract the necessary male parental care. They do that by the manipulation of information available to the males about paternity."

A third possible explanation for the males' parental role arises from what Lancaster calls "the most exciting area of behavioral sciences today— the connection between behavior and biochemistry." Prolactin, a hormone produced by the pituitary gland, has been known for more than a decade to influence maternal behavior of rabbits, rats, and mice. Recently, Alan Dixson, a neuroendocrinologist at the Edinburgh Medical Research Council's Unit of Reproductive Biology, studied prolactin levels in male callitrichids, in particular when caring for their young. He found in common marmosets, a close relative of the tamarin, that males carrying offspring have plasma prolactin levels five times higher on average than males without infants. "It was, I believe, the first demonstration that prolactin is elevated during parental behavior in a male mammal," says Dixson. But he adds a note of caution: "All we know is that males have high prolactin levels when engaged in parental care. We don't know if prolactin actually drives the behavior; we have no proof of cause and effect." Indeed, though prolactin levels may initiate the behavior, it is also possible that close contact with the infant plays a role in raising the hormone level.

Whatever the correct explanation, or combination of explanations, it is evident that within the natural social organization of tamarins, the males of a group take an active interest in the care of the young, making a significant contribution to the survival of their species. And their system of nonmonogamous breeding clearly has its place in the natural order of things.

"We've lived in our culture for a long time with a silly *Ladies' Home Journal* view of maleness," says DeVore at Harvard's Peabody Museum. "You know, now that we've found a polyandrous primate species with a great deal of male caring for the young, it just might, in some people, scratch a deep itch."

6

How Monkeys See the World: A Review of Recent Research on East African Vervet Monkeys

Robert M. Seyfarth and Dorothy L. Cheney

Although laboratory studies have demonstrated that apes can be taught to use symbols to represent objects in the external world (Gardner and Gardner 1969; Premack 1976; Rumbaugh 1977; Patterson 1978), it generally has been assumed that the vocalizations of monkeys and apes under natural conditions convey information only about the motivational state of the signaler (e.g., Smith 1977). This dichotomy between the "semantic" signaling of apes in captivity and the "affective" signaling of the same and related species in the wild has tended to divert attention from two crucial questions: First, what selective forces might have given rise to the potential for representational signaling in nonhuman primates? Second, do we know enough about the signals of monkeys and apes to deny the possibility that such communication occurs under natural conditions? Similarly, there have been almost no comparative studies of communicative development in human and nonhuman species, largely because research on monkeys and apes and research on the language of children have been based on fundamentally different assumptions.

This chapter attempts to bring together research on communication in captive and free-ranging primates and to offer some analogies between nonhuman primate communication and the development of human language. We begin by describing the predator alarm calls of East African vervet monkeys and we discuss how the use of such calls develops during ontogeny. We then use this relatively simple communication system as a model to examine more complex forms of communication, arguing that research on the vocalizations of monkeys and apes, like research on grooming, alliance formation, and other social interactions, should focus on the question of how each communication system functions under natural conditions. The long-term objective of our research is therefore to determine both what monkeys and apes *need* to signal about in their social interactions with each other and how individuals capable of representational signaling might enjoy an evolutionary advantage over others.

Because this chapter attempts to bring together research from a number of fields, we have deliberately borrowed technical terms from human psychology, linguistics, and child development with the intention of applying them to nonhuman primates. In doing so, one must remember that terms such as "semanticity" and "categorization," when applied to humans, carry implications of conscious intent that may not apply to nonhuman species. Thus, when we say, for example, that vervet monkeys have different alarm calls for different predators, we have no evidence that monkeys consciously select different vocalizations in precisely the same way that humans select different words to refer to different objects. Instead, our aim is to emphasize the functional parallels, however rudimentary, between the way monkeys use vocalizations and the way humans use words.

VERVET MONKEY ALARM CALLS

Do nonhuman primates in their natural habitat signal about objects or events in the world around them? A methodological problem confronting any observer who attempts to answer this question is that an animal cannot be interviewed. Instead, the observer must try to arrive at the content of each signal by studying the responses it evokes in other individuals. If the call, for example, conveys subtle information, such responses may not be immediate or obvious (Marler 1961). To draw a parallel with human language, it is as if an observer were attempting to discover the meaning of a conversation by studying only the overt responses of those listening to it. When investigating the possible semantic content of nonhuman primate vocalizations, we therefore began with a subset of vocalizations that might be expected to evoke noticeable and measurably different responses: the predator alarm calls of vervet monkeys. If semantic signaling could be demonstrated in this relatively simple case, vervet alarm calls might serve as a model for research on the more complex and subtle vocalizations used by monkeys in their social interactions with each other.

Vervet monkey alarm calls were first studied by Struhsaker (1967) in Amboseli National Park, Kenya. Struhsaker suggested that acoustically different alarm calls were given by the monkeys in response to different predators and that each call evoked a different and seemingly adaptive response. Our preliminary observations and recordings, made in Amboseli National Park between 1977 and 1978, supported Struhsaker's findings and indicated that adult vervets gave acoustically different alarm calls to at least three classes of predators: large mammalian carnivores, eagles, and snakes. Within each class, alarm calls were largely restricted to a single species: Thus large mammalian carnivore alarms (hereafter called leopard alarms) were given primarily to leopards *(Panthera pardus)*; eagle alarms were given primarily to martial eagles *(Polemaetus bellicosus)*; and snake alarms were given primarily to pythons *(Python sebae)*. The acoustical features of each alarm-call type were such that (1) alarm calls could be assigned unambiguously to one type, both by sound spectrography in the laboratory and by ear in the field, and (2) alarm calls could be distinguished from the nonalarm vocalizations they most closely resembled (Seyfarth, Cheney, and Marler 1980b).

In addition to being acoustically distinct, each alarm-call type was also associated with a different set of responses, each of which seemed to represent an adaptive escape strategy for coping with the hunting behavior of the predator involved. For example, when monkeys were on the ground, leopard alarms caused them to run into trees, where they appeared to be safe from leopard attacks. Eagle alarms caused them to look up or run into bushes, where they seemed to be safe from an eagle stoop, and snake alarms caused them to look down on the ground around them (for further descriptions of predator hunting behavior, see Seyfarth, Cheney, and Marler 1980b).

Both Struhsaker's and our own observations suggested that each alarm-call type effectively represented, or signified, a different class of external danger. However, there remained potential ambiguities in the interpretation of these results. Most serious was the possibility that monkeys apparently responding to an alarm call might in fact have seen the predator. Differences in response might therefore have been due simply to the perception of different predators, in which case acoustical differences among alarms would be irrelevant. Moreover, it was also possible that our perception of the monkeys' responses was affected by our expectations of what a "correct" response should be. With these points in mind, we decided to conduct a series of experiments in which tape recordings of leopard, eagle, or snake alarms given by known individuals would be played to the monkeys in the absence of actual predators.

Playbacks of the alarm-calls of vervet monkeys were conducted on two groups between July 1977 and May 1978. The calls used had been tape-recorded from known individuals during actual encounters with leopards, martial eagles, and pythons. Playbacks were divided among the alarm calls of adult males, adult females, and juveniles. Leopard alarm calls by adult males were longer and contained more acoustical units than alarms to other types of predators. Anticipating the possibility that call length might influence responses, we constructed long and short versions of each call type. Long versions contained a mean of five units and had a mean duration of 3.7 sec (SD = 2.5). Short versions contained a single unit and had a mean duration of 0.3 sec (SD = .2). To control for possible effects of amplitude, calls used in some trials differed naturally in amplitude across alarm types, with leopard alarms being louder than eagle alarms, which, in turn, were louder than snake alarms. In a second subset of trials, calls did not differ significantly in amplitude across alarm types (Seyfarth, Cheney, and Marler 1980b).

In each trial, an alarm call was played to monkeys (at least one adult male, two adult females, and two immatures) from a previously concealed speaker. Subjects were filmed using a sound movie camera for 10 sec preceding and 10 sec following each call playback. Subjects experienced 50 trials on the ground and 38 in the trees. No two playbacks to the same group of monkeys were conducted within 24 hr of each other, nor was any trial run within 15 min of alarming by nearby vervets or by the subjects' own group. Call-type order and speaker position relative to the subjects were varied systematically.

Alarm-call playbacks produced two kinds of response. Subjects in all age-sex classes looked toward the speaker and scanned the surrounding area, more in the 10 sec after playback than in the 10 sec before. They behaved as if searching for additional cues, both from the alarmist and elsewhere. In addition, each alarm-call type elicited a distinct set of responses (Table 10.1). When subjects were on the ground, leopard alarms were more likely than other alarm types to cause them to run into trees. Eagle alarms made them look up and/or run into cover, and snake alarms caused them to look down. When subjects were in trees, eagle alarms were more likely than other alarm types to evoke looking up and/or running out of the tree, whereas snake alarms were more likely to cause subjects to look down. The monkeys behaved as though each alarm-call type designated a different external object or event.

This view of vervet alarm calls as rudimentary semantic signals contrasts with many earlier interpretations, which have tended to regard

Table 10.1 Responses of monkeys to playbacks of leopard, eagle, and snake alarms

Responses of monkeys	Alarm type					
	Leopard (N = 19)	Eagle (N =14)	Snake (N = 19)	Leopard (N = 190)	Eagle (N = 17)	Snake (N - 9)
On ground						
Run into tree	8*	2	2			
Run into cover	2	6**	2			
Look up	4	7**	2			
Look down	1	4	14*			
In tree						
Run higher in tree				4	4	2
Run out of tree				0	5**	0
Look up				3	11	5
Look down				4	12	19*

Note: Entries show the number of trials in which at least one subject showed a given response that was longer in the 10 sec after playback than in the 10 sec before. Asterisks denote cases in which a particular response to a given call type occurred in significantly more trials than with either one or both of the other alarm types.
$*p < .01.$ $**p < .05.$

animal signals simply as manifestations of different levels of arousal, lacking clearly defined external referents (e.g., Smith 1977). If such was the case, we might expect that responses to alarms would have differed in relation to call features that mirror arousal levels, such as call length or amplitude. To test this hypothesis, we compared responses to long and short versions of each call type (see earlier discussion). Responses to leopard, eagle, and snake alarm playbacks were also compared (1) when amplitude differed systematically across alarm type and (2) when amplitude was controlled (see earlier discussion). Results indicated that variation in call length and equation of amplitude, as well as variation in the age-sex class of both alarmists and responders, failed to blur distinctions among major response categories. Variation in the acoustical structure of different call types was the only feature both necessary and sufficient to explain differences in response (Seyfarth, Cheney, and Marler 1980b).

It has also been argued that animal signals do not refer to specific, narrowly defined external referents but that each signal instead encodes one of a small number of very generalized "messages" such as "attack," "escape," or "frustration" (Smith 1977). A few such general signals are thought to be capable of eliciting a wide variety of responses because they are given in different contexts. By this interpretation, the "meaning" of each signal is highly context-dependent. In our experiments, however, context was not a systematic determinant of the responses of vervets to alarm calls. Different alarms evoked different responses in the same context, and responses to some alarms remained constant despite contextual variation. The most parsimonious interpretation is that each alarm represented a certain class of danger and that monkeys responded according to their vulnerability to that danger at the time.

HOW MONKEYS SEE THE WORLD

The Relation between Semantic Signals and Natural Categories

The preceding discussion of vervet alarm calls raises the question of how monkeys classify objects in the world around them. If an organism is to use different signals to represent the virtually infinite number of objects in its environment, it must either employ an infinite number of signals or sort objects into groups. Present indications are that the repertoires of natural, meaningfully distinct signals are limited in animals. Thus any study of representational communication must inevitably consider how a given species "categorizes" objects in its natural habitat. Although research on the "natural categories" of nonhuman species recently has received considerable attention (e.g., Herrnstein, Loveland, and Cable 1976; Cerella 1979; Sandell, Gross, and Bornstein 1979), few studies have gone beyond the phenomenon as it is expressed in the laboratory to consider how such cognitive abilities may have evolved under natural conditions. Category formation is also well documented in humans (e.g., Berlin and Kay 1969; Rosch 1973, 1977), where the ontogeny of word-object associations has been well studied (e.g., Clark 1973; Nelson 1973; Anglin 1977; see also later discussion).

By giving alarm calls to some species but not to others, and by giving acoustically different alarms to different predators, vervet monkeys effectively categorized objects in the world around them. When giving alarm calls, adults were most selective, giving leopard alarms primarily to leopards, eagle alarms primarily to martial eagles, and snake alarms primarily to pythons. In marked contrast to adults, infants (monkeys under 1 year of age) and juveniles (monkeys older than 1 year but not yet adult size) gave alarm calls to a significantly wider variety of species and were significantly more likely to give alarms to nonpredators like warthogs, pigeons, and falling leaves that posed no danger to them (Seyfarth and Cheney 1980; Seyfarth, Cheney, and Marler 1980a).

Intriguingly, however, although infants gave alarm calls to a wider variety of species than did adults, infant alarm-calling behavior was not entirely random. Infants gave leopard alarms primarily to terrestrial mammals, eagle alarms to birds, and snake alarms to snakes or long thin objects (Seyfarth and Cheney 1980). In other words, from a very early age infants distinguished between general predator *classes* (e.g., terrestrial mammal vs. flying bird), whereas adults distinguished between particular predator *species* within such classes (e.g., leopards vs. other terrestrial mammals and martial eagles vs. other birds).

Development in a Social Setting

These data on vervet alarm calls suggest some ways in which nonhuman primate semantic signals, and the categorization they imply, develop under natural conditions in the absence of human training. Moreover, results suggest parallels between the ontogeny of vervet alarms and the ways in which human infants develop an ability to use specific words to refer to specific people or events. At an early stage in development, for example, human infants may use the word "dada" to refer either to (1) any of its adult caretakers or (2) any male adult with whom it comes into contact (Greenfield 1973; Greenfield and Smith 1976). In both cases, the infant's earliest use of "dada" is clearly nonrandom. As the infant grows older, the referential specificity of "dada" increases until, at least in western European culture, the word is generally used to refer exclusively to one person.

Parallels between the ontogeny of human words and the ontogeny of vervet alarm calls become all the more striking when one considers the social mechanisms likely to influence semantic development in human and nonhuman primates. Human infants learn the association between specific words and specific objects or events in a complex social environment, where cues from other individuals play an important developmental role. Observational learning, imitation, subtle reinforcement, and active pedagogy have all been implicated as mechanisms, both for "prelinguistic" social development (Bruner 1976) and for later word-object associations (e.g., Miller 1977).

Similarly, infant vervet monkeys mature in groups of from 10 to 50 individuals, and preliminary data indicate that subtle cues from other group members help infants to sharpen the association between predator species, alarm-call type, and response. Consider first the association between predator species and alarm-call type. As noted earlier, when infants first began to give alarm calls each alarm type was restricted only to a certain broad class of objects (e.g., flying bird vs. terrestrial mammal), whereas the alarms of older individuals were limited to a particular species within each class (e.g., martial eagle vs. other flying bird). Fieldwork currently in progress suggests that subtle reinforcement may be one mechanism by which infants restrict the number of species to which they give alarms. For example, if an infant is the first to alarm at a martial eagle—one of the monkeys' main predators—it is virtually certain that other group members will also give alarms. In contrast, if an infant alarms at a species that does not attack monkeys, the probability of subsequent alarms by adults is much lower.

In an analogous manner, there is evidence for observational learning and/or imitation in the development of alarm-specific escape responses. As noted earlier, adults not only gave different alarm calls to different predators, they also responded differently to each alarm type. In contrast, playback experiments showed that infant responses were more generalized than those of adults and that infants were significantly more likely than adults to respond in ways that were potentially maladaptive (Seyfarth and Cheney 1980). Given that adultlike, alarm-specific responses develop only after experience, it is of interest that infants differed from adults in two further respects. First, infants in playback experiments were significantly more likely than adults to respond in a given way only after first looking at another animal who had already begun that same response and second, infants near their mothers were more likely to show adultlike responses than infants whose mothers had temporarily wandered more than 5 m away. Adults showed no such differences in response depending on the presence of other individuals.

In summary, it seems clear that predator classification by young monkeys improves with age and experience and that the monkeys' social environment plays an important role in this development. Although results thus far suggest intriguing parallels with human language development, further research is needed to determine the precise nature of the process of perceptual categorization that occurs among vervets and the exact roles of early predisposition, experience, and adult tutelage in such development.

How Monkeys Classify Each Other

Although vervet monkeys clearly discriminated among a variety of animal species and divided them into groups, we found no conclusive evidence either for or against the hypothesis that vervets can create a true hierarchical taxonomy with all the formal relations this implies (Kay 1971). Premack (1976), for example, was able to teach the chimpanzee Sarah not only different signs for blue, green, and red but also the relation "blue is a type of color," "red is a type of color," and so on. Although the data are suggestive, they do not prove that vervet monkeys, as they mature, come to understand the relation between specific objects (e.g., martial eagle, tawny eagle) and the higher-order groups to which they belong (e.g., raptor, bird, etc.).

Under what conditions might natural selection confer a reproductive advantage on individuals capable of creating hierarchical taxonomies, and how might such behavior function in the everyday social interactions of group-living monkeys? In an attempt to answer such questions, we conducted a series of experiments that examined how monkeys classify what is perhaps the most important part of their environment: each other.

Perhaps the most ubiquitous examples of hierarchical taxonomy in human societies are found in systems of kinship. Members of a given group are distinguished on one level as individuals and at the same time are grouped together at higher levels, such as the family, clan, and so on. Such classification is not only hierarchical (e.g., Fox 1967; Kay 1971), it also goes beyond a purely "egocentric" view of one's group: Each individual regards others not only in terms of his own relationship with them but also in terms of the relations other individuals have with each other. As applied to nonhuman primates, this view of recognition and social organization suggests the following question: If a group-living monkey, an adult female, for example, can "recognize" her offspring, does this mean she simply divides individuals into two groups (own offspring vs. others), or is there evidence of more subtle individual recognition on the basis of relations that animals other than the adult female are seen to have with each other? Observational data suggest that such complex recognition does indeed occur. Among both baboons and vervet monkeys, for example, individuals not only interact at high rates with members of their own immediate family but also compete with each other to establish bonds with members of high-ranking families (Cheney 1977, 1978; Seyfarth 1980). Individuals seem to "know" not only who ranks higher than they do but also which animals should be grouped together as members of the same kin group (e.g., Kurland 1977).

Experiments that attempt to document the extent to which monkeys recognize the relations that other group members have with each other share at least one methodological problem with experiments on semantic signaling: How can we induce animals to tell us what they know about the identity of another group member? As a first step in this investigation, we conducted a series of playback experiments on maternal recognition of the screams of their 2-year-old offspring. Adult female vervet monkeys and their offspring were selected for study because previous research had indicated that mothers intervened on behalf of their offspring in a large proportion of the offsprings' disputes. We therefore reasoned that playback of juvenile screams could evoke responses from mothers that were both strong and easily distinguishable from the responses of other adults.

Playback experiments were conducted in two groups of monkeys, each of which contained at least seven juveniles between 1 and 3 years of age. We selected for experimentation three to four typical scream bouts from each of four juveniles (two from each of two groups) matched for age, sex, and mother's dominance rank. When conducting an experiment, we first waited until the mother of one of the experimental juveniles was out of sight of her offspring and in proximity to two other "control" females who also had offspring in the group. Control females were also always out of sight of their 2-year-old offspring. A speaker was then concealed in a bush approximately 7 to 15 m from the females. Among trials for each mother, we systematically varied the speaker's position relative to the mother's orientation, so that no mother received all screams from the same direction. Filming of all females began 10 sec before each scream was played and continued for 45 sec after the scream bout had ended. We therefore were able to obtain an accurate record to estimate the probability that each female would look toward the speaker (or show some other response) in the first 10 sec before and after each scream, as well as the latency and duration (up to 45 sec) of each female's response.

Observational data collected before experimentation suggested that the screams of a juvenile often initially attracted wide attention in the group; we therefore predicted that all females would show some response to the playbacks but that mothers' responses would be stronger than controls'. In comparing the behavior of each female before and after screams, we found that playbacks significantly increased the probability that both mothers and controls would look toward the speaker (Cheney and Seyfarth 1980). In general, however, mothers showed both a shorter latency and a longer duration of looking than did controls. In addition, mothers were significantly more likely than controls to move toward the speaker (Cheney and Seyfarth 1980).

The responses of mothers demonstrate that adult female vervets are able to classify juveniles into at least two categories (offspring vs. others) on the basis of voice alone. Are they capable of further discrimination, among the offspring of others? When the responses of control females were compared to their behavior before each experiment, we found that playbacks significantly increased the probability that controls would look at the mother. In contrast, there was no change in the probability that one control would look at another.

There are two possible explanations for the behavior of control females. First, controls may have looked at mothers simply because the stronger response of mothers caused controls to orient toward them. Second, controls may have looked at mothers because they were able to discriminate among the screams of particular juveniles and to associate each juvenile with a particular adult female. To test between these two hypotheses, we examined separately those trials in which mothers did not approach the speaker. Results from these experiments still indicated a significant increase in the probability that controls would look at the mother (Cheney and Seyfarth 1980). Moreover, analysis of the gaze and position of control females in these trials suggested that it is unlikely that the controls' behavior was caused simply by cues from the mother.

The results of these experiments strongly suggest that, in recognizing other group members, individual vervet monkeys go beyond simple discriminations such as "close relatives versus others" and create more complex, hierarchical categories in which individuals are distinguished both on one level as individuals and on higher levels as members of particular kin groups. The ability of monkeys to classify individuals in this manner is almost certainly the result of natural selection acting on animals within a complex social framework, where detailed knowledge of relations among all group members is essential. Indeed, we may speculate that the ability of monkeys to classify predators and their own vocalizations (e.g., Snowdon 1979; Zoloth, Petersen, Beecher, Green, Marler, Moody, and Stebbins 1979), as well as the ability of captive chimpanzees to understand the relation "X is different from Y but both are members of the set A" (Premack 1976), first emerged in the primates' need to classify each other in an analogous manner.

DISCUSSION: FROM SIMPLE TO COMPLEX FORMS OF COMMUNICATION

Language allows us to represent objects in the external world by means of relatively arbitrary, context-independent labels and therefore also reflects the way in which we classify objects for the purpose of representation. In at least a rudimentary sense, certain vocalizations of nonhuman primates function in an analogous manner. The alarm calls discussed in this chapter suggest that, in at least one aspect of their vocal repertoire, free-ranging monkeys are capable of signaling about objects. Moreover, data on both the ontogeny of alarm calls and individual vocal recognition indicate that complex classifications of objects and fellow group members may occur on the basis of vocal cues alone.

There is no reason to assume that such complex signaling abilities are restricted to one relatively simple and narrow subset of the monkeys' vocalizations. Indeed, when thinking about the evolution of language, we frequently assume that the first appearance of rudimentary representational signals brought a considerable selective advantage to its users. If such an assumption is correct, it seems unlikely that animals capable of semantic signaling under a specialized set of conditions (e.g., encounters with predators) will not make use of this ability during more frequently occurring social interactions.

By far the most commonly used vocalizations among vervet monkeys are an apparently graded series of grunts, uttered during a variety of social situations (Struhsaker 1967). Such grunts evoke few immediately obvious responses and at first appear to be simply manifestations of different levels of arousal. Research on the coo vocalizations of Japanese macaques, however, has suggested that subtle variations within the monkeys' graded vocal repertoire are specific to particular social interactions (Green 1975). The same vocalizations also appear to be perceived in a categorical manner (Zoloth et al. 1979). Snowdon and Pola (1978) previously demonstrated that pygmy marmosets categorically responded to synthesized continua of their trills. Moreover, field experiments on the grunts of vervet monkeys now in progress indicate that such calls are not only context-specific but also individually distinctive and in some cases clearly serve to designate different external events (Cheney and Seyfarth, in press). Such results both suggest that we are only beginning to understand how much information is conveyed in animal signals and emphasize the limited usefulness of any strict dichotomy between "semantic" human language and "affective" animal communication.

Premack (1975), for example, has argued that an "affective" signaling system that conveys information only about the signaler's motivational state can become functionally semantic if vocalizations are individually distinctive and if all members of a group "agree" about the level of arousal of different events (see also Marler 1977; Green and Marler 1979). Thus, if a listener can recognize the voice of another individual and also knows how that individual responds to different events, the listener will be able to determine without further cues what that individual is doing, or to what it is reacting, when it vocalizes.

All the assumptions on which Premack's argument is based are satisfied in groups of free-ranging primates. As we have suggested, primate groups are composed of individuals who appear to recognize each other by sight, and, in the absence of visual cues, there is also evidence that monkeys can recognize the vocalizations of others. Even if we accept the suggestion that, for example, different alarm calls are simply manifestations of different levels of arousal, group members seem to "agree" on which predator should be associated with each arousal level.

Premack's argument emphasizes that the apparent dichotomy between "affective" and "semantic" signaling breaks down when we begin to examine how signals function under natural conditions. Whatever the evolutionary history of primate vocalizations, at least some such vocalization can now be said to function in a semantic manner. As research on the social signals of monkeys and apes continues, we think it is important to remember that animals will use complex communicative signals only when it becomes selectively advantageous to do so. Thus, a central question for future research would appear to be: How might the use of semantic signals benefit those who employ them? Research on behavior such as grooming and alliance formation suggest that these interactions are best understood as means by which animals form those social bonds that subsequently bring benefit to them. Similarly, only by studying vocalizations within the broader context of other forms of social interaction and by considering what animals need to signal about will we begin to understand the evolutionary history of representational signaling and the selective forces that may have favored one type of communication over others.

REFERENCES

Anglin, J.M. 1977. *Word object and conceptual development.* New York: Norton.

Berlin, B., and Kay, P. 1969. *Basic color terms: their universality and evolution.* Berkeley: University of California Press.

Bruner, J.S. 1976. From communication to language—a psychological perspective. *Cognition* 3:255–87.

Cerella, J. 1979. Visual classes and natural categories in the pigeon. *Journal of Experimental Psychology: Human Perception and Performance* 5:68–77.

Cheney, D.L. 1977. The acquisition of rank and the formation of reciprocal alliances in free-ranging baboons. *Behavioral Ecology and Sociobiology* 2: 303–18.

_____. 1978. Interactions of male and female baboons with adult females. *Animal Behaviour* 26:389–408.

Cheney, D.L., and Seyfarth, R.M. 1980. Vocal recognition in free-ranging vervet monkeys. *Animal Behaviour* 28:362–7.

_____. In press. How vervet monkeys perceive their grunts: field playback experiments. *Animal Behaviour.*

Clark, E. 1973. What's in a word? On the child's acquisition of semantics in his first language. In *Cognitive development and the acquisition of language.* ed. T. E. Moore, pp. 65–110. New York: Academic Press.

Fox, R. 1967. *Kinship and marriage.* Harmondsworth, Eng.: Penguin.

Gardner, R. A., and Gardner, B. T. 1969. Teaching sign language to a chimpanzee. *Science* 165:664–72.

Green, S. 1975. Communication by a graded vocal system in Japanese monkeys. In *Primate behavior, Vol. 4: Developments in field and laboratory research,* ed. L. A. Rosenblum, pp. 1–102. New York: Academic Press.

Green, S., and Marler, P. 1979. The analysis of animal communication. In *Handbook of behahioral neurobiology. Vol. 3: Social behavor and communication,* ed. P. Marler and J. G. Vandenbergh, pp. 73–158. New York: Plenum.

Greenfield, P.M. 1973. Who is "dada"? Some aspects of the semantic and phonological development of a child's first words. *Language and Speech* 16:34–43.

Greenfield, P.M., and Smith, J.H. 1976. The *structure of communication in language development.* New York: Academic Press.

Herrnstein, R.J., Loveland, D.H., and Cable, C. 1976. Natural concepts in pigeons. Journal *of Experimental Psychology: Animal Behavior Processes,* 2: 285–302.

Kay, P. 1971. Taxonomy and semantic contrast. *Language* 47:866–87.

Kurland, J. 1977. Kin selection in the Japanese monkey. *Contributions* to *Primatology* 12: 1–145.

Marler, P. 1961. The logical analysis of animal communication. *Journal* of *Theoretical Biology* 1:295–317.

_____. 1977. Primate vocalizations: affective or symbolic? In *Progress in ape research.* ed. G.H. Bourne, pp. 85–96. New York: Academic Press.

Miller, G.A. 1977. *Spontaneous apprentices.* New York: Seabury Press.

Nelson, K. 1973. Some evidence for the cognitive primacy of categorization and its functional basis. *Merrill-Palmer Quarterly of Behavior and Development* 19:21–40.

Patterson, F.G. 1978. The gestures of a gorilla: language acquisition in another pongid. *Brain & Language* 5:72-97.

Premack, D. 1975. On the origins of language. In *Handbook of Psychobiology,* ed. M. Gazzaniga and C.B. Blakemore, pp. 591–605. New York: Academic Press.

_____. 1976. *Intelligence in apes and man.* Hillsdale, N.J.: Erlbaum.

Rosch, E. H. 1973. On the internal structure of perceptual and semantic categories. In *Cognitive development and the acquisition of language,* ed. T.E. Moore, pp. 111–44. New York: Academic Press.

_____. 1977. Classification of real-world objects: origins and representations in cognition. In *Thinking: readings in cognitive science,* ed. P.N. Johnson-Laird and P.C. Wason, pp. 212–22. Cambridge University Press.

Rumbaugh, D., ed. 1977. *Language learning by a chimpanzee: the Lana Project.* New York: Academic Press.

Sandell, J. H., Gross, C.G., and Bornstein, M.C. 1979. Color categories in macaques. *Journal of Comparative Physiology and Psychology,* 93:626–35.

Seyfarth, R. M. 1980. The distribution of grooming and related behaviours among adult female vervet monkeys. *Animal Behaviour* 28:798–813.

Seyfarth, R. M., and Cheney, D. L. 1980. The ontogeny of vervet monkeys alarm calling behavior: a preliminary report. *Zeitschrift für Tierpsychologie* 54: 37–56.

Seyfarth, R.M., Cheney, D.L., and Marler, P. 1980a. Monkey response to three different alarm calls: Evidence of predator classification and semantic communication. *Science* 210:801–3.

_____. 1980b. Vervet monkey alarm calls: semantic communication in a free-ranging primate. *Animal Behaviour* 28:1070–94.

Smith, W.J. 1977. Th*e behavior of communicating: an ethological approach.* Cambridge, Mass.: Harvard University Press.

Snowdon, C.T. 1979. Response of non-human animals to speech and to speciesspecific sounds. *Brain, Behavior and Evolution* 16:409–29.

Snowdon, C.T., and Pola, Y.V. 1978. Interspecific and intraspecific responses to synthesized pygmy marmoset vocalizations. *Animal Behaviour* 26:192–206.

Struhsaker, T.T. 1967. Auditory communication among vervet monkeys (*Cercopithecus aethiops*). In *Social communication among primates,* ed. S.A. Altmann, pp. 281–324. Chicago: University of Chicago Press.

Zoloth, S.R., Petersen, M.R., Beecher, M.D., Green, S., Marler, P., Moody, D.B., and Stebbins, W. 1979. Species-specific perceptual processing of vocal sounds by Old World monkeys. *Science* 204:870–3.

7

EXPERIMENTAL APPROACHES TO THE STUDY OF PRIMATE COGNITION IN NATURAL AND NEAR-TO-WILD FIELD SETTINGS

P. A. GARBER AND A. LAVALLEE

INTRODUCTION

Ecological approaches to the study of learning provide important insight into the evolution of sensory capabilities and foraging behavior (Kamil, 1994; Real, 1992; Garber & Dolins, 1996; Tomasello & Call, 1997). In the wild, many species of nonhuman primates exploit resources that vary greatly in their spatial distribution, temporal availability, and ease of acquisition (Fragaszy, 1986; Garber, 1989, 1993). The challenges these foragers face include **where** to travel, **when** to visit and revisit particular feeding sites, and **how** to extract and process food items efficiently. The manner in which these resources are exploited is directly influenced by the species' ability to store, categorize, and associate disparate types of environmental and sensory information, and use this knowledge to generate foraging 'rules' to guide behavior.

In this paper, we examine a series of questions concerning how primates foraging in social groups solve problems of locating and acquiring resources. Specifically, we conducted experimental studies to determine (1) the manner in which wild white-faced capuchins (*Cebus capucinus*) use spatial, temporal, and olfactory information to select feeding sites and (2) strategies of tool selection and tool modification employed by captive brown capuchins (*Cebus apella*) to exploit an otherwise inaccessible food source. The goals of this research are to identify a set of 'learning rules' or 'hypotheses' used by primate foragers to solve novel ecological problems, and to determine the degree to which these solutions are reapplied to successfully obtain food in other ecological and social contexts (Krechevsky, 1932)

Recognizing Cognitive Complexity

We begin by developing a set of criteria for evaluating complex cognitive behavior that can be applied across species. Considering tool use as an example, several insect, bird and mammalian species naturally manipulate objects in specific environmental contexts to extract or obtain resources (Beck, 1980; Visalberghi & Limongelli, 1996). Yet, it is unlikely that tool-using behaviors in each taxon represent comparable levels of cognitive complexity. Specifically, tool use across species is characterized by differences in forethought, the ability to understand cause and effect relationships, and the ability to adjust behavioral patterns according to the present conditions of the foraging task (Beck, 1980; Visalberghi & Limongelli, 1996). Similarly, although many animals use landmarks and other cues to navigate over long distances, there is evidence of species differences in the manner in which spatial information is internally represented, and whether landmarks are remembered associatively (orient to an individual cue) or relationally (knowledge of the spatial relationships of two or more cues to orient in space) (Gallistel, 1990; Dolins, 1993; Dyer, 1994). It is important to recognize that, in the study of animal cognition, it is not the behavior itself that serves as the basis of comparison, but what it reveals about the animal's ability to process information (Visalberghi & Limongelli, 1996). We suggest that there are four primary components to cognitive complexity. These are: (1) an ability to mentally represent spatial and temporal relationships between objects, individuals, and events, (2) an ability to anticipate the consequences of particular actions, (3) an ability to compare and evaluate the results to the desired effect, and (4) an ability to apply information obtained in one context to successfully solve problems in a novel context (Visalberghi & Limongelli, 1996). Cognitive complexity involves the integration of these abilities in the nonrandom application of presolutions or context-appropriate strategies based on an understanding of the causal relationships between actions and consequences. An animal's ability to generalize and extend cause and effect relationships across diverse ecological and social contexts may be one measure of an advanced level of cognitive complexity (Tomasello & Call, 1997).

The Study of Primate Cognition

Studies of primate behavior and cognition have been conducted in two traditional research settings. These are (1) enriched captive environments and (2) natural field environments. Studies in captive settings have often focused on ontogenetic, neural, psychological, experiential, and motor influences on behavior and learning, whereas field studies have traditionally examined the manner in which these behaviors function within a natural ecological and social context (Janson, 1994; Snowdon, 1994). A third research setting, which we term a 'near-to-wild captive environment', has only occasionally been used in the study of primate behavior. Each of these three settings is best suited to address related but different sets of research questions.

We describe **enriched captive** settings as "laboratory environments that model the functional consequences of some of the features of the wild environment without directly duplicating them" (Novak et al., 1994; 238). Naturalistic environments are generally small in horizontal and vertical dimensions, but are designed to stimulate a range of behaviors that are commonly exhibited by a given species in the wild while maintaining experimental control over those variables required to directly test relevant behavioral hypotheses. The majority of studies on primate cognition, tool use, and foraging decisions have been conducted in such a setting.

Near-to-wild conditions offer a unique opportunity to study species in a more complex setting than traditional captive environments, while maintaining greater experimental control than is possible in the wild. One such setting discussed in this paper is the Rainforest Exhibit at Monkey Jungle, Goulds, Florida. This is a 1.6 ha forest enclosure containing hundreds of trees (originally described in DuMond, 1968). In this facility, permanently housed social groups of several primate species including brown capuchins (*Cebus apella*), Peruvian squirrel monkeys (*Saimiri sciureus*), and red howling monkeys (*Alouatta seniculus*) roam free. In near-to-wild conditions, problems associated with testing hypotheses in a large and environmentally complex setting are outweighed by the advantages of studying foraging and learning skills in the context of a more natural physical and social environment (Menzel, 1973; Menzel & Juno, 1982, 1985; Fragaszy & Adams-Curtis, 1991; Menzel, 1991).

Most studies of foraging behavior in nonhuman primates have been conducted in a **natural field setting**. Studying primates in the wild is critical in addressing evolutionary questions concerning the particular environmental conditions that are likely to have shaped the development of species-typical behaviors, the social and ecological contexts in which these behaviors are expressed, their fitness costs and fitness benefits, and how behavior varies in response to changing local conditions. Observations of animals in their natural habitat are essential for identifying the precise challenges a species faces in finding food, locating mates, and avoiding predators, and the set of successful solutions they have developed to meet these challenges. As noted by Janson (1994: 274), however, behavioral-ecological relationships identified in many natural field studies are "necessarily based on correlations, which can mask or confound true causal relationships." In a natural field setting, this is due to the absence of researcher control over the set of conditions that is generally required to distinguish dependent from independent variables and causation from correlation.

Recently, several researchers have successfully examined decision-making in wild primates using carefully designed experimental field studies (Garber & Dolins, 1996; Garber & Paciulli, 1997; Janson, 1996; Janson & Di Bitetti, 1997). In this setting, group members continue to exploit a complex social and ecological environment. However, the information available to the forager is systematically varied and controlled in order to test a series of behavioral and learning hypotheses. "Experimental field studies offer an opportunity to examine species differences in problem solving and perceptual skills, and to identify a set of adaptive challenges that have shaped the evolution of primate sensory systems" (Garber & Dolins, 1996:202).

In order to determine how frequently each of these research settings has been used to study primate cognition, foraging decisions, and feeding behavior, we surveyed all articles published over the past five years (1993–1997) in four major refereed journals. These journals are *The Journal of Comparative Psychology, Animal Behavior, American Journal of Primatology*, and *International Journal of Primatology*. In total, the journals contained 164 relevant articles. The majority of these studies were conducted either in enriched laboratory (52.4%) or natural field conditions (44.5%). Only 1.8% reported on research conducted in near-to-wild environments, and even fewer (1.2%) involved experimental studies in a natural field setting.

WHY STUDY COGNITION IN CAPUCHINS?

Our own work has focused on the problem-solving abilities of two species of capuchin monkeys, *Cebus apella* and *Cebus capucinus*. In this research we have addressed questions related to foraging behavior, tool use, problem-solving, and decision-making. The genus *Cebus* comprises 5 species of primates that range in adult body weight from 2–3.5 kg (Ford & Davis, 1992). Capuchins possess a pseudo-opposable thumb and represent the only group of New World monkeys that is capable of moving each digit independently (Costello & Fragaszy, 1988). Capuchins are characterized by slow life histories (Harvey & Clutton-Brock, 1985; Ross, 1988; Fedigan & Rose, 1995; Fragaszy & Bard, 1997) and have the largest relative brain size of any New World primate (Gibson, 1986, 1990). They are described as exhibiting the "fullest expression of platyrrhine cerebral complexity" (Hershkovitz, 1977: 364) and, for their body size, have brains larger than chimpanzees. Capuchins are among an extremely small number of nonhuman primate species reported to use tools in the wild (chimpanzees: Boesch & Boesch, 1990; orangutans: van Schaik & Sitompul, 1996; baboons: Beck, 1974; Japanese macaques: Tokida et al., 1994; capuchin monkeys: Chevalier-Skolnikoff, 1990).

Capuchins are best described as extractive foragers and expose concealed and embedded prey by breaking open pieces of dead wood, displacing stones and leaf litter, unrolling dead leaf curls, stripping away bark (Oppenheimer, 1968; Terborgh, 1983; Gibson, 1986), and using twigs and branches to probe under loose layers of tree bark (Chevalier-Skolnikoff, 1990) and in tree cavities (Garber per. obs.). They have also been observed cracking hard-shelled nuts or fruits with tough rinds by banging them against hard surfaces (Izawa & Mizuno, 1977; Struhsaker & Leland, 1977). Capuchins clearly possess the cognitive and manipulative skills required for tool-related exploratory behaviors (Parker & Gibson, 1977; Westergaard, 1995). In addition, *Cebus apella* and *Cebus capucinus* have been the focus of many captive studies of tool use, cognition, and learning (for a review see Visalberghi, 1990), natural field studies on feeding ecology and social behavior (Janson, 1985, 1988, 1990; Hall & Fedigan, 1997), and a small number of experimental field studies (Janson, 1996; Janson & Di Bitetti, 1997; Garber & Paciulli, 1997). This previous research provides the theoretical foundation upon which our study is based.

EXPERIMENTAL FIELD STUDY IN A NATURAL ENVIRONMENT

A series of experimental field studies was conducted on a group of 10–13 wild white-faced capuchins inhabiting an advanced, secondary, wet, tropical lowland rain forest in Northeastern Costa Rica. The field site is part of La Suerte Biological Research Station (10°26'N, 83°47'W). In addition to white-faced capuchins, mantled howling monkeys (*Alouatta palliata*) and black-handed spider monkeys (*Ateles geoffroyi*) inhabit the site. The capuchin study group has been the focus of previous field research (Garber & Paciulli 1997; Garber & Rehg, submitted), and was habituated to the presence of observers. Some members of our capuchin study group differed in body size, color markings, and the presence/absence of dependent young. However, it was difficult to reliably identify all or most individuals when they approached the experimental platforms. Therefore data on individual foraging decisions are not presented.

White-faced capuchins frequently forage in a dispersed fashion, with group members often separated by distances of 50–100 meters (Chapman & Fedigan, 1990; Phillips 1995). In large crowned trees many individuals forage simultaneously. In medium or small food patches, foraging party size is typically reduced to 1–3 freely locomoting individuals (Phillips, 1995). Troop integrity is maintained by using a varied repertoire of vocal signals to coordinate and change the direction of group movement and to signal the location of feeding sites (Boinski, 1993; Boinski & Campbell, 1995).

Experimental Design

We constructed two Feeding Stations located 30 meters apart within the home range of our capuchin study group. Feeding Station 1 consisted of seven visually identical platforms arranged in a circular configuration (Figure 1). Three of these seven platforms were each baited with two real bananas. The remaining four platforms each contained a sham reward (two plastic bananas). Feeding Station 2 consisted of six visually identical platforms similarly arranged in a circle. Two of these six platforms were baited with two real bananas each and the remaining four each contained a sham reward (two plastic bananas). Platforms measured 0.8 m^2 and were 1.5 meters in height. The distance between platforms was approximately three meters. In these experiments, Feeding Stations were analogous to the crowns of individual trees each with their own set of feeding sites, pattern of resource distribution, and rate of resource renewal. Feeding activities of the capuchins at a Feeding Station represented within-patch foraging decisions (which platform to visit). Decisions concerning which Feeding Station to visit represent between-patch foraging decisions.

The field experiments were designed to examine the ability of these primates to:

1. remember spatial information and use nearby landmark cues to predict the location of baited feeding sites and

2. solve foraging problems using temporal and spatial rules to locate baited (banana–reward) versus sham (plastic banana–no reward) feeding sites.

During each field experiment, the information available to the forager was controlled, allowing us to test a series of hypotheses regarding the use of spatial information, visual cues, olfactory cues, and foraging rules in selecting feeding sites. Feeding sites were baited at 5:00 am (AM test) and rebaited at 9:00 am (PM test). The capuchins visited the feeding stations during the AM and PM test sessions on each of the 52 days of the study. A visit was scored when a capuchin approached a platform at a distance of ≤ 1 meter and inspected it visually or manually, or sat on the platform and explored it for food. A Chi-square test was used to determine if the frequency of visits to baited platforms and sham platforms differed significantly from expected at a probability of <0.05.

Spatial Information

The first set of experiments was designed to examine the ability of white-faced capuchins to predict the location of baited (real banana) and sham (plastic banana) feeding platforms. The spatial positions of real and sham feeding sites were **constant** over the course of five days (place predictable), and then rotated (changed) on day one of the next test session. This new spatial arrangement remained constant over the course of several days, and then a second rotation was performed. This experiment offered an opportunity to examine the ability of white-faced capuchins to associate the location of a feeding platform with a food reward within a patch, and to test the degree to which spatial information was dominant to visual or olfactory information in selecting a potential feeding site.

The results of three 5-day experiments are presented in Table 1. In condition 1A, the capuchins were provided visual cues (bait not covered), olfactory cues (differences in smell between real and plastic bananas), and spatial information (positions of reward and sham platforms predictable) to locate real banana feeding Sites. On Day 1 of the experiment, the capuchins visited four sham and six real feeding sites (60% correct). Over the next four days of the experiment, the capuchins visited platforms 24 times; 23 of these were to reward platforms and only one visit was to a sham feeding site (96% correct; chance levels at 38.4%; For the 5 days of Experiment 1A: $X^2=19.7$, d.f.=1, p<.001).

In Condition 1B, platforms containing real and plastic bananas were rotated, and the experiment was repeated. If the capuchins were relying on visual or olfactory cues to locate real bananas, then we expected them to travel directly to food rewards placed in new locations. If, however, place or spatial information was the principal cue used to predict the location of baited and sham feeding sites, then we expected them to return to platforms that had previously contained bananas. As indicated in Table 1, on the morning of Day 1 of experiment 1B, the capuchins continued to select those platforms that had contained food rewards in the previous condition. During their initial visit, only four of the eight platforms searched (50%) contained real bananas. By the afternoon of Day 1, however, 80% of platforms searched contained real bananas, and over the remaining four days of this experiment, the capuchins visited reward platforms 90% of the time (For the five days of Experiment 1B: $X^2=21.7$, d.f.=1, p<.001).

We replicated this experiment one additional time. In Condition 1C, however, real and plastic bananas were hidden under large leaves to eliminate direct visual cues, and banana skins were placed alongside the plastic bananas to more closely equalize olfactory information. Place was again held constant, and therefore spatial cues were the only information available to the foragers to locate baited sites efficiently. On the morning of Day 1 the locations of real and sham bananas were rotated. As in Experiments 1A and 1B, the capuchins initially returned to platforms that previously had contained real bananas. During the morning trial of the first day, 5 of 10 platforms visited contained a food reward (50%). In the afternoon, the capuchins' success rate increased to 63%, and over the remaining 4 days of this condition, 77% of the platforms visited by the capuchins contained real bananas (For the 5 days experiment 1C: $X^2=18.8$, d.f.=1, p<.001; Table 1). The results of each experiment indicate that spatial information was more salient than visual and olfactory cues in selecting feeding sites, and that using spatial information alone (Condition 1C), the capuchins could relocate feeding sites at a level significantly greater than chance. In these sets of experiments the capuchins utilized a foraging rule that could be described as WIN-STAY and LOSE-SHIFT. In addition, the capuchins were observed to approach the Feeding Stations from a variety of different directions and to visit individual feeding platforms in different order. Thus, it is likely that they relied on allocentric spatial information (landmark cues) rather than egocentric spatial information (position of their body or physiological effort) in selecting feeding sites.

Experiment 2—Use of Local Landmark Cues

Experiment 1 provides evidence that the capuchins retained spatial information of the locations of 13 individual platforms distributed across two
Feeding Stations, and used this knowledge to make foraging decisions.
However, a question that remains unanswered is whether capuchins associate near-to-site landmarks or distant landmarks with the spatial position of
individual platforms. Although we were unable to test this question directly,
we did examine the ability of white-faced capuchins to use near-to-site
landmarks as associative cues in locating feeding sites. This was accomplished by presenting the foragers with a new set of conditions in which the
locations of real and sham bananas in the AM and PM trials were **random**,
banana skins were placed with plastic bananas to minimize differences in
odor cues, and both real and plastic bananas were covered with large leaves.
In the absence of spatial predictability, salient olfactory cues, and direct
visual sighting of the bananas, we introduced a near-to-site landmark cue
that could be used to predict the location of feeding sites. This cue was a
square 3 x 3 x 1/2 inch yellow block that was placed on individual platforms
only when they contained real bananas. The goal of this experiment was to
determine whether the capuchins would attend to these local cues and use
them in foraging decisions. In the wild, capuchins often forage for concealed
and embedded prey located in microhabitats such as dead wood, bromeliad
whorls, and curled leaves (Oppenheimer, 1968; Fedigan, 1990, 1993). It has
been suggested that decisions regarding which bromeliads to search and
which curled leaves to uncurl are likely influenced by near-to-site cues
which serve to increase foraging success (Garber & Paciulli, 1997).

Experiment 2 was conducted over the course of 12 consecutive days
and consisted of AM and PM trials. The results are presented in Figure 2.
The interpretation of these data is complicated by social factors such as
dominance and access to feeding sites which likely played an important role
in capuchin foraging decisions. Our observations clearly indicated that not
all capuchins arrived at the platforms at the same time, and the presence of
dominant individuals had a marked negative effect on whether subordinates would descend to the platforms to feed. Thus, individual group
members had different experiences and access to different information
concerning which platforms were likely to contain or not to contain food
rewards. Often, the first animals to visit a feeding station went directly to
yellow block/banana platforms, whereas individuals arriving later went
from platform to platform in search of food. In other cases, early arriving
animals waited in the vicinity of the platform but never descended to feed
and therefore had no opportunity to associate food rewards with the

presence of a local landmark (yellow block). An analysis of all capuchin visits to platforms failed to indicate that these near-to-site landmark cues were used by the capuchins to locate feeding sites ($X^2=1.58$, d.f.=1, p>.20).

These data were then reanalyzed using only the first 3 platforms visited at Station 1 and the first two platforms visited at Station 2. This was done because three of seven platforms at Station 1 contained real bananas and two of six platforms at Station 2 contained real bananas, and it appeared that certain capuchins consistently had priority access to reward platforms Analyzing the data this way, 55% of the platforms visited by the capuchins contained a food reward ($X^2=7.87$, d.f.=1, p<.01). This was significantly greater than chance (38.4%) and supports the contention that the first capuchins to visit the platforms relied on the yellow blocks as associative or near-to-site landmark cues to identify feeding sites. In addition, there was evidence of an initial period of trial and error learning. During the first 3 days of this experiment, the capuchins selected real banana platforms on 40.9% (9/22) of all searches (Figure 2). On Days 4-6 however, 58.6% of searches were successful. Overall, during the last nine days of this experiment the first capuchins to visit the platforms selected platforms containing yellow block/food rewards at a rate significantly above chance levels ($X^2=9.19$, d.f.=1, p<.01).

Using Rules of Time and Place

In the next experiment, we examined the ability of white-faced capuchins to apply a set of foraging 'rules' to solve problems associated with spatial and temporal changes in resource predictability. This involved manipulating patterns of **resource renewal**. During the AM baiting session, platforms containing real and sham bananas were assigned **randomly** (place not predictable), banana skins were placed with the plastic bananas to minimize differences in olfactory cues, and visual cues of the plastic or real bananas were eliminated by covering all platforms with large leaves. In the PM baiting session the same conditions were in place, except that positions of real and sham bananas were **predictable** according to the following rule. If a platform had real bananas in the AM it would have plastic bananas in the PM, whereas if a platform had sham bananas in the AM it would have real bananas in the PM. This experiment presented a set of conditions in which spatial-temporal information obtained each morning could be used to predict the location of food rewards in the afternoon, and is analogous to natural situations in which monitoring rates of resource renewal can play an important role in foraging success (e.g. when to return to flowers that have replenished their nectar supply). Solving this resource problem would require a WIN-SHIFT and LOSE-RETURN foraging pattern. This represents a different set of behavioral rules associated with space and time than those required to locate resources in the previous experiments.

In Experiment 3, only Feeding Station 2 was baited using this experimental protocol. An examination of the data indicate that over the 15-day experimental period, there was no significant difference in the ability of the capuchins to locate baited sites during morning and afternoon trials. In both instances the percentage of correct responses did not deviate from chance levels (AM trial–X^2=2.94, d.f.=1 p>05; PM trial–X^2=2.29, d.f.= 1, p>.10). Given that three of six platforms contained real bananas, as in the previous experiment we also analyzed only the first three platform visits. By reanalyzing the data in this way, it became apparent that by day 4 of this field experiment, the first animals to visit feeding platforms were applying a Win-Shift and Lose-Return foraging rule to locate baited feeding sites in the afternoon.

(Figure 3). The frequency of correct responses in the PM trials went from 44% during days 1–3 to 79% during days 4–15 (PM trial–X^2=5.8, d.f.=1, p<.05). However, in the absence of information available from which to predict the location of real and sham sites in AM trials, capuchin performance during days 4–15 did not deviate from chance levels (AM trial–X^2=0.12, d.f.=1, p>.50; 54% correct). Given that the first set of individuals to visit the platforms solved this foraging problem over the course of only three days, it is likely that a Win-Shift and Lost-Return foraging rule was already part of the capuchin behavioral repertoire and was applied successfully in this new feeding context.

Dominance appeared to play a critical role in capuchin foraging strategies. Previous studies of white-faced capuchins (Hall and Fedigan, 1997: 1069), indicate that dominant and subordinate group members adopt different spatial positions within the group and that "subordinates avoid dominant animals as a strategy to reduce contest competition" at feeding sites. In the present study, certain capuchins had priority access to the feeding platforms, whereas other individuals only visited platforms after the dominant animals had already fed or had left the immediate area. There were several cases in which subordinate white-faced capuchins adopted a behavioral strategy of always going to a particular platform while dominant animals were visiting other platforms. Such a pattern, for example, was common for one female capuchin carrying a very young infant. She consistently traveled directly to the same platform during both AM and PM trials. Such a tactic may be analogous to a form of scramble competition in which moving directly to a platform not occupied by others was a successful feeding strategy. The pattern used by this female resulted in obtaining a food reward in approximately 50% of trials. Two other adult females carrying dependent young relied on a similar tactic, and by doing so made it difficult for dominant animals to monopolize food available on all platforms. It is likely, that decisions regarding which platforms to visit are influenced both by social dominance and differences in resource information available to individual group members.

Although the natural field experiments described above highlight the importance of the social environment in capuchin foraging success, they do not examine the degree to which capuchins learn by observing the successful behaviors of others (social learning). Several authors have argued (e.g., Visalberghi & Fragaszy, 1990; Visalberghi, 1993; Visalberghi, et al. 1995) that capuchins do not use conspecifics as models but rely exclusively on trial and error experimentation and knowledge obtained first-hand to solve foraging problems (but see Visalberghi & Fragazy, 1995). We examined this and related issues in an experimental study of extractive foraging and problem solving using tools in captive brown capuchins (*Cebus apella*) in a near-to-wild 1.6 ha forest environment in south Florida's Monkey Jungle Zoological Park. This environmentally and socially complex setting offered the opportunity to examine evidence of the transmission of tool-use information between easily identifiable individuals habituated to the presence of human observers. We also compared the ability of naive vs. experienced tool users to solve foraging problems that required the use of tools.

Tool Use in Captive Capuchins

The results of several laboratory studies have revealed that captive brown capuchins are highly motivated to use tools in the solution of a variety of task-oriented feeding problems (Costello & Fragaszy, 1988; Visalberghi, 1990). Captive capuchins spontaneously use stones to crack nuts (Anderson, 1990), sticks to dig or probe for otherwise inaccessible food rewards (Westergaard & Fragaszy, 1987), and paper towels as sponges to soak up juice (Westergaard & Fragaszy, 1987; Westergaard, 1995). However, their capacity to comprehend tool-task cause and effect relationships has remained the subject of intense debate. Some researchers have argued that, although capuchins use tools to expedite extractive foraging, they fail to recognize the precise properties of a particular tool that make its use effective and context-appropriate (Visalberghi et al.,

1995; Visalberghi & Limongelli, 1996). In this regard, it has been suggested that tool use among captive capuchins is the cognitive equivalent of waving a "magic wand" (i.e., capuchins learn to associate success with a particular behavior or motor pattern without understanding how or why they are successful; Visalberghi & Limongelli, 1994, 1996; Visalberghi et al., 1995), and best interpreted as an artifact of exploratory behavior under laboratory conditions (McGrew, 1993; but see Westergaard & Fragaszy, 1987; Westergaard & Suomi, 1995; Westergaard et al., 1997). However, the fact that under certain ecological conditions wild capuchins do, on occasion, use tools suggesti an advantage associated with analyzing a complex foraging problem and applying an appropriate tool-related solution (it remains uncertain, however, whether all, most, or even more than one individual in a wild group uses tools). Experimental studies that replicate those settings in which the ecological advantages of tool use are high, may provide important insight into cognitive complexity, patterns of learning and patterns of information transmission within a social group.

Experimental Study of Capuchin Tool Use and Problem-Solving

Monkey Jungle Zoological Park provided ideal near-to-wild conditions in which to test questions concerning problem solving and tool use. Test subjects included a group of 11 semi-free ranging brown capuchins (*Cebus apella*), four of which had been involved in a tool use study in a laboratory environment several years earlier (Westergaard & Fragaszy, 1987; Fragaszy & Adams-Curtis, 1991). The remaining seven individuals were considered naive in terms of their experience using tools. The animals were permanent residents of the facility and free to range throughout this forested enclosure.

Research Protocol

The subjects were presented with a feeding device formed from the stump of a recently cut tree. Ten 6.5 cm deep holes were drilled into the stump. Six of these holes were 1.2 cm in diameter and four were 0.8 cm in diameter. During each experimental trial, the holes were filled with honey as a food reward. Access to the honey required the use of tools as probes. Although tools were not provided to the capuchins, they had the opportunity to select natural materials of their own choice and design from a wide variety of sticks, stems, and stones available within their forest enclosure. Wild capuchins are confronted with analogous foraging problems and have been observed using sticks as probes (Chevalier-Skolnikoff, 1990; Garber, pers. obs.) in an attempt to extract food items.

All occurrences of capuchin tool selection, modification, and use were recorded using a focal animal time sampling technique. Each time sample or trial was 15-minutes in duration. The first capuchin to indicate interest by touching the apparatus was designated the focal animal for that particular trial. Thirty-two trials were scored for each focal animal. The percentages of time engaged in probing behaviors and the use of appropriate and inappropriate tools were calculated for each individual.

Results

Three of the 11 capuchins were observed to use natural probes during extractive foraging and consistently selected and modified objects suitable to the particular tool task (Figure 4a,b,c, and d). These included two adult males and one adult female. Tool use was attempted in 22–31 of the possible 32 feeding trials (Table 2). The capuchins used an average 5.7–9.2 tools per trial. On some occasions, effective tools became frayed or broken and were discarded in favor of new tools. On other occasions tools that appeared to function successfully were abandoned for no identifiable reason.

Between 93% and 96% of time spent using tools involved successful probing (Table 3). Approximately 98% of the manufactured or modified tools and 86% of the unmodified tools used by the capuchins were physically appropriate to the task; these tools were of an appropriate shape, size, and flexibility to serve as successful probes. Use of unmodified tools outnumbered modified tools 2.5 to one, and probably reflected the fact that a large number of natural objects in the vicinity of the feeding device were suitable tools. Manufactured tools were produced by detaching fragments from a larger source or subtracting detrimental components from potentially suitable materials (see Beck, 1980). All observed modification strategies appeared to increase the effectiveness of the tool and were therefore interpreted as successful methods of tool manufacture. Our observations are consistent with the assumption that tool use in these capuchins involved an ability to anticipate the consequences of modifying natural objects, compare and evaluate the results to the desired effect, and mentally represent appropriate object characteristics such as tool shape, size, and rigidity. Moreover, the capuchins were able to discriminate appropriate from inappropriate tool materials among the countless objects available within their forest enclosure.

A second experiment tested the capuchins' ability to select tool materials from distant sources. To insure that tools were not immediately available in the vicinity of the feeding device, the apparatus was placed on a bridge over a small ravine. In this experiment, natural objects that could be used as tools were located a few meters below the bridge and at a distance of greater than 5 m. from the bridge. In order to gain access to the honey, the monkeys were required to transport tools from sources that were out of sight of the feeding device. Under these conditions, capuchin foraging success was dependent on the ability to mentally represent the requirements of an out-of sight task, and to select an effective probe from a broad range of potential materials. Two of the three tool-using capuchins were successful at this task. These two capuchins typically chose materials from bushes growing beneath the bridge, and then carried them to the apparatus where final modifications were made. Successful probes were selected 81% of the time.

Discussion

Tomasello & Call (1997: 383) argue that primate cognitive development is noteworthy "not [in] the way they understand and categorize objects, events, and social partners in the environment directly, but rather [in] the ways they understand and categorize how outside objects, events, and social partners relate to one another." An ability to understand tertiary relationships should enable a primate forager to effectively apply cause and effect relationships learned in one context to solve problems in a novel context, as well as to exploit the experience of conspecifics as models of new behaviors with minimal trial-and-error experimentation.

In this paper, we present the results of a series of experimental field studies and near-to-wild captive studies designed to examine the kinds of information white-faced capuchins (*Cebus capucinus*) and brown capuchins (*Cebus apella*) use to locate resources and acquire hidden or embedded foods. These studies have enabled us to identify the degree to which foraging rules used in one ecological context are reapplied to successfully obtain food in other ecological contexts. Our results indicate that wild white-faced capuchins use spatial and temporal information to generate a broad set of foraging rules. These include WIN-RETURN, LOSE-SHIFT, WIN-SHIFT, LOSE-RETURN, as well as the use of nearby associative cues for spatial orientation. Moreover, the patterns of error generated by the capuchins in Experiment 1A, B, and C indicate that individuals form learning sets (Harlow 1949) in which spatial information was more salient than visual and olfactory information in selecting feeding sites. Similarly, platform selections by the capuchins during the first few days of Experiments two and three were indicative of WIN-STAY and LOSE-SHIFT foraging rules. Over time, however, other 'rules' were applied to more efficiently predict the location of reward feeding sites. We argue that the foraging problems presented to the capuchins in these field experiments were ecologically relevant to the kinds of problems they commonly encounter in the wild, and that problem-solving skills used by the capuchins represent a natural ability to store, categorize, and integrate complex cognitive information.

Similarly, three of four captive brown capuchins who had previous tool-using experience in an enriched laboratory setting (Westergaard & Fragaszy, 1987; Fragaszy & Curtis-Adams, 1991), were found to spontaneously use and modify natural objects as tools to solve experimental foraging problems in a near-to-wild setting. Successful probing was observed among all three capuchins during their first set of trials. Given the rapid rate at which these capuchins recognized task requirements and used tools to acquire the food reward, it is likely that these primates applied their previous tool using experience to this new problem-oriented foraging task. Each of these three tool-using capuchins were captive-born and had previous experience in tasks requiring the use of hammers, sponges, probes, and containers (Fragaszy pers. com.). It should be noted, however, that an effective solution in the present experimental setting required both the selection and the modification of natural objects appropriate to the task. This leads us to suggest that these capuchins were guided by an ability to match certain conditions and/or cause and effect relationships of the present task to experiences obtained in previous tool-using experiments, even when those tasks were conducted in different settings, were of different design, and separated in time over a period of several years. The capuchins accomplished this even when the feeding device was out-of-sight.

None of the seven naive capuchins (naive in the sense that we have no evidence that they used tools prior to the experiment) exhibited successful tool-using behaviors under the present experimental conditions. These capuchins failed to pattern their behavior according to successful conspecific 'models' in order to obtain the food reward. It is possible that brown capuchins require personal experience via trial-and-error learning in order to fully understand cause and effect relationships required to solve tool-assisted extractive foraging problems. However, it appears that once an individual has gained such experience, it can generalize and reapply rules or principles learned in one context to solve related problems in novel contexts.

The Effect of the Social Setting on Learning, Foraging, and Problem Solving

In the wild, feeding success among brown capuchins is determined by dominance, with high-ranking group members frequently controlling access to preferred resources (Janson, 1985, 1990, 1996). Social dominance and aggression also were major factors determining individual access to the feeding platforms and feeding device in our experimental studies. Rather than attracting other adult group members, dominant animals rarely tolerated the presence of low-ranking adult capuchins at the experimental feeding sites. We never observed more than one white-faced capuchin on a platform at the same time, or two adult male brown capuchins at the feeding device. Tool-using performance or efficiency was similarly affected by dominance status. The highest ranking male typically worked slowly and methodically when probing for honey, and was consistently more successful across trials than any other individual in obtaining the food reward. In contrast, lower ranking individuals appeared anxious when at the device, were easily distracted as if anticipating displacement, and were less successful in obtaining honey across trials. Thus, access to the feeding device, frequency of tool use, and overall efficiency in extracting resources were influenced by dominance status.

The dominant male, however, often tolerated the presence of juveniles near the feeding device, and these young animals were observed to handle probes discarded by successful adult tool-users. On a few occasions, juveniles would bang or roll these tools across the surface of the device. On another occasion, a young juvenile sitting in front of the device held the end of a stick while the dominant male was using it to probe for honey. Although it is doubtful that this male intended to "teach" the inexperienced capuchin how to use tools, social tolerance may foster the acquisition of such behavior by drawing attention to the tools themselves as well as the contexts in which tool use techniques are applied (Fragaszy & Visalberghi, 1990,1995). In this way, some social relationships may contribute to the development of tool use in young animals.

In group-living animals, locally developed behavioral patterns (i.e., traditions) emerge and are maintained through processes of social learning (Galef, 1995). The acquisition of information through some form of social learning has been suggested to represent a fundamentally different cognitive process than that typically associated with individual learning (Fragaszy & Visalberghi, 1990; but see Heyes, 1994 for a different interpretation). Individual learning often requires repeated exposure to the same problem and a process of trial-and-error experimentation in order to develop an effective solution. Although many individuals within a group may solve the problem in the same way, as suggested by Tomasello and Call (1997: 276) in this type of learning, "each individual [has] reinvented the wheel for itself." In contrast, social learning involves an ability to recognize and associate another's success with a specific motor or behavioral pattern (see Table 4 for a description of the modes of social learning). However, the observer may not necessarily understand the causal relationship between the behavior and the solution of the task (i.e., the principles underlying success; Fragaszy & Visalberghi, 1990; Heyes, 1993; Tomasello and Call, 1997). Under these circumstances, the initial behavior of the observer is expected to be stereotypic and only successful in a limited number of contexts. Since the observer may not initially understand how the elements of the behavioral pattern relate to one another, and how each contributes to the solution of the specific problem, it is limited in its ability to generalize solutions across a range of similar tasks (Tomasello, 1990). A second form of observational learning involves an ability to understand cause and effect relationships of successful behaviors modeled by a conspecific (imitation learning). This is called imitative learning. Imitation is thought to represent a special or cognitively complex form of learning and "is considered to reflect symbolic mental processes because it generates behaviour from mental images created by observation, without direct experience" (Russon, 1997:178). The degree to which imitation is a component of the learning behavior of nonhuman primates remains unclear. Whiten & Ham (1992) reviewed evidence for imitation in nonhuman primates. They conclude that the few examples of imitation in prosimians and monkeys are best explained through simpler learning processes such as priming and ego-based learning (there is evidence of imitative learning in human reared apes; Tomasello and Call, 1997). Similarly, Visalberghi & Limongelli (1996) argue that capuchin monkeys do not learn tool-use techniques by imitation even after repeated exposure to conspecifics that solve tool-task problems. In both our captive and field experiments, there was no evidence that capuchins learned cause and effect problem-solving relationships by imitating the successful behavior of others. Rather, the results support the contention that, although capuchins are keenly aware of, pay attention to, and modify their behavior according to the actions of other group members (i.e., social enhancement and observational learning), foraging problems are solved primarily by individual learning and trial and error experimentation.

As we expand our understanding of primate cognition, it is clear that experimental field studies in conjunction with more traditional field and laboratory research offer highly productive approaches to examining questions of social and individual learning, rule-based foraging, tool use, and the evolution of problem solving behaviors. A next step in addressing issues of problem-solving and learning in wild capuchins is to design experimental field studies that explore the social factors influencing the acquisition of tool use, and to test hypotheses concerning the ecological advantages and fitness benefits associated with such behaviors.

ACKNOWLEDGMENTS

We wish to thank Dr. Francine Dolins for commenting on an earlier draft of this manuscript. Assistance in the field was provided by Lisa Paciulli. Dr. Siân Evans provided logistical support and encouragement during the tool use project at Monkey Jungle. P.A.G. wishes to acknowledge Sara and Jenni for their insight into similarities in cognition and problem-solving capabilities in capuchins and humans.

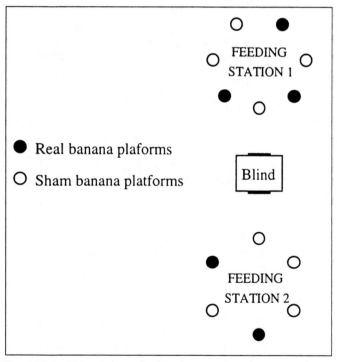

Figure 1–Schematic representation of the position and distribution of feeding platforms and Feeding Stations used in all field experiments on Cebus capucinus in Costa Rica. This figure was reprinted from Garber and Paciulli (1997) with the permission of the authors.

Experiment 2. Local Landmark Cues

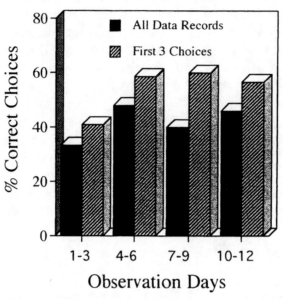

Figure 2–Experiment 2 was designed to test the ability of wild white-faced capuchins to use a local landmark cue (yellow block) to identify baited feeding sites. Data are presented as % correct platform choices over the course of four 3-day intervals. See text for additional details.

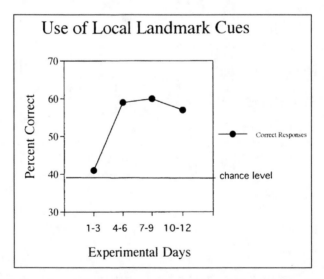

Figure 3–Experiment 3 was designed to test the ability of wild white-faced capuchins to use spatial and temporal information to predict the location of baited feeding platforms. In AM trials place was random. In the PM trials the capuchins used a WIN-SHIFT and LOSE-RETURN foraging rule to locate the bait. Data are presented as % correct platform choices across five 3-day intervals. See text for additional details.

4a–Feeding device used in all of the brown capuchin tool using experiments. Note holes in tree stump. Depth of holes precluded monkeys from obtaining the food reward using their hands or feet, and required the use of a tool.

4b and 4c–A sequence of photographs showing an adult male brown capuchin using a tool to extract honey from the feeding device.

Table 1
Use of Spatial Information in Capuchin Foraging Decisions

Experiment	% Correct Day 1	% Correct Days 2–5	% Correct for Entire Experiment
1A	60	96	85
(N)	6/10	23/24	29/34
1B	62	90	82
(N)	8/13	28/31	36/44
1C	55	77	71
(N)	10/18	34/44	44/62

Table 2
Tool Using Behavior in Cebus apella

Subject	Trials[A]	No. Tools Used	% Time Using Tools[B]
Willie	29	215 (7.4)	38
Erna	22	203 (9.2)	27
Paul	31	179 (5.7)	27

[A] – Number of trials (out of possible 32 trials) during which subject used tools.
[B] – Percentage of time during each 15 minute trial in which tools were used by the subject.
Values in parentheses indicate mean number of tools used per trial.

Table 3
Successful Tool Use and Manufacture in Cebus apella

Subject	% Time Engaged in Successful Probing[A]	% of Unmodified Tools that were Successful[B]	% of Modified Tools that were Successful[C]
Willie	96	93 (N=164/176)	100 (N=39/39)
Erna	94	82 (N=132/161)	95 (N=40/42)
Paul	93	68 (N=80/117)	98 (N=61/62)

[A] – Percentage of total tool use time engaged in successful probing.
[B] – Percentage of unmodified tools that were used successfully to probe for honey.
[C] – Percentage of modified tools that were used successfully to probe for honey.

Table 4
Modes of Social Learning

Social Enhancement	Observational Learning	Imitation
the presence and activity of the model influences the behavior of the observer (e.g., social facilitation and stimulus enhancement)	copying a motor pattern demonstrated by a model while independently learning the rules that make the behavior successful (e.g., mimicking)	gaining some understanding of causal relationships related to novel problem-solving through observation alone (e.g. learning the rules by observing the behavior)

REFERENCES

Anderson, J. R. (1990). Use of objects as hammers to open nuts by capuchin monkeys. *Folia Primatologica, 54,* 138–145.

Beck, B. B. (1974). Baboons, chimpanzees, and Tools. *Journal of Human Evolution, 3,* 509–516.

Beck, B. B. (1980). *Animal Tool Behavior: The Use and Manufacture of Tools by Animals.* New York: Garland STPM Press.

Boesch, C. & Boesch, H. (1990). Tool use and tool-making in wild chimpanzees. *Folia Primatologica, 54,* 86–99.

Boinski, S. (1993). Vocal coordination of group movement among white-faced capuchin monkeys, *Cebus capucinus. American Journal of Primatology, 30,* 85–100.

Boinski, S., & A. F. Campbell. (1995). Use of trill vocalizations to coordinate troop movement among white-faced capuchins: a second field test. *Behaviour, 132,* 875–901.

Chapman, C. A., & L. M. Fedigan. (1990). Dietary differences between neighboring *Cebus capucinus* groups: local traditions, food availability, or responses to food profitability. *Folia Primatologica, 54,* 177–186.

Chevalier-Skolnikiff, S. (1990). Tool use by wild *Cebus* monkeys at Santa Rosa National Park, Costa Rica. *Primates, 31,* 375–383.

Costello, M. B. & Fragaszy, D. M. (1988). Prehension in *Cebus* and *Saimiri:* grip type and hand preference. *American Journal of Primatology, 15,* 235–245.

Dolins, F. L. (1993). *Spatial relational learning and foraging in cotton-top tamarins. Ph.D. thesis.* University of Stirling, Scotland.

DuMond, F. V. (1968). The squirrel monkey in a seminatural environment. In L. A. Rosenblum & R. W. Cooper (Eds.), *The Squirrel Monkey* (pp. 88–145) New York: Academic Press.

Dyer, F. C. (1994). Spatial cognition and navigation in insects. In L. A. Real, (Ed.), *Behavioral Mechanisms in Evolutionary Ecology*, (pp. 66–98). Chicago: University of Chicago Press.

Fedigan, L. M. (1990). Vertebrate predation in *Cebus capucinus*: meat-eating in a Neotropical monkey. *Folia Primatologica, 54*, 196–205.

Fedigan, L. M. (1993). Sex differences and intersexual relations in adult white-faced capuchins, *Cebus capucinus. International Journal of Primatology, 14,* 853–877.

Fedigan, L. M. & Rose, L. M. (1995). Interbirth intervals in three sympatyric species of Neotropical monkey. *American Journal of Primatology,* 37: 9–24.

Ford, S. M & Davis, L. C. (1992) Systematics and body size: implications for feeding adaptations in New World monkeys. *American Journal of Physical Anthropology, 88,* 415–468.

Fragaszy, D. M. (1986). Time budgets and foraging behavior in wedge-capped capuchins (Cebus olivaceus): age and sex differences. In D. M. Taub & F. A. King (Eds.), *Current Perspectives in Primate Social Dynamics* (pp.159–174). New York: Van Nostrand Reinhold Company.

Fragaszy, D. M. & Adams-Curtis, L. E. (1991). Environmental challenges in groups of capuchins. In H. O. Box (Ed.), *Primate Responses to Environmental Change* (pp.239–264). New York: Chapman & Hall.

Fragaszy, D. M. & Bard, K. A. (1997). Comparison of development and life history in Pan and Cebus. *International Journal of Primatology, 18,* 683–701.

Fragaszy, D. M. & Visalberghi, E. (1990). Social processes affecting the appearance of innovative behaviors in capuchin monkeys. *Folia Primatologica, 54,* 155–165.

Galef, B. G. (1995). Why patterns that animals learn socially are locally adaptive. *Animal Behavior, 49,* 1325–1334.

Gallistel, C. R. (1990). *The Organization of Learning.* Cambridge, MA, Bradford Books/MIT Press.

Garber, P. A. (1989). The role of spatial memory in primate foraging patterns: *Saguinus mystax* and *Saguinus fuscicollis. American Journal of Primatology, 19,* 203–206.

Garber, P. A. (1993). Seasonal patterns of diet and ranging in two species of tamarin monkeys: stability versus variability. *International Journal of Primatology, 14,* 145–166.

Garber, P. A. & Dolins, F. L. (1996). Testing learning paradigms in the field: evidence for the use of spatial and perceptual information and rule-based foraging in wild moustached tamarins. In M. A. Norconk, A. L. Rosenberger, & P. A. Garber (Eds.), *Adaptive Radiations of Neotropical Primates* (pp. 210–216). New York: Plenum Press.

Garber, P. A. & Paciulli L. (1997). Experimental field study of spatial memory and learning wild capuchin monkeys *(Cebus capucinus)*. *Folia Primatologica, 68,* 236–253.

Garber, P. A. & Rehg, J. A. (submitted) Tails from the canopy: positional behavior in white-faced capuchins *(Cebus capucinus)*. *American Journal of Physical Anthropology.*

Gibson, K. R. (1986). Cognition, brain size, and extraction of embedded food. In J. G. Else & P. C. Lee (Eds.), *Primate Ontogeny, Cognition, and Social Behavior* (pp. 93–104). Cambridge: Cambridge University Press.

Gibson, K. R. 1990. New perspectives on instincts and intelligence: brain size and the emergence of hierarchical mental constructional skills. In S. T. Parker & K. R. Gibson Eds). *Language and Intelligence in Monkeys and Apes,* (pp. 97–128).Cambridge: Cambridge University Press.

Hall, C. L. & Fedigan L. M. (1997). Spatial benefits afforded by high rank in white-faced capuchins. *Animal Behavior, 53,* 1069–1082.

Harlow, H. F. (1949). The formation of learning sets. *Psychology Review, 56,* 51–65.

Harvey, P. H. & Clutton–Brock, T. (1985). Life history variation in primates. *Evolution, 39,* 559–581.

Hershkovitz, P. 1977. *Living New World Platyrrhines. Volume 1.* Chicago: University of Chicago Press.

Heyes, C. M. (1993). Imitation, culture and cognition. *Animal Behavior, 46,* 999–1010.

Heyes, C. M (1994). Social learning in animals: categories and mechanisms. *Biological Reviews 69,* 207–231.

Izawa, K. & Mizuno, A. (1977). Palm-fruit cracking of wild black-capped capuchin *(Cebus apella)*. *Primates, 18,* 773–792.

Janson, C. H. (1985). Aggressive competition and individual food consumption in wild brown capuchin monkeys *(Cebus apella)*. *Behavioral Ecology and Sociobiology, 18,* 125–138.

Janson, C. H. (1988). Intra-specific food competition and primate social structure: a synthesis. *Behaviour, 105,* 1–16.

Janson C. H. (1990). Ecological consequences of individual spatial choice in foraging groups of brown capuchin monkeys *Cebus apella. Animal Behavior, 40,* 922–934.

Janson, C. H. (1994). Naturalistic environments in captivity: a methodological bridge between field and laboratory studies in primates. In: E. F. Gibbons, Jr., E. J. Wyers, E. Waters, and E. W. Menzel, Jr. (Eds.), *Naturalistic Environments in Captivity for Animal Behavior Research,* (pp. 271–279), Albany, NY: State University of New York Press.

Janson, C. H. (1996). Toward an experimental socioecology of primates. In M. A. Norconk, A. L. Rosenberger, & P. A. Garber (Eds.), *Adaptive Radiations of Neotropical Primates,* (pp. 309–325). New York: Plenum Press.

Janson, C. H. & M. S. Di Bitetti. (1997). Experimental analysis of food detection in capuchin monkeys: effects of distance, travel speed, and resource size. *Behavioral Ecology and Sociobiology, 41,* 17–24.

Kamil, A. C. (1994). A synthetic approach to the study of animal intelligence. In L. A. Real (Ed.), *Behavioural Mechanisms in Evolutionary Ecology,* (pp. 11–45). Chicago: University of Chicago Press.

Krechevsky, I. A. (1932). "Hypotheses" versus "chance" in the presolutional period in sensory discrimination-learning. *University of California Publications in Psychology, 6,* 27–44.

McGrew, W. C. (1993). The intelligent use of tools: Twenty propositions. In K. R. Gibson & T. Ingold (Eds.), *Tools, Language, and Cognition in Human Evolution* (pp. 151–170). Cambridge: Cambridge University Press.

Menzel C. R. (1991). Cognitive aspects of foraging in Japanese monkeys. *Animal Behavior, 41,* 397–402.

Menzel, C. R. & Juno, C. (1985). Social foraging in marmoset monkeys and the question of intelligence. *Philosophical Transactions of the Royal Society of London, B308,* 145–157.

Menzel, E. W. (1973). Chimpanzee spatial memory. *Science, 182,* 943–945.

Menzel, E. W. & Juno, C. (1982). Marmosets (*Saguinus fuscicollis*): are learning sets learned? *Science 217,* 750–752.

Novack, M. A., O'Neil, P., Beckley, S. A. & S. J. Suomi (1994). Naturalistic environments for captive primates. In: E. F. Gibbons, Jr., E. J. Wyers, E. Waters, & E. W. Menzel (Eds.), *Naturalistic Environments in Captivity for Animal Behavior Research,* (pp. 236–258), Albany, NY: State University of New York Press.

Oppenheimer, J. R. (1968). *Behavior and ecology of the white-faced monkey, Cebus capucinus, on Barro Colorado Island.* Ph.D. dissertation, University of Illinois, Urbana.

Parker, S. T. & Gibson, K. R. (1977). Object manipulation, tool use, and sensorimotor intelligence as feeding adaptations in cebus monkeys and great apes. *Journal of Human Evolution, 6,* 623–641.

Phillips, K. A. (1995). Resource patch size and flexible foraging in white-faced capuchins *(Cebus capucinus). International Journal of Primatology, 16,* 509–519.

Real, L. A. (1992). Information processing and the evolutionary ecology of cognitive architecture. *American Naturalist, 140 (suppl.),* 108–145.

Ross, C. (1988). The intrinsic rate of natural increase and reproductive effort in primates. *Journal of Zoology, 214,* 199–219.

Russon, A. E. (1997). Exploiting the expertise of others. In: A. Whiten & R. W. Byrne (Eds.), Machiavellian Intelligence II: Extensions and Evaluations, (pp. 174–206), Cambridge: Cambridge University Press.

Schaik, van C. P. & Sitompul, A. (1996). Manufacture and use of tools in wild Sumatran orangutans. Naturwissenschaften, 83, 186–188.

Snowdon, C. T. (1994). The significance of naturalistic environments for primate behavioral research. In: E.F. Gibbons, Jr., E. J. Wyers, E. Waters, & E. W. Menzel, Jr. (Eds.), *Naturalistic Environments in Captivity for Animal Behavior Research,* (pp. 217–235). Albany, NY: State University of New York Press.

Struhsaker, T. T. & Leland, L. (1977). Palm-nut smashing by *Cebus a. apella* in Colombia. *Biotropica, 9,* 124–126.

Terborgh, J. (1983). *Five New World Primates: A Study in Comparative Ecology.* Princeton: Princeton University Press.

Tokida, E., Tanaka, I., Takefushi, H., & Hagiwara, T. (1994). Tool-using in Japanese macaques: use of stones to obtain fruit from a pipe. *Animal Behavior, 47,* 1023–1030.

Tomasello, M. (1990). Cultural transmission in the tool use and communicatory signaling of chimpanzees? In S. T. Parker & K. R. Gibson (Eds.), *Language and Intelligence in Monkeys and Apes* (pp. 274–311). Cambridge: Cambridge University Press.

Tomasello, M. & Call, J. (1997). *Primate Cognition.* Oxford: Oxford University Press.

Visalberghi, E. (1990). Tool use in *Cebus. Folia Primatologica, 54,* 146–154.

Visalberghi, E. (1993). Capuchin monkeys: a window into tool use in apes and humans. In K. R. Gibson & T. Ingold (Eds.), *Tools, Language, and Cognition in Human Evolution* (pp.138–150). Cambridge: Cambridge University Press.

Visalberghi, E. & Fragaszy, D. M. (1990). Do monkeys ape? In S. T. Parker and K. R. Gibson (Eds.), *"Language" and Intelligence in Monkeys and Apes* (pp. 247–273). Cambridge: Cambridge University Press.

Visalberghi, E. & Fragaszy, D. M. (1995). The behavior of capuchin monkeys, *Cebus apella,* with novel food: the role of social context. *Animal Behavior,* 49, 1089–1095.

Visalberghi, E., Fragaszy, D. M., & Savage-Rumbaugh, S. (1995). Performance in a tool-using task by common chimpanzees *(Pan troglodytes),* bonobos *(Pan paniscus),* an orangutan *(Pongo pygmaeus),* and capuchin monkeys *(Cebus apella). Journal of Comparative Psychology,* 109, 52–60.

Visalberghi, E. & Limongelli, L. (1994). Lack of comprehension of cause-effect relations in tool-using capuchin monkeys *(Cebus apella). Journal of Comparative Psychology, 108,* 1–8.

Visalberghi, E. & Limongelli, L. (1996). Acting and understanding: Tool use revisited through the minds of capuchin monkeys. In A. E. Russon, K. A. Bard, & S. T. Parker (Eds.), *Reaching Into Thought. The Minds of the Great Apes* (pp. 57–79). Cambridge: Cambridge University Press.

Westergaard, G. C. (1995). The stone tool technology of capuchin monkeys: Possible implications for the evolution of symbolic communication in hominids. *World Archaeology, 27,* 1–9.

Westergaard, G. C. & Fragaszy, D. M. (1987). The manufacture and use of tools by capuchin monkeys (Cebus apella). *Journal of Comparative Psychology, 101,* 159–168.

Westergaard, G. C., Lundquist, A. L., Kuhn, H. E., and Suomi, S. J. (1997). Ant-gathering with tools by captive tufted capuchins *(C. apella). International Journal of Primatology,* XX, 95–103.

Westergaard, G. C. & Suomi, S. J. *(1995).* The production and use of digging tools by monkeys: a nonhuman primate model of a hominid subsistence activity. *Journal of Anthropological Research, 51,* 1–8.

Whiten, A. & Ham, R. (1992). On the nature and evolution of imitation in the animal kingdom: reappraisal of a century of research. In: P. J. B. Slater, J. S. Rosenbatt, C. Beer, & S. Milinski (Eds), *Advances in the Study of Behavior,* Vol. 21 (pp. 239–283). New York: Academic Press.

8

Infant Killing as an Evolutionary Strategy: Reality or Myth?

Robert W. Sussman, James M. Cheverud, and Thad Q. Bartlett

The students nodded. They had all studied animal behavior, and they knew, for example, that when a new male took over a lion pride, the first thing he did was kill all the cubs. The reason was apparently genetic: the male had evolved to disseminate his genes as widely as possible, and by killing the cubs he brought all the females into heat, so that he could impregnate them.

(Michael Crichton, Jurassic Park)

Infanticide (as seen in lions) also occurs in the entellus langur (Presbytis entellus). Marauding bands of nomadic males raid a troop, drive off the resident males, kill all the juveniles, and quickly mate with the females.

(The Oxford Companion to Animal Behavior)

Among many primate biologists, infant killing by conspecific males is thought of as an evolutionary strategy giving adaptive advantage to the infanticidal male.[1,2] In fact, as can be seen from the above, the use of the sexual selection hypothesis to explain infanticide has become a widespread, almost mythological belief, even in the popular literature. The theory is as follows. An infanticidal male gains reproductive advantage by selectively killing the unweaned offspring of his male rival. In addition to the relative gain in genetic representation, the infanticidal act terminates lactational amenorrhea, shortening the interbirth interval of the infant-deprived female. This ensures the earliest possible opportunity for the infanticidal male to mate with and inseminate the infant-deprived female. Theoretically, the most likely context for this to occur is during male takeover in species with one male groups.

Recently, this theory has been expanded to include seasonally breeding species, such as the ring-tailed lemur (*Lemur catta*), in which the infanticidal male cannot immediately mate with the dead infant's mother. If a male's infant is the subject of infanticide, he is unlikely to be chosen again as a mate in subsequent years (he becomes an "incompetent father").[3,4] Thus, females select infanticidal males to father their offspring.

There are two major problems with the sexual selection explanation for infant killing among primates. The first involves the data; the second the theory itself.

THE DATA

Recently, we examined the literature to determine precisely how many cases of infant killing actually have been observed by primate researchers. Further, we examined the context of these incidences of infanticide.[5] We found that there were only 48 cases in which the death of the infant was observed. These cases occurred in thirteen species of primate, and almost half of the killings (21) were done by Hanuman langurs. More than half of the langur deaths occurred at one Indian site, Jodhpur.[6]

One might argue that predation also is rarely observed and yet it is an important cause of death among primates. But the numbers are not comparable. First, the database for predation is quite broad relative to that for infanticide.[7,8] A review of the literature reveals a large number of observed cases,[9] even though documenting predation is very difficult.[10] Second, primatologists rely on studies of very small prey populations (e.g., one or two primate groups) rather than studies on predators. Field studies of predators indicate that primates are important prey items for many species.[8,11,12] Finally, primates display typical antipredator defense behaviors outlined by Endler.[13] Yet no such mechanisms exist to deter infanticidal attacks by males. A fixed action pattern towards specific predators is quite different from males associating with infants, females protecting their infants from strange males, or monogamy. In fact, Sommer notes that mothers sometimes "allowed even infanticidal males to come so close to their infants that a sudden jump would have been sufficient to grasp the hopping infant from the ground or from the mother's breast."[14]

A second, even more serious problem with the data is the fact that the context rarely fits the pattern predicted for sexual selection. In only eight of the 48 cases was the infanticidal male observed mating with the mother. In two of these, the male was the most likely father of the infant that he killed! Only six cases involved direct attacks on independent infants, and in an additional three cases a mother-infant pair was the subject of direct repeated attacks. The majority of infant deaths occurred during general aggressive episodes. There is evidence among Hanuman langurs in particular,[15] that in these situations infants often place themselves into danger by their own actions (e.g., clinging to their mother during attacks, or being attracted to action and excitement). Thus, of the 48 cases, only 12.5% fit the requirements of the sexual selection hypothesis. In 87.5% of observed infant killings, the context is not compatible with this hypothesis.

There appears to be no underlying consistent context in which infanticide takes place, such as group take over. The circumstances surrounding infant deaths are highly variable and the use of a single term, with all its implications, to refer to the numerous phenomena involved in infant killing misrepresents the complexity of primate social behavior.

THE THEORY

The fundamental assumption of the sexual selection hypothesis concerns the genetic basis for infant killing behavior. Although the inheritance of the "infanticidal trait"[16-18] is crucial for the operation of the sexual selection model, there is no evidence supporting its genetic inheritance. Are the sons of infant-killing males more likely to be infant killers themselves because of genes they inherit from their fathers?

In addition to the lack of data on genetic inheritance, selection for infant killing has never been demonstrated. Selection can be measured by quantifying the covariance between the character and relative fitness in a population that includes infanticidal males.[19-21] Relative fitness is the relative intrinsic rate of increase of the individual compared to that of the population as a whole. When lifetime relative fitness is unavailable, its time specific components can be analyzed, with the caveat that the selection measure may be counteracted at other life stages. What is the increase in relative fitness associated with infanticide behavior?

Selection for infant killing, if it exists at all, is likely to be weak. First, variance in infant killing is low because it is a rare event[5] and low variance limits the covariance of the trait with relative fitness. Second, the only indication of fitness differences we have are a few cases of small decreases in interbirth intervals for females who lost infants relative to those who did not.[14] However, a large proportion of infants die within the first months of life regardless of infant-killing males.[22-24] Some of these infants would have died anyway. The shortening of the interbirth interval due to infant killing needs to be discounted by the underlying death rate so that selection is much weaker than indicated by interbirth interval differences reported in the literature. Furthermore, differences of a few months in the timing of offspring born to infant killers compared to non-killing males who take over a group will only have a slight effect on relative lifetime intrinsic rate of increase. In fact, the necessity of using year-long age intervals in primate demography makes the likely effect smaller than measurable error. It is important to remember that the fitness increase due to infant killing would only be the slightly earlier production of offspring, since the benefits of controlling a breeding group would also accrue to non-killing males.

Even given a slight increase in fitness for infant-killing males, this increase could well be due to selection on other, correlated traits.[25] We must avoid considering individual traits as independent evolutionary entities rather than parts of integrated character complexes. Differences in fitness associated with infant killing may actually be due to direct selection on other functionally related characters such as overall aggression.[25,26] If there is direct selection on aggressiveness, and aggression and infant killing are correlated, infant-killing males may have the same or lower fitness than nonkillers. In this instance, infant killing would increase as a correlated response to selection for increased overall aggressiveness not due to independent adaptation.

Most witnessed cases of infant killing appear to be simply genetically inconsequential epiphenomena of aggressive episodes. At this stage, there is little evidence to suggest that infant killing is anything but a rare and evolutionary trivial phenomenon. No evidence of genetic inheritance or direct selection for the trait has been provided, just non-quantitative plausibility arguments based on anecdotes. Until more specific evidence is available, the concept that infanticide in nonhuman primates is a widespread, adaptive behavior must be approached with appropriate caution. The burden of proof remains, as it always has, with those who favor the sexual selection hypothesis.

It is both important and enjoyable to formulate scientific hypotheses, and it is not difficult to fit them into an evolutionary framework. However, this in itself is not science. Good science begins when one collects the relevant data needed to test these hypotheses. Hypotheses that are untestable or that cannot be disproved are not useful to science. As we have indicated, there are a number of ways the sexual selection hypothesis can be tested, and we urge those interested in these questions to collect the necessary data. An infant killing or disappearance does not in itself support the hypothesis of selection and selection does not cause cases of infanticide. Selection is the relationship between relative fitness and a character caused by environmental factors, and these factors, fitness, and the character itself must be measured to determine whether or not infant killing is an evolutionary strategy.

ENDNOTES

1. Hardy SB. (1977). Infanticide as an evolutionary strategy. Am Sci 65:40–40.

2. Hausfater G, Hardy SB (eds) (1984). *Infanticide: comparative and Evolutionary Perspectives*. New York: Aldine.

3. Pereira ME, Weiss ML (1991). Female mate choice, male migration, and the threat of infanticide in ringtailed lemurs. Behav Biol Sociobiol 18:141–152.

4. Kappeler PM (1993). Sexual selection and lemur social systems. In Kappeler PM, Ganzhorn JU (eds) *Lemur Social Systems and Their Ecological Basis*, pp. 223–240. New York: Plenum.

5. Bartlett TQ, Sussman RW, Cheverud JM (1993). Infant killing in primates: a review of observed cases with specific reference to the sexual selection hypothesis. Am Anthropol 95:958–990.

6. Sommer V (1994). Infanticide among the langurs of Jodhpur: Testing the Sexual selection hypothesis with a long–term record. In Parmigiani S, vom Saal F (eds) *Infanticide and Parental Care*, pp 155–198. London: Harwood Academic Publishers.

7. Anderson CM (1986). Predation and primate evolution. Primates 27:15–39.

8. Hart DL (in prep). *Primates as Prey: Ecological, Morphological, and Behavioral Interrelations Between Primates and Their Prey*. Ph.D. Thesis, Washington University, St. Louis.

9. Sussman RW, Hart DL, Rehg J (in prep). Predation on primates: a review of observed cases.

10. Isbell LA (1994). Predation on primates: Ecological patterns and evolutionary consequences. Evol Anthropol 3:61–71.

11. Rettig NL (1978). Breeding and behavior of the harpy eagle (*Harpia harpyja*). Auk 95:629–643.

12. Goodman SM, O'Connor S, Langrand O (1993). A review of predation on Lemurs: implications for the evolution of social behavior in small, nocturnal primates. In Kappeler PM, Ganzhorn JU (eds) *Lemur Social Systems and Their Ecological Basis,* pp. 51–66. New York: Plenum.

13. Endler JA (1991). Interactions between predators and prey. In Krebs JR, Davies NB (eds) *Behavioural Ecology,* pp. 169–196. London: Blackwell Scientific.

14. Sommer V (1987). Infanticide among free-ranging langurs (Presbytis entellus) at Jodhpur (Rajasthan/India): Recent observations and a reconsideration of hypotheses. Primates 28:163–197.

15. Dolhinow PP (in press). A mystery: Explaining behavior. In Strum SC, Lindburg DG, Hamburg DA (eds) *The New Physical Anthropology.*

16. Hardy SB (1979). Infanticide among animals: A review, classification, and examination of the implications for the reproductive strategies of females. Ethol Sociobiol 1:13–40.

17. Hardy SB (1984). Assumptions and evidence regarding the sexual selection hypothesis: a reply to Boggess. In Hausfater G, Hrdy SB (eds) *Infanticide: Comparative and Evolutionary Perspectives,* pp. 315–319. New York: Aldine.

18. Newton PN (1988). The variable social organization of Hanuman langurs (*Presbytis entellus*). Infanticide and the monopolization of females. Int J Primatol 9:59–77.

19. Arnold S, Wade M (1984). On the measurement of natural selection: Theory. Evolution 38:709–719.

20. Phillips P, Arnold S (1989). Visualizing multivariate selection. Evolution 43:1209–1222.

21. Schluter D (1988). Estimating the form of natural selection of a quantitative trait. Evolution 45:849–861.

22. Sade DS, Cushing K, Cushing P, Dunaif J, Figueroa A, Kaplan J, Laner C, Roades D, Schneider J (1976). Population dynamics in relation to social structure on Cayo Santiago. Yrbk Phys Anthropol 20:253–262.

23. Jaquish C, Gage T, Tardif S (1991). Reproductive factors affecting survivorship in captive Callitrichidae. Am J Phys Anthropol 84:291–306.

24. Sussman RW (1991). Demography and social organization of free-ranging *Lemur catta* in the Beza Mahafaly Reserve, Madagascar. Am J Phys Anthropol 84:43–58.

25. Lange R, Arnold S (1983). The measurement of selection on correlated characters. Evolution 37:1210–1226.

26. Moore A (1990). The evolution of sexual dimorphism by sexual selection: The separate effects of intrasexual selection and intersexual selection. Evolution *44*:315–331.

9

INFANTICIDE: LET'S NOT THROW OUT THE BABY WITH THE BATH WATER

SARAH BLAFFER HRDY, CHARLES JANSON, AND CAREL VAN SCHAIK

As originally defined by Darwin[1] sexual selection refers to a struggle between members of one sex for access to the other with the result for the unsuccessful competitor being not death, but few or no offspring. The sexual selection hypothesis for infanticide proposes that a male increases his reproductive success by killing unrelated infants if the infant's death makes the female return to receptivity sooner than would otherwise have been the case and if it does not decrease his likelihood of subsequently mating with her. Sussman et al.[2] first dispute the observational evidence for this hypothesis. Second, they argue that no genetic basis for infanticide has been demonstrated. Last, they assert that the proposed genetic benefits to infanticidal males are not sufficient to be subject to selection. Instead, they argue that infant deaths are incidental byproducts of generalized aggressions.

Before we address Sussman et al.'s objections, let's be clear on where we agree. First, we agree that the sexual selection hypothesis is perhaps too readily invoked in both the popular and scientific literature. In the first general review of infanticide in animals[3] the first sentence of the abstract reads: "Infanticide among animals is a widespread phenomenon with no unitary explanation." Five explanatory hypotheses for infanticide, each generating a different set of predictions concerning who would kill whom when, were laid out. The possibility that infanticide would occasionally occur as an unsolicited by product of inter-group aggression or other social conflict was one of those five possibilities (see Table 1). If Sussman et al. wish to argue that not every case of infanticide in nature is due to sexual selection, or even natural selection, who disagrees?

Secondly, we concur that we need more field data, and that larger sample sizes as well as experimental data collected under controlled conditions as exist for rodents[4] are scientifically—if not always ethically—desirable.

THE OBSERVATIONAL EVIDENCE

Now for the disagreements. In an effort to underscore how limited the evidence for infanticide is, Sussman et al.[2] point out that half of all 48 (their tally) published cases of observed infanticide come from just a single species, *Presbytis entellus,* and that half of these all come from a single site, Johdpur—the implication being that infanticide is not so widespread after all, and may largely be peculiar to some langur populations. However, this representation is misleading. First, what counts are rates of infanticide. Without information on how many animals were monitored and for how long, it is meaningless to say more killings were witnessed at one study site than another. Roughly 1,000 langurs were studied at Jodhpur, over 18 years (1969–1987), by more than ten full-time doctoral or post-doctoral observers working together with local assistants in the largest scale project ever undertaken for any colobine. Second, infanticide is very widespread, having now been observed in conditions predicated by the hypothesis in species of five of the six primate radiations (the exception being tarsiers), in both captive and field conditions. Infanticidal attempts can predictably be provoked by removing a group's resident male(s). Reported differences in rates of infanticide are found at least in part because species and populations vary in how often they meet the conditions in which male infanticide is likely.[5] Indeed, this variation could be put to use in future comparative tests of the sexual selection hypothesis.

Sussman et al.[2] compare the evidence for infanticide with that for predation, another rare behavior, for which, they argue, the evidence is much better. However, we would ague that, if one uses the same standards of evidence, infanticide is, if anything, better documented than predation on wild primates. Forty-eight observed cases of infanticide is far greater than the number of witnessed cases of predation upon primates that made it into the professional literature. Most published estimates of predation rates for primate populations are inferred (sudden disappearance of healthy animals, cries in the night, bones under a nest, monkey hairs in a scat).[6,7] For example, in her landmark study of relative effects of predation and resource competition on the social systems of vervet monkeys, Isbell[7] did not witness a single predation event even though the disappearance rate for females and juveniles was 65%, and the rate of predation was estimated at 45%.

Despite the paucity of direct observations, it is widely accepted (and Sussman et al. concur) that predation has been an important selection pressure on primates who have accordingly evolved anti-predator strategies that range from careful selection of sleeping locations and avoidance of dangerous habitats to vigilance, predator-specific alarm calls and sometimes cooperative defense.[6] Arguing from the larger samples of observed infanticides, we note that there is a range of male, female, and even infant behaviors that only begin to make sense when we assume that infanticide, like predation, is a recurring threat, even if the actual events are rarely witnessed. These include adult males who closely associate with the infants they have sired,[8] females with unweaned infants holding back in encounters with strange males or avoiding the boundaries of ranges altogether,[8,9] mothers who attempt to abandon their infants in the company of familiar ousted males rather than take infants with them back to a troop with an interloper in it, transformations of laissez-faire mothers into obsessively restrictive ones in the presence of strange males, mothers avoiding and even attacking such interlopers,[10] female migrations into groups coinciding with lowest vulnerability to infanticide.[11] These examples suggest to us that behavioral counter-strategies against infanticide are common and successful, and help account for its infrequent occurrence in many species. Sussman et al. contest these behavioral observations by citing cases such as some langur females, who, under extreme pressure from an infanticidal male, abandon or cease to defend an infant. Instead we view such cases as analogous with the well-documented Bruce effect in rodents, whereby a female mouse exposed to an alien male spontaneously resorts the fetus; such females cut their losses by ceasing to invest on behalf of an infant almost certain to be killed.

THE GENETIC BASIS

So far the criticism has focused on the quality and quantity of the evidence for infanticide in wild primates. Sussman et al.[2] also argue that for the sexual selection hypothesis to make sense infanticidal tendencies must have some genetic basis, and that we know virtually nothing about this in primates. Indeed, the genetic basis for almost any behavioral trait in primates is unknown. However, experimental studies on infanticidal behavior in small-bodied, short-lived, and fast-breeding rodents[12] provide strong evidence that genes are involved.

Among rodents marked differences exist in tendencies to commit infanticide that vary between wild-caught and lab-bred strains.[13,14] Even in strains known to be highly infanticidal, researchers find pronounced intra- as well as inter-strain differences in probability that a male or female in a given test situation will kill an infant.[12,14] Hence a male mouse belonging to the highly inbred C57B1/6KJ strain in which individuals are almost genetically identical, introduced at the age of 65 days to a pup, responds infanticidally 70% of the time compared to 25% of the time in the case of males from another strain (e.g., DBA/2J). However, even in the extremely infanticidal lines, infanticidal behavior is still facultatively expressed according to circumstances. In a male mouse social status (e.g., dominant versus subordinate), reproductive status, as well as seemingly random developmental factors such as intrauterine position, can be critical.[15] Interestingly, exposure to testosterone in utero appears to have a sensitizing effect on the neural area mediating infanticide,[15] suggesting, as some of us have long suspected, that although some infant killing may well result as an incidental byproduct of aggressive thrashing about as Sussman et al. argue, the kind of goal-directed infanticidal behavior being described[10,16,17] may best be understood as a separate motivational system from aggression.

As in primates, a male mouse's response towards infants is very context-specific, changing predictably from benevolent, soon after ejaculating with a given female, to infanticidal after the number of light/dark cycles needed to wean the pups has elapsed.[12] While the mechanisms may not be exactly similar in primates, the wealth of evidence from rodents underscores the presence and variability of genetic and other mechanisms underlying infanticide in a group that is more amenable to experimental manipulation. Sussman et al.[2] ignore these experimental results, while deploring the absence of similar rigor among wild primates. Although it would be scientifically very satisfying to have similar data for primates, various constraints (time, money, and ethical concerns) will probably dictate that advances in this area will continue to come from non-primates.

THE RESOLUTION OF SELECTION

As their final exhibit in the case against sexually selected infanticide, Sussman et al.[2] claim that no selection on infanticide has been demonstrated, and "if it exists at all, is likely to be weak."[18] True, selection on the infant-killing phenotype has never been measured. The selection gradient, commonly used to predict evolutionary change in a trait, can be estimated as the regression of the relative fitness of individuals on their trait values within a population.[19] In practice, there is a major hurdle, because its estimation requires complete behavior records over a male's adult life as well as estimated lifetime reproductive success. No primate data set even comes close to producing these data. Sussman et al. considered this demonstration important because they felt that infanticide is "but a rare and evolutionary trivial phenomenon."[18] However, their assertion that selection on infanticidal behavior must be weak because infanticide is rare flied in the face of abundant evidence for strong selection on rare alleles. Furthermore, for some primate species infanticide is neither rare nor inconsequential.

The question is, will the average adult male ever have the opportunity to commit infanticide during his lifetime? Among Jodhpur langurs, one third of infants born are killed by males invading the breeding unit from outside it.[16] Similarly, 14% of infant mountain gorillas are killed by males[20] as are 12% of red howler infants.[21] While the relative mortality risk due to infanticide may be lower in many other species and populations, such numbers indicate that males successful in gaining access to females will have multiple opportunities for infanticide, and that selection could therefore act on infanticidal behavior. These percentages are quite comparable to those of other mammals in which infanticide is common and in which the evidence that it is a significant selection pressure is overwhelming, such as lions[22] (27% of all cub deaths in first year due to infanticide) and prairie dogs[23] (39% of litters partly or totally killed). In lions, DNA fingerprinting reveals that all cubs born in a pride are sired by the resident,[24] so there can be little doubt that the reproductive benefits of infanticide accrue to the infanticidal males. These studies complement the primate studies, and demonstrate that the perpetrators of infanticide can derive significant fitness benefits from it.

Infanticide may be a common cause of mortality, but if natural infant mortality is high or reduction in inter-birth intervals is modest, benefits to infanticidal males will be diluted. However, among mammals, primates are characterized by slow life histories and relatively low infant mortality rates. Sussman et al.[2] claim that the only indication of fitness differences we have are small decreases in interbirth intervals for females who lost infants relative to those who did not. They arrive at this conclusion largely on the basis of the Jodhpur results.[16] However, because of provisioning, the Jodhpur langurs have the shortest interbirth interval of which the species is capable, virtually identical to captive animals fed ad lib. By contrast, in wild red howlers, females that lose their infants to observed and inferred infanticide have interbirth intervals 37% shorter than other females.[21] Because of the typically short breeding tenure of males in most infanticidal primate species, even a small reduction in interbirth interval increases the likelihood that a new male will sire offspring before he is ousted, or his progeny are old enough to escape infanticide by the next male. Additional advantages may accrue, as an infanticidal male eliminates offspring sired by rivals as well as future competitors.

ARE THERE PLAUSIBLE ALTERNATIVES?

The alternative proposed by Sussman et al.[2] is that "most cases of infant killing appear to be simply inconsequential epiphenomena of aggressive episodes." This implies that there has been no selection for any increased tendency for males to eliminate unrelated infants. No doubt, infanticide might once have occurred as a byproduct of males encountering unfamiliar females and some infanticides may still be explained as incidental aggression. However, the deliberate targeting and stalking of infants belonging to unfamiliar females,[10,16,17,22] the widespread occurrence of the male takeover/infanticide pattern, as well as the experimental data on the timing of infanticide in relation to ejaculation in rodents, imply selection for specific response. Hence, in various rodents, the act of ejaculation with a female partner (spontaneous ejaculation does not suffice) provides a male mouse with a neural failsafe system for timing when it is safe versus possibly genetically suicidal to destroy pups that he encounters.[15] Such calibrations simply do not strike us as the stuff that "genetically inconsequential epiphenomena" are made of.

CONCLUSION

Where infanticide is a major source of mortality, there is very reason to expect it to affect parental behavior and even social systems. Regardless of the functional significance, infanticide is likely in certain circumstances and if a particular behavior minimized their occurrence, we expect selection to favor the behavior. But can such selection actually shape primate social systems?[8] The idea remains controversial for primates, but consider data for the dung beetle *Nichophorus orbiocollis*.[25] After preparing a dung ball, parents deposit the eggs. Guarding by both biological parents dramatically reduces the probability that conspecifics will usurp the resource, kill the newly hatched brood and produce a replacement clutch. Such data strongly suggest that infanticide selects for bi-parental care in this species.

The continuing debate over infanticide among primates reflects two different world views, both of them defendable. Consider the following summation from Bartlett et al.:[18] "Clearly, proponents of the sexual selection hypothesis accept the fact that there is variation in takeover events, yet they maintain that there is an underlying consistency—infant killing follows group takeover. Yet, while this may be true in general terms for many cases (emphasis ours) the use of a single term to refer to the numerous phenomena described above misrepresents the complexity of primate social behavior. . .". Precisely. While some are interested in emphasizing the uniqueness of each case—a valid position—others are driven by the need to seek for general patterns and to use theory to explain them. For the former it is an insult to the sanctity of the individual and the sacredness of context that generalizations should extend beyond the specifics of the case in hand. The latter drive their greatest pleasure from noting that so many findings could have been correctly predicted on the basis of pitifully incomplete datasets merely by relying on logic, comparisons, and extrapolations guided by evolutionary theory.

ENDNOTES

1. Darwin C (1871). *The Descent of Man, and Selection in Relation to Sex.* London: John Murray.

2. Sussman RW, Cheverud JM, Bartlett TQ (1955). Infant killing as an evolutionary strategy. Evol Anthropol 3:149–151.

3. Hrdy SB (1979). Infanticide among animals: a review, classification, and examination of the implications for the reproductive strategies of females. Ethol Sociobiol 1:13–40.

4. Parmigiani S, vom Saal F (1994). *Infanticide and Parental Care.* London: Harwood Academic Publishers.

5. Newton PN (1986). Infanticide in an undisturbed forest population of manuman langurs, *Presbytis entellus.* Anim Behav 34:785–789. For effects of male replacement, see Sugiyama Y (1965). On the social change of Manuman langurs (*Presbytis entellus*) in their natural conditions. Primates 6:213–217. See also Washburn S, Hamburg D (1968). Aggressive behavior in Old World monkeys and apes. In Jay P (ed). Primates. New York: Holt, Rinehart, & Winston.

6. Cheney D L, Wrangham R W (1987). Predation. In Smuts, B, Chaney D, Sefarth R, Wrangham RW, Struhsaker TT (eds). *Primate Societies,* pp. 227–239. Chicago: University of Chicago Press.

7. Isbell L (1990). Sudden short-term increase in mortality of vervet monkeys (*Cercopithecus aethiops*) due to leopard predation in Amboseli National Park, Kenya. Am J Primatol 21:41–52.

8. van Schaik CP, Dunbar RIM (1990). The evolution of monogamy in large primates: a new hypothesis and some crucial tests. Behavior 115:30–62.

9. Goodall J (1986). *The Chimpanzees of Gombe: Patterns of Behavior.* Cambridge: Harvard University Press.

10. Hrdy SB (1977). *The Langurs of Abu: Female and Male Strategies of Reproduction.* Cambridge: Harvard University Press.

11. Sterck EHM (submitted). Determinants of females transfer in Thomas' langurs.

12. Perrigo G, vom Saal F (1994). Behavioral cycles and the neural timing of infanticide and parental behavior in male house in ice. In Parmigiani S, vom Saal F (eds). *Infanticide and Parental Care,* pp. 365–396. London: Harwood Academic Publishers.

13. Jakubowski M, Terkel J (1982). Infanticide and caretaking in non-lactating *Mus musculus*: Influence of genotype, family group and sex. Amin Behav *30*:1029–1035.

14. Svare B, Broida J, Kinsley C, Mann M (1984). Psychobiological determinants underlying infanticide in mice. In Hausfater G, Hrdy SB (eds). *Infanticide: Comparative and Evolutionary Perspectives.* New York: Aldine, pp. 387–400. See also Elwood R, Kennedy HF (1994). Selective allocation of parental and infanticidal responses in rodents: A review of mechanism. In Parmigiani S, vom Saal F (eds). *Infanticide and Parental Care.* Switzerland: Harwood, pp. 397–426.

15. vom Saal F (1984). Proximate and ultimate causes of parental behavior in male house mice. In Hausfater G, Hrdy SB (eds). *Infanticide: Comparative and Evolutionary Perspectives,* pp. 401–424. new York: Aldine

16. Sommer V (1994). Infanticide among the langurs of Jodhpur. Testing the sexual selection hypothesis with a long-term record. In Parmigiani S, vom Saal F (eds). *Infanticide and Parental Care,* pp. 155–198. London: Harwood Academic Publishers.

17. Leland L, Struhsaker TT, Butynski T (1984). Infanticide by adult males in three primate species of Kibale Forest, Uganda. In Hausfater G, Hrdy SB (eds). *Infanticide: Comparative and Evolutionary Perspectives.* New York: Aldine, pp. 151–172

18. Bartlett TQ, Sussman RW, Cheverud JM (1933). Infant killing in primates: a review of observed cases with specific reference to the sexual selection hypothesis. Am Anthropologist *95*:958–990.

19. Arnold SJ, Wade MJ (1984). On the measurement of natural and sexual selection: applications. Evolution *38*:720–734.

20. Watts DP (1989). Infanticide in mountain gorillas. New cases and a reconsideration of the evidence. Ethology *81*:1–18.

21. Crockett CM, Sekulic R (1984). Infanticide in red howler monkeys (*Alouatta seniculus*). In Hausfater, G., Hrdy, S. B. (eds). *Infanticide: Comparative and Evolutionary Perspectives*. New York: Aldine.

22. Pusey AE, Packer C (1994). Infanticide in lions: Consequences and counter strategies. In Parmigiani, S., vom Saal, F. (eds). *Infanticide and Parental Care*, pp. 277–300. London: Harwood Academic Publishers.

23. Hoogland JL (1994). Nepotism and infanticide among prairie dogs. In Parmigiani S, vom Saal F (eds). *Infanticide and Parental Care*, pp. 321–377. London: Harwood Academic Publishers.

24. Gilbert D, Packer C, Pusey AE, Stephen's JC, O'Brien SJ (1991). Analytical DNA fingerprinting in lions: parentage, genetic diversity, and kinship. J Hered 82:378–386.

25. Scott MP (1990). Brood guarding and the evolution of male parental care in burying beetles. Behav Ecol Sociobiol 26:31–39.

26. Hrdy SB, Hausfater G (1984). Comparative and evolutionary perspectives on infanticide: Introduction and overview. In Hausfater G, Hrdy SB (eds). *Infanticide: Comparative and Evolutionary Perspectives*, pp. xiii–xxxv. New York: Aldine.

10

THE PULSE THAT PRODUCED US

ELISABETH S. VRBA

*Two major global coolings may have prodded
antelopes and humans to evolve*

Earth's crust and atmosphere change constantly, and wedged in between
them like a sandwich filling, life revolves as well. To what extent are
extinction and speciation—the evolution of new species out of ancestral
populations—tied to geophysical changes? Did humans originate in response to some identifiable cosmic or climatic event?

Charles Darwin, in an 1838 notebook, noted that "man is a species
produced like any other—lawfully." To learn more about our own origins,
I have looked for evolutionary patterns in other organisms that lived at the
dawn of humanity. Antelopes are good animals to examine for clues because they are reliable indicators of past environments and shared the
African savanna with our early ancestors, the australopithecines, or man-
apes. Conveniently, antelopes make up 60 to 80 percent of all large mammal fossils found in the same strata as hominids, the family of primates that
includes australopithecines and humans.

About twenty years ago, as a South African paleontologist studying the
Transvaal's limestone caves, I first noticed that somewhere in the fossil deposits
between 2.5 million and 2 million years ago, antelopes and other animals
changed strikingly. Anatomical features such as teeth indicated that antelopes
living before 2.5 million years ago had occupied moist woodlands. Shortly
afterwards, however, these forest antelopes disappeared and were replaced by
many new species that graze only in dry, open savannas.

But because the Transvaal cave strata were jumbles of washed-in bones,
the sequence was not reliable and had to be dated by being compared with

deposits elsewhere. Some years later, in East Africa, other researchers found similar fossils in deposits that could be dated by radiometric techniques. Several independent studies have since confirmed that the same kind of faunal change that took place in South Africa also occurred in Ethiopia, Kenya, and Tanzania close to 2.5 million years ago.

Such a dramatic change in large fauna, and by inference in vegetation, is one line of evidence that southern Africa became significantly drier about 2.5 million years ago. I wondered if this was a purely local phenomenon and whether the change was slow or rapid. A 1980s study of deep-sea cores near Greenland by Nick Shackleton, of Cambridge University, contributed some answers. Shackleton discovered abundant evidence for an extensive arctic glaciation dated close to 2.5 million years ago.

During that period, global temperatures may have plummeted by as much as 10° to 20° F, and the world became colder than at any time in the past 65 million years. The continents became much more arid, and the steppes advanced toward the equator. The earliest fossils of Oryx, the most arid-adapted antelopes of all, appeared along with other grazers of open savannas, such as the giant buffaloes *Pelorovis* and giant hartebeests *Megalotragus*. These species soon extended their ranges from southern and eastern Africa toward the equator where we find fossils testimony of their presence. Steppe and grassland horses, *Equus*, from Europe moved east into India and Pakistan. They also migrated south into Africa, together with Asian forms like the Indian black buck, *Antelope cervicapra*, but while the horses evolved into several varieties of zebras, the Asian antelopes did not last long in Africa.

A similar, earlier cooling also seemed to affect all of sub-Saharan Africa about 5 million years ago, close to the Miocene-Pliocene boundary. Climatologist John Mercer and James Kennett and paleoanthropologist C. K. Brain have documented marked swings in the global climate at that time, with wide-spread continental cooling and the lowering and retreat of oceans. We also know that the Mediterranean dried up, leaving massive salt deposits, and that thousands of miles of savannas opened up at the expense of forest on several continents. This earlier cooling also produced waves of extinctions and radiations of species, giving rise to the seven major groups of antelopes that still dominate the African savannas today. Within these groups, however, many species went extinct at the later cooling 2.5 million years ago.

How did our primate ancestors fare during these climatic changes in South Africa? About 5 million years ago, the first proliferation of antelope species coincided with the occurrence of the first australopithecines in East Africa—perhaps their first appearance on the planet. Before that time, large primates were apish forest dwellers that shared their leafy refuges with ancestral antelopes. In between the 5-million-year-old deposits and those 2.5 million years old, the only known hominids are the lightly built australopithecines, five-foot-tall, bipedal primates with ape-sized brains and upright posture. After 2.5 million years ago, however, we see evidence of an explosive radiation among hominids. Apparently several different species appeared; paleoanthropologists are still arguing about how many. Clark Howell, of the University of California at Berkeley, for instance, thinks there were five or six. Among them were the large, vegetarian man-ape *Paranthropus* and various members of the human genus, *Homo*—who thrived with the further spread of dry grasslands and the continued shrinking of forest habitats. Other evidence of new kinds of hominids include the first-known robust australopithecines fossil, the Black Skull, found by Richard Leakey and Alan Walker near Kenya's Lake Turkana and the oldest-known fragment of a *Homo* species, from Lake Beringo, Kenya, dated by Andrew Hill's group at Yale to 2.5 million years ago.

The archeological record of artifacts offers additional corroboration of dramatic change. Stone tools from Ethiopia—the earliest yet discovered—date to between 2.4 and 2.6 million years ago. Using tools to obtain and prepare food was an important innovation for hominids and indicates increased brain size and function.

The British ecologist Evelyn Hutchinson once referred to the "evolutionary theater and ecological play." Halfway through the hominid play that began 5 million years ago, something happened that pushed most of the old cast members (including the small-bodied australopithecines) off the stage and introduced new ones (such as *Homo* species)—a process I call turnover-pulse. I believe that when we better understand the events at the Miocene-Pliocene boundary, we will find that the appearance of the australopithecines was only one part of a global turnover of species, one of the recurrent pulses in the history of life.

New species of primates, antelopes, birds, and carnivores may all have originated in response to several successive cooling plunges during the later Miocene. Many African lineages survived the climatic changes intact, but those that underwent extinctions and speciations appear to have done so in concert with others: plants, hominoids, antelopes, rodents, and such marine invertebrates as snails and foraminifera. All the evidence, as I see it, indicates that the lineage of upright primates known as australopithecines, the first hominids, was one of the founding groups of the great African savanna biota.

My hypothesis that the same climatic pulses dramatically stimulated both antelope and human evolution has increasingly gained support from specialists studying many disparate creatures. A decade ago, paleontologist Hank Wesselman discovered a rapid pulse of extinctions and speciations in

African rodents at the 2.5-million-year mark. In addition, Raymonde Bonefille, of Marseille, has found that pollens in Ethiopia show that there was a simultaneous "turnover" of many plant species. In each case, the pattern is wholly consistent with global cooling, increased glaciation, a shrinking of wet, forested country, and the rise of vast, dry grasslands. Animal species everywhere either moved, bowed out, or evolved into new groups, as Italian paleontologist Augusto Azzaroli has demonstrated for many lineages of Eurasian mammals, including deer, cattle, various carnivores, and rodents.

According to the classic Darwinian view, the "engine" that drives the evolution of species is competition between organisms; extinctions occur when species outcompete others for the same resources. If one were to represent each species as a star that lights up in the sky, the Darwinian model would show some stars appearing and others going dark in a fairly random pattern. But the fossil record appears to tell a different tale. Species seem to arise and vanish in pulses of varying intensities, with many appearing and others disappearing at the same time. Some of these pulses would appear to be dim, while others would light up the heavens.

As a rain forest or grassland shifts or disappears, diminishing animal populations can remain unchanged within the shrinking habitats in which they evolved, perhaps expanding again when and if a favorable climate returns. On the other hand, if conditions are right, evolution within the threatened population may produce a new species. According to the new scenario first proposed by Harvard biologist Ernst Mayr in the 1940s, an animal species may occupy an extensive geographic range until major changes in rainfall, temperature, or geographical boundaries break the population into smaller, isolated groups. These "island populations" cease to trade genes, and eventually some may diverge sufficiently to form the cores of new species. Without the impetus of environmental pulses, most species and ecosystems seem to remain in equilibrium most of the time and resist change until they are pushed.

I see the biosphere as a living layer, stretched thinly over the globe, responding rhythmically to the beat of the earth. During a climatic shift, species may either find some safety as generalists, able to tolerate a wide range of foods and conditions, or they may cling unchanged to the shrinking habitats in which they evolved. In the long run, however, both of these strategies may lead to dead ends. If a lineage's evolutionary success is measured by the production of many diverse species, then the successful gamblers on speciation are the big winners. Our ancestral species, the early australopithecines, entered a narrow genetic corridor about 2.5 million years ago. They disappeared, but as the progenitors of novelty—ultimately including the most ubiquitous large mammal species on earth—they hit the jackpot.

11

OUR GREATEST EVOLUTIONARY STEP

STEPHEN JAY GOULD

In my previous book, *Ever Since Darwin*, I began an essay on human evolution with these words:

> New and significant prehuman fossils have been unearthed with such unrelenting frequency in recent years that the fate of any lecture notes can only be described with the watchword of a fundamentally irrational economy—planned obsolescence. Each year, when the topic comes up in my courses, I simply open my old folder and dump the contents into the nearest circular file. And here we go again.

And I'm mighty glad I wrote them, because I now want to invoke that passage to recant an argument made later in the same article.

In that essay I reported Mary Leakey's discovery (at thirty miles south of Olduvai Gorge in Tanzania) of the oldest known hominid fossils—teeth and jaws 3.35 to 3.75 million years old. Mary Leakey suggested (and so far as I know, still believes) that these remains should be classified in our genus, *Homo*. I therefore argued that the conventional evolutionary sequence leading from small-brained but fully erect *Australopithecus* to larger-brained *Homo* might have to be reassessed, and that the australopithecines might represent a side branch of the human evolutionary tree.

Early in 1979, newspapers blazed with reports of a new species—more ancient in time and more primitive in appearance than any other hominid fossil—*Australopithecus afarensis*, named by Don Johanson and Tim White. Could any two claims possibly be more different—Mary Leakey's argument that the oldest hominids belong to our own genus, *Homo*, and White's decision to name a new species because the oldest hominids possess a set of apelike features shared by no other fossil hominid. Johanson and White must have discovered some new and fundamentally different bones. Not at all. Leakey and Johanson and White are arguing about the same bones. We are witnessing a debate about the interpretation of specimens not a new discovery.

Johanson worked in the Afar region of Ethiopia from 1972 to 1977 and unearthed an outstanding series of hominid remains. The Afar specimens are 2.9 to 3.3 million years old. Premier among them is the skeleton of an australopithecine named Lucy. She is nearly 40 percent complete—much more than we have ever possessed for any individual from these early days of our history. (Most hominid fossils, even though they serve as a basis for endless speculation and elaborate storytelling, are fragments of jaws and scraps of skulls.)

Johanson and White argue that the Afar specimens and Mary Leakey's fossils are identical in form and be long to the same species. They also point out that the Afar and bones and teeth represent everything we know about hominids exceeding 2.5 million years in age—all the other African specimens are younger. Finally, they claim that the teeth and skull pieces of these old remains share a set of features absent in later fossils and reminiscent of apes. Thus, they assign the Laetoli and Afar remains to a new species. *A. afarensis*.

The debate is just beginning to warm up, but three opinions have already been vented. Some anthropologists, pointing to different features, regard the Afar and specimens as members of our own genus, *Homo*. Others accept Johanson and White's conclusions that these older fossils are closer to the later south and east African *Australopithecus* than to *Homo*. But they deny a difference sufficient to warrant a new species and prefer to include the Afar and fossils within the species *A. africanus*, originally named for South African specimens in the 1920s. Still others agree with Johanson and White that the Afar and fossils deserve a new name.

As a rank anatomical amateur, my opinion is worth next to nothing. Yet I must say that if a picture is worth all the words of this essay (or only half of them if you follow the traditional equation of 1 for 1,000), the palate of the Afar hominid certainly says "ape" to me. (I must also confess that the designation of *A. afarensis* supports several of my favorite prejudices. Johanson and White emphasize that the Afar and Laetoli specimens span a million years but are virtually identical. I believe that most species do not alter much during the lengthy period of their success and that most evolutionary change accumulates during very rapid events of splitting from ancestral stocks. Moreover, since I depict human evolution as a bush rather than a ladder, the more species the merrier. Johanson and White do, however, accept far more gradualism than I would advocate for later human evolution.)

Amidst all this argument about skulls, teeth, and taxonomic placement, another and far more interesting feature of the Afar remains has not been disputed. Lucy's pelvis and leg bones clearly show that *A. afarensis* walked as erect as you or I. This fact has been prominently reported by the press, but in a very misleading way. The newspapers have conveyed, almost unanimously, the idea that previous orthodoxy had viewed the evolution of larger brains and upright postures as a gradual transition in tandem, perhaps with brains leading the way—from pea-brained quadrupeds to stooping half brains to fully erect, big-brained *Homo*. *The New York Times* writes (January 1979): "The evolution of bipedalism was thought to have been a gradual process involving intermediate forerunners of modern human beings that were stooped, shuffle-gaited 'ape-men,' creatures more intelligent than apes but not as intelligent as modern human beings." Absolutely false, at least for the past fifty years of our knowledge.

We have known since australopithecines were discovered in the 1920s that these hominids had relatively small brains and fully erect posture. (*A. africanus* has a brain about one-third the volume of ours and a completely upright gait. A correction for its small body size does not remove the large discrepancy between its brain and ours.) This "anomaly" of small brain and upright posture has been a major issue in the literature for decades and wins a prominent place in all important texts.

Thus, the designation of *A. afarensis* does not establish the historical primacy of upright posture over large brains. But it does, in conjunction with two other ideas, suggest something very novel and exciting, something curiously missing from the press reports or buried amidst misinformation about the primacy of upright posture. *A. afarensis* is important because it teaches us that perfected upright gait had already been achieved nearly four million years ago. Lucy's pelvic structure indicates bipedal posture for the Afar remains, while the remarkable footprints just discovered at Laetoli provide even more direct evidence. The later south and east African australopithecines do not extend back much further than two and a half million years. We have thus added nearly one and a half million years to the history of fully upright posture.

To explain why this addition is so important, I must break the narrative and move to the opposite end of biology—from fossils of whole animals to molecules. During the past fifteen years, students of molecular evolution have accumulated a storehouse of data on the amino acid sequences of similar enzymes and proteins in a wide variety of organisms. This information has generated a surprising result. If we take pairs of species with securely dated times of divergence from a common ancestor in the fossil record, we find that the number of amino acid differences correlates remarkably well with time since the split—the longer that two lineages have been separate, the more the molecular difference. This regularity has led to the establishment of a molecular clock to predict times of divergence for pairs of species without good fossil evidence of ancestry. To be sure, the clock does not beat with the regularity of an expensive watch—it has been called a "sloppy clock" by one of its leading supporters—but it has rarely gone completely haywire.

Darwinians were generally surprised by the clock's regularity because natural selection should work at markedly varying rates in different lineages at different times: very rapidly in complex forms adapting to rapidly changing environments, very slowly in stable, well-adapted populations. If natural selection is the primary cause of evolution in populations, then we should not expect a good correlation between genetic change and time unless rates of selection remain fairly constant—as they should not by the argument stated above. Darwinians have escaped this anomaly by arguing that irregularities in the rate of selection smooth out over long periods of time. Selection might be intense for a few generations and virtually absent for time thereafter, but the net change averaged over long periods could still be regular. But Darwinians have also been forced to face the possibility that regularity of the molecular clock reflects an evolutionary process not mediated by natural selection, the random fixation of neutral mutations. (I must defer this "hot" topic to another time and more space.)

In any case, the measurement of amino acid differences between humans and living African great apes (gorillas and chimpanzees) led to the most surprising result of all. We are virtually identical for genes that have been studied, despite our pronounced morphological divergence. The average difference in amino acid sequences between humans and African apes is less than one percent (0.8 percent to be precise)—corresponding to a mere five million years since divergence form a common ancestor on the molecular clock. Allowing for the slop, Allan Wilson and Vincent Sarich, the Berkeley scientists who uncovered this anomaly, will accept six million years, but not much more. In short, if the clock is valid, A. afarensis is pushing very hard at the theoretical limit of hominid ancestry.

Until recently, anthropologists tended to dismiss the clock, arguing that hominids provided a genuine exception to an admitted rule. They based their skepticism about the molecular clock upon an animal called *Ramapithecus*, an African and Asian fossil mainly from jaw fragments and ranging back to fourteen million years in age. Many anthropologists claimed that *Ramapithecus* could be placed on our side of the ape-human split—that, in other words, the divergence between hominids and apes occurred more than fourteen million years ago. But this view, based on a series of technical arguments about teeth and their proportions, has been weakening of late. Some of the strongest supporters of *Ramapithecus* as a hominid are now prepared to reassess it as an ape or as a creature near to the common ancestry of ape and human but still before the actual split. The molecular clock has been right too often to cast it aside for some tentative arguments about fragments of jaws. (I now expect to lose a $10 bet I made with Allan Wilson a few years back. He generously gave me seven million years as a maximum for the oldest ape-human common ancestor, but I held out for more. And while I'm not shelling out yet, I don't really expect to collect.*)

We may now put together three points to suggest a major reorientation in views about human evolution: the age and upright posture of *A. afarensis,* the ape-human split on the molecular clock, and the dethroning of *Ramapithecus* as a hominid.

We have never been able to get away from a brain-centered view of human evolution, although it has never represented more than a powerful cultural prejudice imposed upon nature. Early evolutionists argued that enlargement of the brain must have preceded any major alteration of our bodily frame. But *A. africanus,* upright and small brained, ended that conceit in the 1920s, as predicted by a number of astute evolutionists and philosophers from Ernst Haeckel to Friedrich Engels. Nevertheless, "cerebral primacy," as I like to call it, still held on in altered form. Evolutionists granted the historical primacy of upright posture but conjectured that it arose at a leisurely pace and that the real discontinuity—the leap that made us fully human—occurred much later when, in and unprecedented burst of evolutionary speed, our brains tripled in size within a million years or so.

Consider the following, written ten years ago by a leading expert: "The great leap in cephalization of genus *Homo* took place within the past two million years, after some ten million years of preparatory evolution toward bipedalism, the tool-using hand, etc. Arthur Koestler has carried this view of a cerebral leap toward humanity to an unexcelled height of invalid speculation in his latest book, *Janus.* Our brain grew so fast, he argues, that the outer cerebral cortex, seat of smarts and rationality, lost control over emotive, animal centers deep within our brains. This primitive bestiality surfaces in war, murder, and other forms of mayhem.

I believe that we must reassess fundamentally the relative importance we have assigned to upright posture and increase in brain size as determinants of human evolution. We have viewed upright posture as an easily accomplished, gradual trend and increase in brain size as a surprisingly rapid discontinuity—something special both in its evolutionary mode and the magnitude of its effect. I wish to suggest a diametrically opposite view. Upright posture is the surprise, the difficult event, the rapid and fundamental reconstruction of our anatomy. The subsequent enlargement of our brain is, in anatomical terms, a secondary epi-phenomenon, an easy transformation embedded in a general pattern of human evolution.

*Jan., 1980. I just paid. Might as well start off the new decade right.

Six million years ago at most, if the molecular clock runs true (and Wilson and Sarich would prefer five), we shared our last common ancestor with gorillas and chimps. Presumably, this creature walked primarily on all fours, although it may have moved about on two legs as well, as apes and many monkeys do today. Little more than a million years later, our ancestors were as bipedal as you or I. This, not later enlargement of the brain, was the great punctuation in human evolution.

Bipedalism is no easy accomplishment. It requires a fundamental reconstruction of our anatomy, particularly of the foot and pelvis. Moreover, it represents an anatomical reconstruction outside the general pattern of human evolution. As I argue in essay 9, through the agency of Mickey Mouse, humans are neotenic—we have evolved by retaining juvenile features of our ancestors. Our large brains, small jaws, and a host of other features, ranging from distribution of bodily hair to ventral pointing of the vaginal canal, are consequences of eternal youth. But upright posture is a different phenomenon. It cannot be achieved by the "easy" route of retaining a feature already present in juvenile stages. For a baby's legs are relatively small and weak, while bipedal posture demands enlargement and strengthening of the legs.

By the time we became upright as *A. afarensis*, the game was largely over, the major alteration of architecture accomplished, the trigger of future change already set. The later enlargement of our brain was anatomically easy. We read our larger brain out of the program of our own growth, by prolonging rapid rates of fetal growth to later times and preserving, as adults, the characteristic proportions of a juvenile primate skull. And we evolved this brain in concert with a host of other neotenic features, all part of a general pattern.

Yet I must end by pulling back and avoiding a fallacy of reasoning—the false equation between magnitude of effect and intensity of cause. As a pure problem in architectural reconstruction, upright posture is far-reaching and fundamental, an enlarged brain superficial and secondary. But the effect of our large brain has far outstripped the relative ease of its construction. Perhaps the most amazing thing of all is a general property of complex systems, our brain prominent among them—their capacity to translate merely quantitative changes in structure into wondrously different qualities of function.

It is now two in the morning and I'm finished. I think I'll walk over to the refrigerator and get a beer; then I'll go to sleep. Culture-bound creature that I am, the dream I will have in an hour so when I'm supine astounds me ever so much more than the stroll I will now perform perpendicular to the floor.

12

EARLY HOMO

R. LEWIN

Two distinct groups of hominids coexisted 2 million years ago, in Africa. One group was made up of small-brained species, the australopithecines; in the second included the large-brained hominids, members of the genus *Homo*. In this unit we will discuss what is known of the anatomy and biology of early *Homo* and consider some of the uncertainties that surrounded the origin and composition of this group.

The definition of the genus *Homo* has always been somewhat contentious, not least because it is tied—consciously or unconsciously—to the state of 'being human'. There is a series of anatomical characters that are to be found uniquely in *Homo*—some aspects of the pelvis, thigh bones, teeth, face and cranium, for instance—but what has always stood out prominently in scholars' definitions is the size of the brain. To be *Homo* is to be a large-brained hominid, one presumably more technologically accomplished than the australopithecines. The question is, how big a brain qualifies for admission to the genus *Homo*?

The average modern human brain is 1350 cm^3 in capacity, with a range of 1000 cm^3 to about 2000 cm^3. How much smaller than 1000 cm^3 can a hominid's brain be, and still be counted as *Homo*? Before 1964 there were several estimates of this 'cerebral rubicon', ranging from 700 to 800 cm^3. In the late 1940s the British anthropologist Sir Arthur Keith proposed a figure of 750 cm^3, which lies midway between the largest known gorilla brain and the smallest human brain. Keith's proposal was widely accepted until 1964, when Louis Leakey, Philip Tobias and John Napier advanced a new definition of the genus *Homo*, which included a cerebral rubicon of 600 cm^3.

Leakey and his colleagues' new definition was associated with the announcement of a new species of Homo—Homo habilis—fossils of which had been recovered from Olduvai Gorge between 1960 and 1963. The reason for the reduction in the cerebral rubicon in this definition of Homo was that the fossil cranium that was part of the new species had a capacity of only 680 cm^3, a figure that would have failed under Keith's standard.

Leakey's fossils came from the same site where Zinjanthropus had been discovered, and were therefore of the same age, 1.75 million years old. Homo habilis was therefore the earliest member of the Homo lineage to be recognized, and Leakey considered it to be directly ancestral to Homo sapiens, Homo erectus being a sidebranch, not an intermediate species. By contrast, most other scholars see a continuous evolutionary line, going from Homo habilis, through Homo erectus, to Homo sapiens.

The announcement of Homo habilis occasioned tremendous objections from the anthropological community, some of which are still voiced today. In an article published in 1986, British anthropologist Christopher Stringer explained the substance of the negative reaction as follows: 'The two main arguments against the existence of Homo habilis have centered on the supposed lack of 'morphological space' between Australopithecus africanus and Homo erectus for such a species, and the sheer variation of specimens assigned to the species.' The title of Stringer's article, 'The credibility of Homo habilis', gives some idea of the depth of current uncertainties surrounding the putative species of Homo habilis.

The first of the two arguments—the question of morphological space—is based on the proposal that Australopithecus africanus is ancestral to Homo erectus. The argument is that, although there are some clear anatomical differences between these two species—notably a larger brain in the latter—they are in fact very similar in many ways. They are so similar the argument runs, that it is hard to imagine something that is intermediate between the two that could not readily be described as being a normal variant of either the putative ancestor or the putative descendant. (The phrase 'morphological space' simply refers to the extent of anatomical difference between the two species.) Indeed, at least half of the specimens that have been assigned to Homo habilis by some scholars have been variously attributed to Australopithecus africanus or Homo erectus by others.

The second argument centers on the range of anatomical variation among the specimens that have variously been said to belong to Homo habilis. This variation has to do with cranial and dental shape as well as brain size, which ranges from close to 600 cm^3 to more than 800 cm^3. Interpretations of this anatomical variability differ. Some scholars say that the range of anatomical differences within this group of fossils is nothing more than normal variability within a single species, including differences between large males and small females.

Others follow the line of the morphological space objection, and say there is no such species as *Homo habilis*. Still others consider that the fossils represent two species, one of which is *Homo habilis* while the other is a second species of *Homo*, which so far has not been formally named. No wonder that Stringer titled his article as he did.

We will now cover briefly some of the anatomy that separates early *Homo* from the contemporary australopithecines, and consider how this might be related to new behavioral adaptations. Finally we will discuss the discovery of a new fossil that has been attributed to *Homo habilis* and explore how it throws further light on the biology of this species and on the tempo of human evolution as a whole.

First, as we have already noted, the brain capacity is larger than in australopithecines, a change that produces several associated characteristics. For instance, the temple areas in australopithecines narrows markedly, forming what is known as the postorbital constriction. In early *Homo* this constriction is much reduced because of the expanded brain. In addition, in australopithecines the face is large relative to the size of the cranial vault, a ratio that is reduced in the larger-brained *Homo* species. The cranial bone itself is thinner in *Homo* than in *Australopithecus*.

The tooth rows are tucked under the face as in other early hominids, a feature that becomes even more exaggerated in later species of *Homo*. The jaw and dentition of *Homo habilis*, however, is less massive than in the australopithecines. Although the teeth are capped with a thick layer of enamel, their overall appearance is less of a grinding machine than appears in the small-brained hominids: the cheek teeth are smaller, and the front teeth larger than in australopithecines, and the premolars are narrower. The patterns of wear on *Homo habilis* teeth are, however, distinguishable from those of the australopithecines: the pattern is that of a generalized fruit eater. Only with the evolution of *Homo erectus* 1.6 million years ago does the tooth-wear pattern make a dramatic shift, a change that might indicate the inclusion of a significant amount of meat in the diet.

The original set of *Homo habilis* fossils from Olduvai Gorge included a relatively complete hand, the structure of which was compatible with an ability to make and use tools, concluded John Napier. Indeed, the name *Homo habilis* means handy man. Stone artifacts—'choppers', 'scrapers', and sharp flakes of the Oldowan technology—first appear in the record about 2.5 million years ago, which, according to some estimates, coincides with the evolution of *Homo habilis*. Such a coincidence falls in neatly with the long-established tendency to view stone-tool making as a uniquely human—that is *Homo*—ability. But both the gracile and robust australopithecines may also have had the ability to make and use stone artifacts.

The evolution of technological skill associated with stone-tool making has always appeared to be a satisfactory explanation for the expansion of brain capacity in the *Homo* lineage. If australopithecines were in fact equally skillful, then this explanation falls. There must, presumably, have been some selection pressure on mental skills that separated the *Homo* and australopithecine lineages. Whether this was associated with the development of more complex subsistence activities, or was instead in the realm of more complex social interaction is difficult to determine.

Whatever was the behavioral complex that included a demand for greater brain power, *Homo habilis* apparently retained the tree-climbing ability that was evident in the anatomy of the earlier hominid, *Australopithecus afarensis*. In 1982 Randall Susman and Jack Stern of the State University of New York at Stony Brook published an analysis of the foot and hand bones that were part of that initial *Homo habilis* discovery at Olduvai Gorge. 'The skeleton represents a mosaic of primitive and derived features, indicating an early hominid which walked bipedally and could fabricate stone tools but also retained the generalized hominoid capacity to climb trees,' they said. This conclusion is questioned by some scholars, as too is the contention that the foot and hand belonged to the same, 13-year-old, individual.

In absolute terms, fossil hominid collections are fairly sparse, in spite of the several spectacular finds of 'partial skeletons'—of *Australopithecus afarensis* and *Homo erectus*—in recent years. Nevertheless, it has seemed fairly clear that in the earliest hominid, and in australopithecines in general, there was considerable difference in body size between males and females of each species. It has also seemed clear that in *Homo erectus*, which evolved about 1.6 million years ago, this marked sexual dimorphism is greatly reduced, largely by an increase in the size of the female. And it has often been assumed that the first member of the *Homo* lineage would be somewhat intermediate between these two states.

The discovery by Donald Johanson and his colleagues in 1986 of a highly fragmented partial skeleton of Homo habilis from Olduvai Gorge effectively abolished this perception. In fact, as British anthropologist Bernard Wood commented at the time of publication of the fossil: 'The new find rudely exposes how little we know about the early evolution of *Homo*.'

The 1.8 million-year-old fossil—some 300-plus fragments of it—was that of a mature female, and yet she stood only a meter tall, slightly less than the diminutive Lucy. Her arms were very long: the ratio of arm length to leg length was 95 per cent—a little higher than *Australopithecus afarensis*—

as compared with 70 per cent in modern humans. Although the fossil, code-named OH 62, is very similar in many ways to *Australopithecus afarensis*, its discoverers argue that it is *Homo habilis*, on the basis of comparison with a specimen from Sterkfontein in South Africa. The cranium of OH 62 is too fragmented and incomplete to allow a reliable estimate of brain size, but the assumption is that it would have been considerably larger than Lucy's.

The discovery of OH 62 shows that sexual dimorphism is just as marked in *Homo habilis* as it is in earlier and contemporary australopithecines: the species is not neatly intermediate between a 'primitive' australopithecine ancestor and an 'advanced' *Homo erectus* descendant. 'The very small body size of the OH 62 individual suggests that views of human evolution positing incremental body size increase through time may be rooted in gradualistic preconceptions rather than fact', note Johanson and his colleagues in their 1987 publication. 'This reinforces the view that encephalization in the terminal Pliocene played a key role in hominid evolution.'

It should be noted that not all anthropologists agree that OH 62 is a member of *Homo habilis*. Indeed, some take it as evidence that there were two *Homo* species in Africa 2 million years ago, not one. The debate continues.

If OH 62 is *Homo habilis*, and if, as most people agree, this species gave rise to *Homo erectus*, then the evolutionary transition must have been abrupt. The time gap between OH 62 (dated at 1.8 million years) and the earliest *Homo erectus* (dated at 1.6 million years) is relatively small.

Fossils attributed to *Homo habilis* have been recovered from various sites in South and East Africa, and include the famous 1470 man from Koobi Fora, in Kenya. The oldest specimen dates to a little more than 2 million years, and the youngest about 1.8 million years. Even if the species originated somewhat earlier than this, say 2.5 million years ago, it apparently was still relatively short lived. Although there are some fragmentary indications of a perhaps earlier origin of the *Homo* lineage, a date of 2.5 million years coincides with a major climatic event that engendered speciation in a wide variety of organisms. The robust australopithecine lineage also seems to have its origin at this event. The habitat fragmentation generated by the climatic event therefore appears to have sundered the hominid group in several different adaptive directions.

KEY QUESTIONS

- Apart from direct anatomical information, what other evidence might help determine that early *Homo* pursued different subsistence strategies from the australopithecines?

- Is it more or less likely that there could have been several coexisting species of Homo than several coexisting species of *Australopithecus*?

- How could one resolve the question of who made the tools?

- Are there special reasons why the origin of *Homo erectus* might have been an abrupt event?

KEY REFERENCES

Donald C. Johanson *et al.*, 'New partial skeleton of *Homo habilis* from Olduvai Gorge, Tanzania', *Nature*, vol 327, pp. 205–209 (1987).

D. E. Lieberman, *et al.*, A comparison of KNM-ER 1470 and KNM-ER 1813,' *Journal of Human Evolution*, vol 17, pp. 503–512 (1988).

Christopher B. Stringer, 'The credibility of *Homo habilis*' in *Major topics in primate and human evolution*, edited by B. Wood, L. Martin, and P. Andrews, 1986.

Randall L. Susman and Jack T. Stern, 'Functional morphology of *Homo habilis*', *Science*, vol 217, pp. 931–934 (1982).

Bernard Wood, 'Who is the 'real' *Homo habilis*?' *Nature*, vol 327, pp. 187–188 (1987).

13

Self-Awareness in Primates

Gordon G. Gallup, Jr.

*The sense of identity distinguishes man from
most but perhaps not all other forms of life*

In spite of the widespread acceptance to Darwinian theory, when it comes
to himself man still conceives of man as being fundamentally different
from other animals and endowed with special psychological qualities. But
based in part on what we now know about chimpanzees (*Pan troglodytes*),
many of the apparent differences between man and animals are matters of
degree, not kind. One of the first claims for a uniquely human trait was
the use of tools. Jane Goodall, however, discovered that under natural
conditions chimpanzees make and use tools in ingenious ways and that,
consistent with the concept of culture, such information can be passed on
from one generation to the next. Chimpanzees even seem capable of
fabricating tools in anticipation of their future use (Teleki 1974).

Also a surprise to many anthropologists was the discovery that,
unlike many other primates, chimpanzees eat meat and seem willing to
share it with companions (Teleki 1973). Chimpanzees are not merely
opportunistic predators. Their source of meat, which can occasionally
include human infants, is derived from what appears to be deliberate and
cooperative hunting by adult males. Male-oriented, cooperative hunting
patterns which terminate in sharing have long been held to be an evolutionary precursor to the development of modern man.

Evidence for the representational capacity of chimpanzees is their
ability to deal with objects and events that are separated in time and space
(Menzel 1973). It appears that with proper training chimpanzees can
even master many of the rudiments of symbolic communication and

syntax (Gardner and Gardner 1969; Premack 1971), and they can use learned symbols to communicate with one another (Savage-Rumbaugh, Rumbaugh, and Boysen 1978). Since chimpanzees are capable of learning to use various nonvocal forms of language in ways that parallel the language development of both deaf and speaking children, the question whether language is uniquely human has come to depend more and more on how one defines language—for example, whether or not it must be spoken. The issue, however, is not one of form but one of underlying mental capacity.

In the last analysis, the widely held view of language as our defining characteristic may turn out to be a straw man. Syntax, reconstitution, and displacement, which are essential ingredients of language, also appear to be part and parcel of the complex motor and intellectual skills underlying tool use and tool fabrication (Hewes 1973). The ability to utter articulate speech sounds is a motor skill not fundamentally different from learning to brachiate through tall trees, and both sets of activities are an expression of a deep structure. Just as the exact words and their sequences are for the most part irrelevant to the facts to be transmitted, so are the movements involved in getting from point A to point B. But in each case a basic "grammar" governs the way in which elements can be combined to achieve a particular goal. Just as the elements contained in a message can be reconstituted to form new messages, the fabrication of tools also requires reconstituting aspects of the environment as a means to an end. Language enables organisms to communicate about objects and events from which they themselves are displaced in time and/or space. But fashioning tools in advance of their intended use, as well as retaining tools for use on other occasions, also involves elements of displacement.

In support of this analysis, sign language does not appear to provide chimpanzees with any new concepts but merely gives them a means of expressing what they already know. A more substantive issue is whether animals share cognitive, conceptual, and representational processes in common with man. Language represents one, but, as I will show in this paper, certainly not the only, means of mapping such capacities.

The similarities between chimpanzees and humans continue to obtain when analysis penetrates to the level of anatomical and even molecular phenomena. Comparative neuroanatomical studies show that the chimpanzee brain closely resembles our own, and that chimpanzees even have temporal-lobe asymmetries similar to those in the human brain (Yeni-Komshian and Benson 1976). Chimpanzees show isoagglutination reactions which are indistinguishable from those of human blood (Chiarelli 1973), and a sequence analysis of hemoglobin reveals an identical order of amino acid molecules (Wilson and Sarich 1969). In terms of complex polypeptides humans and chimpanzees are more than 99 percent identical (King and Wilson 1975). Genetically and biochemically chimpanzees are so much like people that we have been characterized by King and Wilson as being as similar to one another as are sibling species of other organisms.

SELF-AWARENESS

One of the last remaining holdouts for human distinction is man's sense of identity, his capacity to conceive of himself, to think about himself, and to contemplate his own existence. The concept of self occupies a central position in many areas of the social and behavioral sciences, yet the sense of self has been an elusive topic. Some philosophers argue that the concept of self poses a logical impossibility. How can the self be aware of itself without raising the specter of an infinite regress of perceptive selves? In other words, how can both the subject and object of perception be one and the same? If consciousness is taken as equivalent to pointing at something, then by analogy it is held that the index finger cannot point at itself.

This problem can be tackled in a number of ways. In the first place, logical problems or not, the sense of self is real. Most people can conceive of themselves. The distinction between subject and object mainly poses a problem in a temporal sense, because you always think about yourself as you were or will be. You can think about yourself, but you cannot always be thinking about yourself. Finally, to return to our analogy, a mirror can be used to circumvent the philosopher's dilemma. In front of a mirror the index finger can indeed be the object at which it is pointing. When a person observes his own image in a mirror, both the subject and object of perception are necessarily one and the same.

Another problem is how to define and measure self-awareness. The fact that most people have an implicit sense of self has perpetuated a certain laziness about defining and objectifying the phenomenon. In fact, as traditionally conceived, the concept of self is intellectually bankrupt because, as Epstein (1973) points out, practically all definitions lack meaningful referents or tend to be tautological. Moreover, a prevailing view in psychology has been that the related issues of self-awareness and consciousness are simply not amenable to objective analysis in animals. In this article I propose to show that, just as mirrors can be used to resolve some of the logical problems of self-awareness, they can also be used to give concrete meaning to self-awareness and render it more objectively analyzable. Does man have a monopoly on the concept of self? Are we evolution's only experiment in self-awareness?

SELF-RECOGNITION

In front of a mirror any visually capable organism is ostensibly an audience to its own behavior. However, most animals react to themselves in a mirror as if they were seeing other animals, and engage in a variety of social responses, typical of the particular species, directed toward the reflection (Gallup 1968). Although mirrors enable organisms to see themselves as they are seen by others, many animals seem incapable of recognizing the dualism implicit in such stimulation, and even after prolonged exposure fail to discover the relationship between their behavior and the reflection of that behavior in a mirror. Yet mirrors hold a peculiar fascination for them. Some animals have been taught to make a variety of responses simply to gain brief access to their own reflection, and goldfish and parakeets show a strange preference for looking into mirrors instead of at other members of the same species (Gallup 1975).

Self-recognition in humans is learned. For example, people with congenital visual defects who undergo corrective operations later in life initially react to themselves in mirrors in exactly the same way as do animals. Infants also show such behavior and often respond to their reflection as if it were a playmate. Children begin to respond to mirrors as if confronted with other infants before 6 months of age, but do not show signs of self-recognition until they reach 18 to 24 months (for a critical review of this literature see Gallup 1979). Profoundly retarded children and adolescents and comparably handicapped adults sometimes seem totally incapable of learning to recognize themselves in mirrors. Thus, the capacity for self-recognition requires a degree of intellectual functioning which even exceeds that of some humans. It is also interesting that prolonged mirror gazing has been associated with the onset of schizophrenia in man. In fact, some schizophrenics appear to have lost their capacity for self-recognition and can be found talking to themselves in mirrors and laughing at the reflection (see Gallup 1979).

After pondering the possibility of an evolutionary discontinuity between animals and man in their ability to recognize themselves, I did a study (1970) to see whether chimpanzees were capable of deciphering mirrored information about themselves. In spite of the fact that many of us were told about the identity of our own reflection by our parents, we probably required prolonged exposure to mirrors before being able to recognize it ourselves. To examine the effects of extended exposure I gave four pre-adolescent chimpanzees individual access to a mirror for ten consecutive days. Invariably their initial reaction consisted of responses which would ordinarily be made in the presence of another chimpanzee, and for the first few days they engaged in a variety of social gestures while watching the reflection. After about three days, however, the tendency to treat the reflection as a companion disappeared, and they began using the mirror to respond to themselves. They used the reflection to gain visual access to and experiment with otherwise inaccessible information about themselves, such as grooming parts of the body they had not seen before, inspecting the inside of their mouths, and making faces at the mirror.

In an attempt to satisfy skeptics and clarify my own impressions of what had transpired, I devised an unobtrusive and more rigorous test of self-recognition. After the last day of mirror exposure, each chimpanzee was anesthetized and the mirror was removed. Once the chimpanzee was unconscious, I painted the uppermost portion of an eyebrow ridge and the top half of the opposite ear with a bright red odorless, nonirritating dye. The animal was then placed back into its cage and allowed to recover in the absence of the mirror. The significance of this approach is threefold. First, the chimpanzee had no way of knowing about the application of the marks since the procedure was accomplished under deep anesthesia. Second, the dye was carefully selected because of its lack of tactile and olfactory properties. Finally, the marks were strategically placed at predetermined points on the chimpanzee's face so that it would be impossible for them to be seen without a mirror.

Following the chimpanzee's recovery from anesthesia the mirror was reintroduced as an explicit test of self-recognition. Upon seeing the reflection all the chimpanzees attempted to touch the marked areas on themselves while looking into the mirror and showed a renewed interest in the reflection. In addition there were several noteworthy attempts to examine visually and smell the fingers which had been used to touch marked portions of the face. I suspect that most people would react in much the same way if, upon awakening one morning, they saw themselves in a mirror with red marks on their face. In fact, variations of this technique have now been adopted for use with humans (Gallup 1979).

In a further attempt to eliminate any doubt about the source of these reactions, I anesthetized and marked several comparable chimpanzees which had never seen themselves in mirrors. However, when the animals were presented with the mirror they made no responses whatsoever to the marks, exhibited no patterns of self-recognition, and ostensibly ignored the dye. Marked chimpanzees without prior exposure to a mirror all responded to the reflection as if confronted with another chimpanzee.

ABSENCE OF SELF-RECOGNITION IN MONKEYS

The findings with chimpanzees have now been replicated several times and have been extended by a group of investigators in Germany to include orangutans (Lethmate and Dücker 1973). With the exception of man and the great apes, however, all other primates (referred to here as monkeys) have failed to exhibit self-recognition even after extended exposure to mirrors. Thus, in the process of trying to resolve one apparent evolutionary discontinuity I appear to have uncovered another. To date, spider monkeys, capuchins, squirrel monkeys, stump-tailed macaques, rhesus monkeys, crab-eating macaques, Java monkeys, pig-tailed macaques, lion-tailed macaques, mandrill, olive, and hamadryas baboons, as well as two species of gibbons, have all been systematically tested, and none has shown any indication of an ability to realize that its behavior was the source of the behavior depicted in the mirror. Contrary to claims for an underlying evolutionary continuity to mental functioning (e.g. Griffin 1976), only man and the great apes seem capable of extracting this information from mirrors.

In an attempt to salvage the conceptual integrity of monkeys, several years ago I went so far as to expose a crab-eating macaque to a mirror for over 2,400 hours during a period of five months. But to no avail. At the end of that time it failed to show any signs of self-recognition and continued to respond to its image as if it were seeing another monkey. Robert L. Thompson and Suzanne C. Radano at Hunter College (pers. comm.) recently completed a study in which a pig-tailed macaque was kept in a cage containing a polished metal mirror for a period of one year, but the monkey never showed evidence of self-recognition, and social responses directed toward the reflection continued at a diminished rate for the entire year. Finally, a French psychologist, Mireille Bertrand (pers. comm.), has made systematic observations of a home-reared pig-tailed macaque that has had daily access to mirrors for almost seven years, and she finds that it is till incapable of recognizing itself and even now makes an occasional social response to the image. Chimpanzees, in contrast, begin to show signs of self-recognition after as few as three or four days of mirror exposure!

Since, admittedly, it is difficult to deal with negative instances, we tried to devise a means of making the identity of the reflection more explicit in an effort to increase the monkey's opportunity to show self-recognition. It occurred to me that one possibility might be to capitalize on the well-developed capacity of monkeys for recognizing individuals. Any species capable of forming and maintaining a dominance hierarchy must have the capacity to recognize and differentiate among individuals.

Even chickens and crayfish form dominance hierarchies. But how does one use individual recognition to facilitate self-recognition? Larry B. Wallnau, Susan D. Suarez, and I (in press) gave familiar cagemates paired access to a common mirror. In principle, each member of the pair should be able to identify and recognize the reflection of its companion, and thus the question about the source of the remaining unfamiliar individual they see in the mirror is posed in a more direct way.

To assess the effects of paired access to mirrors we conducted two experiments. In the first, a feral adult rhesus monkey and her six-month-old infant were given over 1,000 hours of paired mirror exposure. Mother and infant were then anesthetized, the mirror was removed, and red dye was applied to an eyebrow and the abdomen of both animals. Marks on the stomach were used as a basis for comparing the reaction to marks of facial features, which could be seen only in the mirror, and to document the rhesus monkey's motivation to touch and inspect marked portions of the body that could be seen directly. After recovery each animal was tested individually for its reaction to the mirror. Following the individual tests, the mother and infant were reunited and tested again under conditions of paired access to the same mirror.

Both the adult female and a control animal without prior mirror experience touched and inspected the marked area on their own stomachs, but none of the monkeys, including the infant, showed responses to these marks while looking into the mirror. When mother and infant were placed together again in front of the mirror the infant repeatedly attempted to groom and inspect the marked portion of its mother's eyebrow, but neither animal showed evidence of self-recognition. We also tried the same procedure with a pair of 6-month-old rhesus monkeys, separated from their mothers shortly after birth, and maintained together in front of a mirror for a period of 14 consecutive weeks. While both animals touched and groomed marked portions of their cagemate's face on the test of self-recognition, neither monkey showed signs of self-recognition or reacted to marks on its own face in response to the reflection. We are currently keeping both of these animals together in front of a mirror and plan to see what effects, if any, a lifetime of exposure to mirrors may have.

For the time being, however, these experiments extend previous findings and converge to suggest that monkeys, in contrast to great apes, are incapable of recognizing themselves in mirrors. Our data also demonstrate that the failure to find self-recognition in rhesus monkeys is not due to a lack of the monkeys' interest in the marks which have been used to assess self-recognition. Although monkeys can learn to use mirrored cues to manipulate objects they cannot otherwise see, they appear incapable of learning to sufficiently integrate features of their own reflection to use mirrors to respond to themselves. Again, it is not that they cannot learn to respond to mirrored cues. When looking at the reflection of a human or a bit of food they can detect the inherent dualism as it pertains to objects other than themselves and, after adequate experience, do respond appropriately by turning away from the mirror to gain more direct access to the object of the reflection. Yet they completely fail to interpret mirrored information about themselves correctly.

My interpretation of these results, taken collectively, is that most primates lack a cognitive category that is essential for processing mirrored information about themselves, and the nature of this cognitive deficit may be tied to the sense of self (Gallup 1977). One of the unique features of mirrors is that the identity of the observer and his reflection in a mirror are necessarily one and the same. Therefore, if you do not know who you are, how could you possibly know who it is you are seeing when you look at yourself in a mirror? The capacity to infer correctly the identity of the reflection presupposes a sense of identity on the part of the organism making that inference. Perhaps the monkey's inability to recognize itself is due to the absence of a sufficiently well integrated self-concept.

Some people may object to this conclusion on the grounds that, although lacking a visual self, monkeys and other animals may have an olfactory or even an auditory sense of self. This, however, is a mistaken distinction. One's concept of self is not modality specific. Your sense of self does not disappear when you close your eyes, cover your ears, or hold your nose. Self-awareness is a multimodal phenomenon, and as such presupposes considerable intermodal equivalence.

To date, no one has attempted to specify a neurological basis for the sense of self. However, rather than being localized in a particular part of our neuroanatomy, self-recognition may present an emergent phenomenon which occurs only when a species acquires a certain number of cortical neurons with sufficiently complex interconnections. Alternatively, one could argue for a threshold model. Different organisms may have different degrees of self-awareness, but only with an explicit sense of self does self-recognition become possible. The threshold for self-recognition, in other words, may be quite high compared to the threshold for other ways of conceiving of oneself. It is also possible that the capacity for self-recognition may be an indirect consequence of selection for other cognitive skills, and as such would represent a correlated trait.

Because of their unusually large, complex brains the cetaceans (porpoises and whales) may represent another group of mammals that have a concept of self. However, because cetaceans lack arms and fingers, procedures requiring these mammals to respond to marks would not be applicable. An interesting alternative approach is to use videotape and underwater probes. For example, on some occasions a porpoise would be allowed to view its own live image on an underwater television screen, while on other occasions it would see the videotape of another porpoise in the same situation. The porpoise's ability to recognize itself could be tested by introducing a probe into the background. If the porpoise is presented with the probe while it is viewing the image of another porpoise, it would have no ostensible reason to turn around. (When we watch a television program that depicts someone sneaking up on someone else from behind, we normally do not turn around.) On the other hand, if the porpoise had succeeded in recognizing its own televised image, presentation of the probe should cause the porpoise to turn around in the presence of its image to confront and inspect the probe. Elephants are another class of big-brained mammals that might be interesting to test for self-recognition. Their unique prehensile trunks seem ideally suited for assessing their reactions in front of a mirror to surreptitiously applied facial marks.

SPECIES IDENTITY AND THE CONCEPT OF SELF

A prevailing view in social psychology is that the concept of self in humans develops only out of a social milieu and as such is dependent upon interaction with others. For instance, George Herbert Mead (1934) argued that in order for the self to emerge as an object of conscious inspection a person must have the opportunity to examine himself from another's point of view. In order to conceive of yourself you may need to be able to see yourself as you are seen by others. Knowledge of self, in other words, may presuppose knowledge of others. In keeping with this idea, we found that chimpanzees reared by themselves under conditions that prevented interaction with others seemed incapable of recognizing themselves in a mirror (Gallup et al. 1971).

The notion that explicit self-awareness may require the opportunity to examine oneself from another's point of view raises some intriguing possibilities. Jung (1958) believed that a truly objective view of man would require the opportunity to see ourselves from another species' perspective. But what if one could see oneself only from another species' point of view? It has been reported that when the chimpanzee Washoe, who had been taught sign language and reared with humans, first saw other chimpanzees she referred to them as "black bugs" (Linden 1974). Moreover, while being reared in social isolation can seriously impair primates sexual behavior, human-reared chimpanzees are more impaired than those reared in complete social isolation (Rogers and Davenport 1969). Why? Maybe it is because they think they are human.

Then there is the famous informal experiment conducted with another home-reared chimpanzee named Vicki (Hayes and Nissen 1971). Among other things, Vicki was taught to sort stacks of snapshots into a human and an animal pile. One day Vicki's own photograph was placed in the stack, and when she came to it she picked it up and without hesitation placed it on the human pile. There are at least two ways to interpret her action. One is that man may not be the only one to appreciate the similarities between chimpanzees and men. The other is that maybe Vicki thought she was human.

Temerlin (1975) reported that as a result of rearing a chimpanzee in his home, his young son began to develop doubts about his own species identity. The imprinting literature shows that affiliation tendencies for many species are often tied to early social experiences. For you and me and the rest of the great apes, the content of our individual identity may similarly by subject to social influences. Just as the presence or absence of social interaction may determine the formation of one's concept of self, the quality and nature of those interactions appear to influence the content, or ingredients, of the concept.

While the behavioral or functional consequences of imprinting are much the same for any species, my data suggest that the cognitive consequences may be quite restricted. Although under natural conditions it is true that "birds of a feather flock together," the apparent limits of self-awareness among many species pose a serious challenge to widely held views of species identity. The issue is basically whether species-specific affiliation patterns result from a sense of species identity or from more fundamental familiarity effects, simple associative factors, and/or genetic predispositions. Figuratively speaking, do goldfish tend to aggregate with other goldfish because they know they themselves are goldfish? If they do, it would require a sense of belonging or membership and the cognitive capacity to equate themselves with other organisms. Such a capacity represents the intellectual equivalent of thinking "I am one of them." But that presupposes a sense of "I." If an organism is incapable of identifying itself in a mirror, how can it possibly identify itself as being a member of some particular class of organisms? Species identity as such presupposes an individual identity and may therefore be highly restricted.

It is also intriguing that, while the development of an individual identity in great apes requires social interaction with others, the others need not be of the same species. For instance, most chimpanzees reared exclusively with humans show obvious signs of being able to recognize themselves in mirrors but an active avoidance, or even disdain, for members of their own species. Thus, the existence of self-awareness in chimpanzees would not appear to depend on a particular or even an accurate species identity.

Finally, some people assert that man is unique in his capacity to contemplate his own death. However, I think the capacity for self-awareness in chimpanzees renders this very much an open question. In principle, once you can conceive of yourself, you can begin to think about yourself. Once you can become the object of your own attention, you can begin to contemplate your own existence. If you can contemplate your own existence, then it is a fairly simple and maybe even logical next step to begin contemplating your nonexistence. Indeed, this might be a particularly compelling next step upon witnessing the transition between life and death in a companion. In principle it ought to be possible to educate the chimpanzee about its inevitable demise, but at least one psychologist has already expressed hesitation about doing so (Premack 1976). Is ignorance, in this instance, bliss? Adrian Desmond (pers. comm.) feels that, perhaps, just as for man, every time a healthy, well-adjusted great ape dies a universe blinks out of existence.

The development of an individual identity represents a conceptual leap for several other reasons. One of the unique by-products of self-awareness is that, in principle, it makes it possible for the brain to begin thinking about the brain and speculating about the mechanisms of its own functioning. An evolutionary biologist has argued recently that self-awareness has the potential to emancipate organisms intellectually from some of the deterministic forces of evolution (Slobodkin 1978). Certainly without some kind of intellectual emancipation, the concept of evolution would be impossible. After all, without the capacity to reflect on oneself, how could a product of evolution ever begin to comprehend evolution? Ultimately, an organism capable of contemplating its own existence may find itself in the rather peculiar and certainly precarious position of being able to take steps to modify that existence.

REFERENCES

Chiarelli, A. B. 1973. *Evolution of the Primates*. Academic Press.

Epstein, S. 1973. The self-concept revisited, or a theory of a theory. *Am. Psychol.* 28:404–16.

Gallup, G.G., Jr. 1968. Mirror-image stimulation. *Psych. Bull.* 70:782–93.

____. 1970. Chimpanzees: Self-recognition. *Science* 167:86–87.

____. 1975. Towards an operational definition of self-awareness. In *Socioecology and Psychology of Primates*, ed. R. H. Tuttle. Mouton.

____. 1977. Self-recognition in primates: A comparative approach to the bidirectional properties of consciousness. *Am. Psychol.* 32:329–38.

____. 1979. Self-recognition in chimpanzees and man: A developmental and comparative perspective. In *Genesis of Behavior*, vol. 2: *The Child and Its Family*, ed. M. Lewis and L. Rosenblum. Plenum Press.

Gallup, G. G. Jr., M. K. McClure, S. D. Hill, and R. A. Bundy. 1971. Capacity for self-recognition in differentially reared chimpanzees. *Psych. Rec.* 21:69–74.

14

THE EXPANDED BRAIN

R. LEWIN

This unit focuses on the context and consequences of human brain evolution. The context will expose some of the biological constraints under which this extraordinary evolutionary event occurred. And the consequences should help illuminate some of the selection pressures which fueled that event.

The question to be answered is: how did humans come to possess such extraordinary powers of creative intelligence, powers that surely outstrip what would have been necessary in the practical day to day life of technologically primitive hunter-gatherers? In exploring this conundrum we will cover three aspects of human mental evolution: the expansion of the brain and intelligence, consciousness, and language. Inevitably, these three qualities are tightly intertwined.

Although the hominid lineage stretches back some 6 million years, fossil evidence for brain size goes back only 3 million years, to the specimens of *Australopithecus afarensis* at the Hadar, Ethiopia. Given this somewhat limited view of hominid history, it is nevertheless apparent that brain expansion has been great and rapid: a threefold increase occurred in that 3 million years, going from around 400 cm^3 to 1350 cm^3, the average of modern populations. Impressive in itself, it is the more so when, as pointed out by Harry Jerison of the University of California, Los Angeles, 'there is no evidence of a change in any other mammals in [this same period]'. In other words, brain expansion among hominids was not just part of a recent, general mammalian pattern.

To understand this expansion more fully we will look first at some of the characteristics of the human brain in the context of primate biology; we will then turn to the fossil evidence of this expansion; finally, we will consider some of the ideas currently offered to explain the phenomenon.

First of all, the brain is a very expensive organ to maintain. In adult humans, for instance, even though it represents just 2 per cent of the total body weight, the brain consumes some 18 per cent of the energy budget. 'One might therefore ask,' says Robert Martin, 'how, in the course of human evolution, additional energy was made progressively available to meet the needs of an ever-increasing brain size.'

Life-history factors—gestation length, metabolic rate, precociality versus altriciality, and so on—have important bearings on the size of brain a species can develop. In this context, two major ideas have been advanced in recent years that bear on the special problem faced by hominids in underpinning brain expansion.

The first, proposed by Martin, is that the mother's metabolic rate is key to the size of brain a species can afford: the higher the metabolic rate, the bigger the potential brain size. The second, proposed by Mark Pagel and Paul Harvey of Oxford University, is that gestation time and litter size are the determining factors: long gestation, with a litter of one is optimal for a large-brained species. Both hypotheses are said by their authors to have empirical support, but a debate continues as to which is the more germane. Whichever case proves to be correct, both pathways require the same kind of environmental context: stable, high-energy food supply, with minimum predation pressure.

In being well endowed mentally, humans and other primates are a part of a very clear pattern among vertebrates as a whole. Depending somewhat on the measure you use, mammals are about 10 times brainier than reptiles, and in their turn, reptiles are about 10 times brainier than amphibians. Underlying this stepwise progression, which represents successive major evolutionary innovations and radiations, is the building of more and more sophisticated 'reality' in species' heads.

So, being mammals, primates by definition are better equipped mentally than any reptile. However, two orders of mammal have significantly larger brains than the rest: they are Primates and Cetaceans (toothed whales). And among primates, the anthropoids (monkeys and apes) are brainier still. Only humans lie off that monkey/ape axis: the brain of *Homo sapiens* is three times bigger than that of an ape of the same body size.

The need to grow such a large brain has distorted several basic life-history characteristics seen in other primates. For instance, the adult ape brain is about 2.3 times bigger than the brain in the newborn (neonate); in humans the difference is 3.5 times. More dramatic, however, is the size of the human neonate compared with ape newborns. Even though humans are of similar body size to apes (57 kilograms, compared to 30 to 100 kilograms) and have a similar gestation period (270 days, compared to 245 to 270 days), human neonates are approximately twice as big and have brains twice as big as ape newborns. 'From this it can be concluded that human mothers devote a relatively greater quantity of energy and other resources to fetal brain and body development over a standard time than do our closest relative, the great apes', notes Martin.

Another major difference is the pattern of growth. In mammals with precocial young—which includes primates—brain growth proceeds rapidly until birth, whereupon a slower phase ensues for about a year. In humans, the prenatal phase of rapid brain growth continues until well after birth, a pattern that is seen in altricial species. One difference with altricial species, however, is that in humans the rapid postnatal phase (fetal rate) brain growth continues for a relatively longer period than is typical of such species. The effect is to give humans the equivalent of a 21 month gestation period (9 in the uterus, 12 outside).

This unique pattern of development has been called secondary altriciality. One important consequence is that human infants are far more helpless and for a much longer time than the young of the great apes. This extended period of infant care and of subsequent 'schooling' must have had a major impact on the social life of hominids.

Fossil evidence of brain evolution is of two types: an indication of absolute size, and information about the surface features—convolutions and fissures of the brain. Both pieces of evidence can be obtained from either natural or artificial endocasts, which show the convolutions of the brain as they had become impressed on the inner surface of the cranium.

Brain size is the first and most obvious piece of information to be gleaned, and this can often be gained even with partial crania. There is therefore a fair amount of data about the expansion of brain size, beginning with *Australopithecus afarensis,* a little more than 3 million years ago. Measured at a little less than 400 cm³, this early australopithecine brain is often said to be about the same as that of modern gorilla and chimpanzee brains. However, this is misleading, for two reasons: first, early australopithecines were smaller in body size than modern gorillas; second, modern ape brains almost certainly are expanded over what their 3 million-year-old ancestors' brains would have been. It is therefore safe to say that brain expansion had already been established by the time *Australopithecus afarensis* appeared.

In bold terms, then, brain size for the australopithecines was close to 400 cm³, and it never really increased throughout the tenure of this genus. More marked expansion is seen with the origin of the genus *Homo,* specifically *Homo habilis,* which existed from about 2.5 million to 1.6 million years ago and had a range of brain size of about 650 to 800 cm³. The range for *Homo erectus,* 1.6 million to about 300,000 years ago, is 850 to a little more than 1000 cm³. Archaic *Homo sapiens,* including Neanderthals range from 1100 to more than 1400 cm³, which is larger than in modern humans.

By looking at overall brain structure as revealed in endocasts, it is possible to differentiate between an apelike and a humanlike brain organization. The four lobes in each hemisphere are as follows: the frontal, the temporal, the parietal, and the occipital. Very briefly, a brain in which the parietal and temporal lobes predominate is humanlike, whereas in apelike brains these areas are much smaller.

Ralph Holloway of Columbia University has examined in detail a wide range of hominid fossil endocasts, including *Australopithecus afarensis.* The conclusion was a surprise: the brain had apparently been reorganized into a humanlike configuration right from these earliest times of the hominid lineage. Even though it is not possible to see clearly the humanity in the humanlike brain organization, this result implied that something special was happening, very early on in hominid evolution.

Just recently Holloway's conclusions have been challenged by Dean Falk of Purdue University. Although she agrees with Holloway that brains of *Homo* species are reorganized in the human direction, she contends that australopithecine brains are essentially apelike. The precise location of some of the key fissures and divisions between lobes is often very difficult and open to interpretation. In this case the differences of opinion continue unresolved.

It is relatively easy to plot brain expansion through hominid history, but how are we to measure the rise of intelligence through time? The archeological record is notoriously sparse with tangible indications of the working of the mind: tales told around a camp fire, complex and drawings, dances embodying social mythology leave no trace, and yet are the essence of humanity in a hunter-gatherer society. Yes, paintings and engravings betoken mental activities beyond basic subsistence, something we can identify as quintessentially human, but these come very late in our history.

What we are left with are the stone tools and other clues to economic activity. The imposition of standardization and expansion of complexity were very slow to develop in prehistoric stone-tool industries. Using the criteria of psychological theory (that of Piaget), archeologist Thomas Wynn of the University of Colorado has analyzed some of the early stone-tool industries, looking for signs of humanlike intelligence. 'The evolution of a uniquely hominid intelligence had not occurred by Oldowan times', he concludes, referring to the fossil and archeological remains at Olduvai Gorge, dating between 1.9 and 1.6 million years. This was the time of *Homo habilis* but prior to *Homo erectus*. 'This suggests that selection for a complex organizing intelligence was not part of the original hominid adaptation.'

One last insight that fossil evidence might allow in relation to expanding brain size concerns its impact on social organization, specifically in infant care. Once hominids shifted from the basic primate pattern of brain growth, producing instead a much more helpless infant whose brain continued to grow at the fetal rate, then great allocation of time and resources would be needed for rearing offspring. It is theoretically possible, as Robert Martin points out, that no change in infant care would be needed until after the adult human brain size exceeded 873 cm^3, which is the transition size between *Homo habilis* and *Homo erectus*. The argument is as follows.

Suppose that hominids had been able to make all the other changes in fetal development—speeding up body and brain growth—but then reverted to the basic primate pattern in the neonate. This pattern would have allowed for the doubling (actually, x 2.3) of brain growth at birth. Now, the brain size of human infants is 384 cm^3: multiply this by 2.3 and you get 873 cm^3. This theoretical calculation depends on the assumption that the birth canal in the pelvis of *Homo habilis* or early *Homo erectus* females would be able to accommodate a neonate's head the size of a modern infant's.

From the fossil evidence available so far, it is clear that the hominid birth canal was smaller than the modern female's at this point in our history. Which means that a shift to humanlike postnatal brain growth patterns would have had to have occurred already in *Homo habilis,* presumably with the concomitant impact on social organization.

From fossils we turn to theories; theories about the selection pressure (or pressures) that powered hominid brain expansion. Popular for a very long time was the notion that the very obvious difference between hominids and apes—that humans made and used stone tools—was the most likely cause: the tripling of hominid brain size was accompanied by an ever increasing complexity of tool technology. 'Man the tool maker' was the encapsulation of this approach in the 1950s, to be followed a decade later by 'Man the hunter'. In either case, the emphasis was on the mastering of practical affairs as the engine of hominid brain expansion.

In more recent times new ideas have emerged, which might be encapsulated in the phrase 'Man the social animal'. Part of the reason for this shift of opinion has come from primate field studies, which are now reaching an important point of maturity. In addition, there has been a greater introspection about the human mind itself, particularly consciousness.

The new insight into 'Man the social animal' begins with a paradox, similar in nature to the human paradox: laboratory tests have demonstrated beyond doubt that monkeys and apes are extraordinarily intelligent, and yet field studies have revealed that the daily lives of these creatures is relatively undemanding, in the realm of subsistence at least. Why, then, did this high degree of intelligence develop?

The answer may lie in the realm of primate social life. Although, superficially, a primate's social environment does not appear to be more demanding than that of other mammals—the size and composition of social groups is matched among antelope species, for example—the *interactions* within the group are far more complex. In other words, for a nonhuman primate in the field, learning the distribution and probable time of ripening of food sources in the environment is intellectual child's play compared with predicting—and manipulating—the behavior of other individuals in the group. But why should social interactions be so complex, so Machiavellian in primate societies?

When you observe other mammal species and see instances of conflict between two individuals it is usually easy to predict which will triumph: the larger one, or the one with bigger canines or bigger antlers, or whatever is the appropriate weapon for combat. Not so in monkeys and apes. Individuals spend a lot of time establishing networks of 'friendships' and observing the alliances of others. As a result, a physically inferior individual can triumph over a stronger individual, provided the challenge is timed so that friends are at hand to help the challenger and while the victim's allies are absent.

'Alliances are far more complex social interactions than are two-animal contests', says Alexander Harcourt of Cambridge University. 'The information processing abilities required for success are far greater: complexity is geometrically, not arithmetically, increased with the addition of further participants in an interaction. ... In sum, primates are consummate social tacticians.'

In a recent survey of much of the field data relevant to primate social intelligence, Dorothy Cheney, Robert Seyfarth (both of the University of Pennsylvania), and Barbara Smutts (of the University of Michigan) posed the question 'are [primates] capable of some of the higher cognitive processes that are central to human social interactions?' The question is important, because if anthropoid intellect, honed by complex social interaction, is merely sharper than the average mammal's and more adept at solving psychologist's puzzles, then it doesn't match the *creative* intelligence in which we are interested.

Cheney and her colleagues had no difficulty in finding many examples of primate behavior that appear to reflect humanlike social cognition. The researchers conclude that 'primates can predict the consequences of their behavior for others and they understand enough about the motives of others to be able to be capable of deceit and other subtle forms of manipulation'. So, if, as seems to be the case, nonhuman primate intellect has been honed, not in the realm of practical affairs but in the hard school of social interaction, one is still left with the question: why? Why have primates found it advantageous to indulge in alliance building and manipulation? The answer, again from field studies, is that individuals who are adept at building and maintaining alliances are also reproductively more successful: making alliances aids in access to potential mating opportunities.

Once a lineage takes the evolutionary step of using social alliances to bolster reproductive success, it finds itself in what Nicholas Humphrey, a Cambridge University psychologist, calls an evolutionary ratchet. 'Once a society has reached a certain level of complexity, then new internal pressures must arise which act to increase its complexity still further,' he explains, 'for, in a society [of this kind], an animal's intellectual "adversaries" are members of his own breeding community. And in these circumstances there can be no going back.'

And where in all this does consciousness fit in? Humphrey describes it as an 'inner eye', with pun intended. Consciousness is a tool—the ultimate tool—of the social animal. Through being able to look into one's own mind and 'see' its reactions to things and other individuals, one can more precisely predict how others will react to those same things and individuals. Consciousness builds a better reality, one that is attuned to the highly social world humans inhabit.

KEY QUESTIONS

- What limitations are there in measuring differences in intelligence from differences in brain size and overall organization?

- How might one infer levels of intelligence from different stone-tool technologies?

- What key pieces of information might lend Support to the 'Man the social animal' hypothesis?

- How would one test whether nonhuman primates possessed a humanlike consciousness?

KEY REFERENCES

D. Cheney et al., 'Social relationships and social cognition', *Science*, pp. 1361–1366 (1986).

D. Falk, 'The petrified brain', *Natural History*, September 1984, pp. 36–39.

A.H. Harcourt, 'Alliances in contests and social intelligence', in *Social expertise and the evolution of intellect*, edited by R. Byrne and A. Witen, Oxford University Press, 198.

R.L. Holloway, 'Human brain evolution', *Canadian Journal of Anthropology*, vol 3, pp. 215–230 (1983).

N.K. Humphrey, 'The social function of intellect', in *Growing points in ethology*, edited by P.P.G. Bateson and R.A. Hinde, Cambridge University Press, 1976.

N.K. Humphrey, *The inner eye*, Faber and Faber, 1986.

R.D. Martin, 'Human brain evolution in an ecological context', *Fifty-second James Arthur Lecture*, American Museum of Natural History, 1983.

M.D. Pagel and P.H. Harvey, 'How mammals produce large-brained offspring,' *Evolution*, pp. 948–957 (1988).

T. Wynn, 'The intelligence of Oldowan hominids', *Journal of Human Evolution*, pp. 529–541 (1981).

15

CRACKING THE BRAIN CASE

IRA B. BLACK

In the past decade, new approaches and emancipating discoveries have revolutionized our understanding of the brain and mind. Recombinant DNA technology, new brain-imaging techniques, brain cell culture, and the computer revolution are yielding information at an explosive rate. We are beginning to understand the relationship that exists between brain genes and cognition. The physical bases of learning and memory are emerging. New and ingenious experiments are revealing the overall organization of cognitive life and our emotions.

How did the human brain evolve? Indeed, what cognitive capacities and personality traits, if any, are uniquely human? What is the broader evolutionary context for the biology of brain and mind function? These are just some of the questions that paleoanthropologists in general, and Dean Falk in particular, have taken as their challenge.

In *Braindance*, Falk employs a conversational, frequently polemical vehicle to present her views of hominid brain evolution, treating the reader to a generous subtext concerning the sociopolitics of paleoanthropology. While her use of hyperbole, loose analogy, and anecdote are often distracting, she does provide a much-needed orientation to the contentious field of hominid brain evolution. Even her subjective, sometimes rancorous accounts of controversies with intolerant, competitive adversaries provide a glimpse of the rough-and-tumble of science.

In Falk's view, human brain evolution is predicated on the emergence of frontal lobe function, the development of associational cortex, and the lateralization of brain function—that is, the growing asymmetry of the two cerebral hemispheres. The frontal lobes lying above the brow at the front of the brain, are essential for creativity, initiative, personality and subjective awareness. The associational cortex, on the other hand, builds up ever more complex associations of information relayed from the sensory areas. This is where, for example, the appearance, sound, and emotion attached to an experience are associated in memory. Not surprisingly, Falk focuses on frontal lobe function and associational cortex evolution to explain hominid evolution.

Falk traces frontal and associational phylogeny in the lineage from *Australopithecus africanus* to *Homo habilis, H. erectus,* and the present keeper of the flame, *H. sapiens.* While her formulation provides a useful neuroanatomical and anthropological road map, it misses a central conceptual mark. Her account implies that hominid brain evolution is about the selection of an ever better, all-purpose thinking machine. In contrast, modern cognitive and neuroscientific discoveries suggest that the primate (and human) brain is composed of diverse, highly specialized cognitive subsystems, not a single universal thinking engine (*see* "Mozart and Modularity," page 8). But we're jumping ahead. Let's describe Falk's views in greater detail.

Assailing the paleoanthropological "old guard" and "old boys club," Falk argues that Raymond Dart's Taung "child" actually had an apelike brain, not the human-like brain claimed by the discoverer (*see* "Taungs and Its Significance," *Natural History,* April 1980). Similarly, Donald Johanson's 3-million-year-old Lucy (*A. afarensis*) is excluded as the link to the genus *Homo.* In Falk's view, the real point of departure is Mary Leakey's startling discovery in 1978: fossilized footprints at Laetoli, dating from 3.5 million years ago (*see* "The Pitted Pattern of Laetoli Feet," *Natural History,* March 1990). And here Falk begins an engrossing epic.

Falk is at her best inferring that the hominid brain began its explosive growth 1.5 million years after the walk at Laetoli. In other words, the bipedal Laetoli hominid had an apelike brain and was probably the common ancestor of modern hominids. Moreover, the dissociation of bipedalism and brain growth prompts Falk to dismiss a host of theories that have related hominid brain evolution to erect posture. In place of the scenarios that she now finds implausible, Falk enunciates "the radiator theory of brain evolution."

Setting the stage for her theory, she notes that normal brain function requires a rather narrow temperature window. She then takes us for a walk in the sun-baked savanna, with the solar orb beating down on the heads of our upright ancestors. The combination of the hot sun and the new stresses on cerebral blood flow induced by gravity acting on a now-erect animal places limits on brain growth.

In Falk's view, the evolution of "a cranial radiator system of veins" allowed cooling of the brain and removed the major limitation on brain growth (*see* "The Petrified Brain," *Natural History,* September 1984). Falk also notes common features in the brain venous sinuses of gracile australopithecines and hominids, which differ from those of *A. africanus* and *A. robustus,* and she constructs the lineage accordingly. *A gracilis* led to the hominid line in which brain size increased so dramatically.

Emancipated by the brain vein drain, the cerebral organ was free to respond to selective pressures. Falk asserts:

> Since the time of Darwin, there have been many speculations about possible prime movers of human brain evolution. Some of these have been rather fanciful. Among the nominees are warfare, work language, tool production, throwing, and hunting. Despite all the speculation about prime movers, there seems to have been resistance to the simple possibility that brain size increased as a result of selection for general intelligence.

Here Falk gets into neuroscientific difficulty by treating the brain as a single system.

In fact, the particular mechanisms mediating the expansion of the frontal cortex and associational areas and the elaboration of lateralization, so important to Falk, are never adequately explicated. Yet the particulars of the evolution of specific subsystems lie at the crux of the scientific problem. To appreciate potential difficulties with Falk's stance, let's place paleoanthropology in a neuroscientific context.

A sampling of some recent advances in neuroscience may put this enormous task in perspective. The human brain contains approximately 100 billion neurons, each with about 10,000 specialized junctions, or synapses, that communicate with other neurons. Activation of billions of synapses at a time results in body movement, a perception, or thought.

Chemical signals, or neurotransmitters, transfer information from one neuron to another in thousandths of a second. Neurons convert the transmitter signals into electrical impulses that are carried along neural cables to the next synaptic junction. There, another transmitter jumps the gap, communicating with the next neuron in line. These basic, building-block synaptic mechanisms are present even in such simple life forms as coelenterates.

In humans, the synaptic networks are organized into diverse systems serving different, highly specific functions. We now know that individual neurons use multiple transmitter signals to convey information to other neurons. In effect, each of the 100-billion neurons can act as a picocomputer, integrating vast amounts of information. Even at the level of the single neuron, complexity and the capacity for sophisticated processing are apparent.

Recent discoveries indicate that the genes that produce transmitters are controlled by the environment. For example, stressful environmental events elicit the well-known fight-or-flight response by activating genes that trigger adrenaline and noradrenaline secretion. In essence, the neuron translates environmental events into behavior through gene action. Thus, the environment shapes neural function during an individual's lifetime, while selecting for neural functions during evolutionary time. Falk misses the opportunity to integrate these new insights.

Startling discoveries now indicate that brain neurons use chemical growth factors, as well as transmitters, to communicate. These factors, also secreted in response to environmental stimuli and nerve impulses, cause growth of new and stronger nerve pathways. In other words, environmental activation of a neural circuit may increase its size and effectiveness by causing growth factor secretion. Growth factors may also play a role in evolution, regulating expansion of old neural systems and eliciting growth of new systems and functions. Unfortunately, Falk does not explore these emerging relationships between the environment, the individual, brain genes, growth factors, and evolution.

How has selection organized these molecular and cellular mechanisms into functioning cognitive systems? How is the functioning cognitive system organized? Converging evidence from neurology, psychology, and neuroscience suggests that cognitive function is organized into discrete modules, which were well summarized by Michael Gazzaniga, professor of psychiatry at Dartmouth, in his article "Organization of the Human Brain" (*Science*, vol. 245, 1989). Apparently unified mental life is actually composed of multiple, distinct components. Different brain areas perform different mental function, and disconnection of areas prevents normally integrated mind function. Mentality literally disintegrates.

For example, the curious and tragic syndrome of alexia without agraphia—when a person cannot read but is able to write—owes its existence to modularity. In this disorder, visual areas become separated (as a result of strokes) from the receptive language area (Wernicke's area), preventing reading. However, since language is *expressed* by the separate motor language area (Broca's area), writing is not impaired.

Of course, modularity is apparent in normal sensory processing as well. For example, when we look at an object, we analyze color, motion, and depth perception along separate synaptic pathways, but the result is a unified perception.

Modularity of cognitive function represents one organizing principle of brain action. In turn, modularity is one manifestation of lateralizaton, the asymmetry of right and left brain function that Falk perceptively cites as a key to hominid brain evolution. In chapter 5 of *Braindance*, Falk summarizes the work of Roger Sperry, professor of biology at the California Institute of Technology, who studied brain asymmetry in animal models in the 1960s. Gazzaniga, a graduate student, applied the research to humans, with astounding results.

In the 1960s and 1970s, Gazzaniga performed landmark studies of so-called split-brain patients. These individuals had intractable epilepsy, which caused electrical seizures to spread from one cerebral hemisphere to the other. They were helped by surgical separation of the two halves of the brain, which transected the massive fiber bundle connecting the hemispheres. The procedure prevented seizure spread, but it also prevented the interhemispheric transfer of information. The stage was set for some fascinating observations.

In one series of experiments Gazzaniga flashed a frightening scene of a burning building to the mute right hemisphere of a patient's brain (only the left had language function). The patient became anxious and agitated. When asked what was wrong, the verbal left brain, not having observed the scene, made up stories. In experiment after experiment, the verbal left brain fabricated explanations, theories, and hypotheses to explain experiences originating in the inaccessible, mute right brain.

These landmark studies led to a number of insights, some directly relevant to human brain evolution. The obvious asymmetry of the brain's left and right hemispheres argues for the differential localization of function as a general principle of brain (and mind) organization.

In addition, a specific module that Gazzaniga terms the interpreter is found only in the dominant left verbal hemisphere. The interpreter constantly attempts to bring unity to a modular consciousness and to the discontinuities of internal and external reality. Apparently, the mind prefers an incorrect explanation to no explanation at all.

In the split-brain patients, the interpreter was always found in the dominant left hemisphere, along with language. In some deep, yet unrecognized manner, therefore, interpreter function and language may be closely related. And few would argue with the contention that language function is uniquely human.

In spite of some controversial claims in the 1960s, most scientists agree that chimpanzees never learn the human equivalent of language. After three decades of work, David Premack, professor of psychology at the University of Pennsylvania, one of the leaders in the field, points out that although chimps can learn a type of artificial representation system, it is distinct from human language. Children use words as representations, employing both abstract and imaginal codes that result in syntactic constructions inaccessible to chimps. By comparison, chimp "language" is invariant and impoverished. Falk tends to gloss over these critical differences, thereby missing central points concerning the nature of human intelligence and the type of evolutionary processes that must have occurred.

In her enthusiasm for the cleverness of chimps, Falk confounds general intelligence and language. To disentangle the two and get back on the evolutionary track, we must understand the message of language scientists. Simply stated, language is a highly specialized cognitive capacity, not a characteristic of a generalized cognitive machine.

In his classic work, *Syntactic Structures,* MIT linguist Noam Chomsky pointed out that in spite of the apparently endless variations among some 4,000 extant languages, a common grammar seems to be built into the human brain. (Linguists use the term grammar to denote a mental structure for mapping meaning onto sound for the production of speech, and conversely for decoding.) An Oxford don, a South Foré tribesman in New Guinea, and a !Kung bushman obey the same underlying grammatical rules.

The implications of Chomsky's formulation for hominid brain evolution are profound. The human brain has a subsystem specialized for language. Extensive clinical evidence supports the contention that language and general cognition are dissociable. Animals and infants exhibit normal cognition without language. Aphasic stroke patients display normal intelligence. Conversely, demented patients are often able to speak relatively normally but are virtually void of the most rudimentary problem-solving ability. An explanation of human brain evolution based on the phylogeny of a general intelligence, as invoked by Falk, just won't do. Any account must describe mechanisms governing the emergence of a specialized language system in the human brain.

Falk does, however, acquaint the reader with some important introductory material. The general scheme of cortical organization is outlined, the potential evolutionary roles of prefrontal and associational cortices are summarized, and the concept of lateralization is introduced. This information may equip the reader to deal with some of the thornier issues of human evolution.

Ira B. Black is professor and chairman of the Department of Neuroscience and Cell Biology at the Robert Wood Johnson Medical School/UMDNJ and author of Information in the Brain: A Molecular Perspective.

16

MOZART AND MODULARITY

STEPHEN JAY GOULD

*How could a mere child be so transcendent in one arena
but so ordinary in all other ways?*

Daines Barrington (1717–1800), an English lawyer and wealthy member of
the lesser nobility, published so many short articles on such a variety of
subjects that he could scarcely avoid a reputation as a dilettante. In numerous communications to the Royal Society of London, he discussed the
landing place of Caesar in Britain, the nonuniversality of Noah's flood, the
antiquity of playing cards, and the death of Dolly Pentreath, the last native
speaker of Cornish (an extinct branch of Celtic languages). Some of his
colleagues considered him superficial and overly credulous. One detractor
even composed a heroic couplet in his dishonor:

Pray then, what think ye of our famous Daines?
Think of a man denied by Nature brains!

Then, in 1764, Barrington happened upon something truly important.
But stung by rebukes for his previous carelessness and hyperbole, he
proceeded cautiously. He waited six years before publishing his observations as a note in the *Philosophical Transactions of the Royal Society of
London,* Britain's leading scientific journal, then and now. And he began his
article by invoking the classical literary form for understatement—litotes.
(These Greek terms for parts of speech and forms of rhetoric have paralyzed
generations of schoolchildren who can't remember the difference between a

dactyl and a synecdoche. Monty Python got back at professorial pedants by making great merriment with "litotes" and its improbable sound.) Litotes (from the Greek *litos*, meaning "small" or "meager") is a form of understatement that expresses an affirmative by the negative of its contrary—as in "not bad" for "good." In his opening paragraph, Barrington used litotes in a near apology to readers for taking their time:

> If I was to send you a well attested account of a boy who measured seven feet in height when he was not more than eight years of age, it might be considered as not undeserving the notice of the Royal Society.

In his second paragraph, Barrington sneaked up a bit further upon his actual discovery:

> The instance which I now desire you will communicate to that learned body, of as early an exertion of most extraordinary musical talents, seems perhaps equally to claim their attention.

The third paragraph, although only in historical retrospect, drops the bombshell:

> Joannes Chrysostomus Wolfgangus Theophilus Mozart, was born at Saltzbourg [sic] in Bavaria [*sic* again], on the 17th of January, 1756 [*sic* thrice, for Mozart was born on January 27]. ... Upon leaving Paris [in 1764 at age eight] he came to England, where he continued more than a year. As during this time I was witness to his most extraordinary abilities as a musician, both at some public concerts, and likewise by having been alone with him for a considerable time at his father's house; I send you the following account, amazing and incredible almost as it may appear.

Litotes had ceded to overt wonderment.

Mozart's skills were so astounding that Barrington even doubted his extreme youth; could father Leopold's game be an elaborate ruse, passing off a well-trained adult midget as a young son? Barrington delayed publication for six years until he could obtain proof in the form of Mozart's birth certificate from the register of Salzburg, "procured from his excellence Count Haslang, envoy extraordinary and minister plenipotentiary of the electors of Bavaria and Palatine" (you just gotta believe somebody with a title like that).

Leopold Mozart made quite a business of showing off his precocious son. Barrington, graced with a private visit, proceeded as any intellectual would: he tested eight-year-old Wolfgang for a variety of musical skills in reading, memory, and improvisation, and his letter to the Royal Society is a report of his impressions. (I learned about this publication at a special exhibit of the British Museum. Barrington's article, entitled "Account of a very remarkable young musician," appeared in 1770, in volume 60 of the *Philosophical Transactions*. The notion that young Mozart had served as subject for a scientific paper in England's leading journal was too much to resist for this forum. What better symbol could we possibly advance for the fruitful interaction of art and science?)

One issue, above all, intrigued Barrington as he observed Mozart and affirmed in spades all the reports he had heard about the young child's precocity (for Barrington sought, in this article, to plumb the nature of genius itself, not merely to explicate Mozart, who, remember, was then just a remarkable little boy, not yet an icon of Western achievement): apparent "wholeness" must be decomposable into separate modules, each subject to independent development. How else could a mere child be so transcendent in one particular arena but ordinary in all other ways? This idea of dissociability must provide a key to understanding human talents: genius is not integral but must result from a hypertrophy of particular modules.

Barrington cites two examples of dissociation in grasping the nature of genius. First, he marvels at Mozart's musical sophistication in an otherwise ordinary and rambunctious eight-year-old boy. If young Wolfgang had been a miniature adult, as adept in manners as in music, then genius might be portrayed as integral, but he acted like an ordinary kid in all areas outside his special talent:

> I must own that I could not help suspecting his father imposed with regard to the real age of the boy, though he had not only a most childish appearance, but likewise had all the actions of that stage of life. For example, wilst he was playing to me, a favorite cat came in, upon which he immediately left his harpsichord, nor could we bring him back for a considerable time. He would also sometimes run about the room with a stick between his legs by way of horse.

Second, Barrington gained some insight about the dissociability of basic emotions. He asked Mozart to improvise songs expressing particular emotions—a song of love and a song of anger. Again, Barrington took refuge in litotes to express his wonder at the successful results:

> [The love song] had a first and a second part, which ... was of the length that opera songs generally last: if this extemporary composition was not amazingly capital, yet it was really above mediocrity, and showed most extraordinary readiness of invention.

The song of rage was even more dramatically successful:

> This lasted also about the same time with the Song of Love; and in the middle of it, he had worked himself up to such a pitch, that he

beat his harpsichord like a person possessed, rising sometimes in his chair.

But how could an eight-year-old boy, with presumably limited experience, at least of sexual love, so abstract and distill these basic modules of our emotional repertoire? This could only be possible, Barrington reasoned, if the fundamental emotions themselves are genuinely dissociable packages. Our totality must be an amalgam of separable components.

We have, before and ever since, been fascinated with such "splinter skills"—extraordinary talents in otherwise undistinguished or even severely handicapped people—for the same reason that so intrigued Barrington: such dissociation seems to argue for separate origin and causation of talents that we would prefer to view—but cannot on this evidence—as expressions of a more general genius. We all know that standard examples of chess grandmasters who cannot balance their check books and mentally handicapped people with prodigious skills in apparently instantaneous numerical calculation or reckoning the day of the week for any date over centuries or millennia.

For all the criticism that Barrington received as an injudicious dilettante, this time he chose well—both in subject and argument. For the principle of dissociation, and construction from separable modules, is central to our understanding of any complex system that arises by natural evolution. Barrington chose the right issue for his wonderment—and the breadth of application extends well beyond divine Mozart to the evolution of any complex organism and the structure of mind. Integral wholeness may sound warm, fuzzy, and romantic, but dissociability is the necessary way of the world.

Since principles are often best illustrated by exposing the fallacy of their contraries, I present the most important, and probably most intelligent, argument ever raised against evolution by a great scientist in the turbulent generation before Darwin. In the *Discours préliminaire* to his four-volume work on fossil vertebrates, published in 1812, Georges Cuvier denied the possibility of evolution by affirming the doctrine of intrinsic and nondissociable wholeness.

Cuvier designated his principle as "the correlation of parts," maintaining that all features of an organism are intricately designed and coordinated to function in a certain optimal way. No part can change by itself. Any conceivable alternation in one organ would require the redesign of every other feature, for optimal function requires complete integration:

> Every organized individual forms an entire system of its own, all the parts of which mutually correspond, and occur to produce a certain definite purpose, by reciprocal reaction, or by combining towards

the same end. Hence none of these separate parts can change their forms without a corresponding change in the other parts of the same animal, and consequently each of these parts, taken separately, indicates all the other parts to which it belonged.

As the last phrase shows, Cuvier used this principle primarily to argue that he could reconstruct entire organisms from fossil fragments, since one bone implied a necessary shape for all other (see my column of June 1990). But Cuvier had a second and even grander motive—the denial of evolution. How can transmutation occur if parts cannot alter separately or at least with some degree of independence? If each tiny modification required a redesign of every other feature, then inertia itself must debar evolution. How can we imagine a coordinated change of all parts every time some minute advantage might attend a slight alteration in one feature? Cuvier continued:

Animals have certain fixed and natural characters, which resist the effects of every kind of influence, whether proceeding from natural causes or human interference: and we have not the smallest reason to suspect that time has any more effect upon them than climate.

I call this argument intelligent because its logic is impeccable. If parts were not dissociable, then evolution could not occur. "All for one" might be good morality for a Musketeer but cannot describe the pathway of natural change in complex systems.

Logical arguments are only as good as their premises. The chain of inference may be irrefutable, but if the premise be false, then the conclusion must fail as well. To cite the harsh motto of our computer age: GIGO, or garbage in, garbage out (no matter how phenomenal the inner workings of the machine).

Cuvier's logic was correct, but his premise of total integrity is false. Evolution does proceed (as it must) by dissociating complex systems into parts, or modules, made of a few correlated features, and by altering the various units at differing rates and times. Biologists refer to this principle as "mosaic evolution," and we need look no further than the history of our own species. Human ancestors, like Lucy and her early australopithecine cousins, evolved an upright posture of nearly modern design before any substantial enlargement of the brain had occurred.

This cardinal principle of dissociability works just as well for the mental complexities of emotions and intelligence as for designs of entire bodies. As he began to compile the notes that would lead to his evolutionary theory, Charles Darwin recognized that he could not give an evolutionary account of human emotions without the principles of modularity and dissociation.

He wished, for example, to trace facial gestures to antecedent states in ancestral animals. But if the human set is an integrated array, locked together by our unique consciousness, then a historical origin for simpler systems becomes impossible. Darwin recognized that two principles must underlie the possibility of evolution. First, gestures cannot be subject to fully conscious control; some, at least, must represent automatic, evolved responses. As evidence for ancestral states, Darwin cited several gestures that make no sense with our modern morphology but that must have served our forebears well. In sneering, we tighten our upper lips and raise them in the region of our canine teeth. This motion once exposed the fighting weapons of our ancestors (as it uncovers the long and sharp canines in many modern mammals that perform the same gesture), but human canines are no bigger than our other teeth and this inherited reaction has lost its original function.

Second, just as young Mozart could separate and abstract single emotions, Darwin realized the standard facial gestures must be modules of largely independent action—and that the human emotional repertoire must represent a concatenation of separate links rather than facets of an unbreakable totality. Evolution can mix, match, and modify independently. Otherwise we face Cuvier's dilemma: if all emotions are inextricably bound by their status as interacting, optimal expressions, then how can anything ever change?

Late in his life, Darwin wrote an entire book on this subject *The Expression of the Emotions in Man and Animals* (1872). But his youthful jottings in the so called M Notebook of 1838, hastily scribbled in the months before he codified his theory of natural selection in September of that year, are even more compelling for their telegraphic expression of excitement in discovery and novel explanation. Darwin later labels this notebook as "full of Metaphysics on Morals and Speculations on Expression." His notes on emotional gestures center on modularity and its importance for evolutionary explanation. Each feeling is linked to a gesture (often quite complex); we have limited control over the form of a gesture, and its evolutionary meaning must often be sought in a lost ancestral function. Darwin wrote:

> He may despise a man and say nothing, but without a most distinct will, he will find it hard to keep his lip from stiffening over his canine teeth.—He may feel satisfied with himself, and though dreading to say so, his step will grow erect and stiff like that of turkey. ... With respect to sneering, the very essence of an habitual movement is continuing it when useless,—therefore it is here continued when ... uncovering the canine [is] useless.

Darwin then speculates on the further evolution of emotions treated as separate entities. He argues that sighing is still directly useful in humans "to relieve circulation after stillness." Yet we might retain the gesture as a sign for an accompanying emotion even if the physiological benefit disappeared: "If organization were changed, I conceive sighing might yet remain just like sneering does."

I received my clearest insight into the modularity of facial expressions not from any scientific writing but from viewing the world's greatest sculpture: Michelangelo's Moses in the church of San Pietro in Vincoli (Saint Peter in Chains), in Rome. Moses, bearing the tablets of the Ten Commandments, has just come down from Mount Sinai. Suffused with holiness and with joy at the gift he may now bestow upon his people, he looks around only to see the Israelites worshipping the golden calf. His face is a maelstrom of emotions: zeal and ardor for what he has witnessed on the mountain, rage at his people for their transgression, deep sorrow for human weaknesses. The sublimity of the statue lies in the richness of this mixture upon one face—as if Moses is truly Everyman (and in every major state of feeling).

I visited this statue several times and felt its power but could not grasp how Michelangelo had put so much into one face. On my last trip, and largely by chance, I think that I found guide to the solution. Michelangelo understood—whether viscerally or explicitly, I do not know—the principle of modularity. When I focused on one feature and covered the rest of the face, I saw only one emotion each time. The eyebrows speak one message, the nose another, the lips a third. The rich face can be decomposed into modules of feeling, but the totality stuns us by integration.

Many of the most famous experiments in animal ethology affirm and extend the principle of modularity. Consider Niko Tinbergen's classic work on begging for food in newly hatched gulls (so beautifully described in his charming book *The Herring Gull's World*). The newborns peck vigorously at their parent's beak, apparently aiming for a red spot near the tip of the mandible. If an infant makes proper contact, the parent regurgitates a parcel of food and the baby gull gets is first meal.

But what inspired the pecking behavior? The baby gull has no conscious understanding of a reward to be gained. It has never eaten before and cannot know what a knock on a parent's bill will provide. The behavior must be innate and unlearned.

At what, then, does the baby bird direct its pecks? At first consideration, one might conjecture that the entire form or gestalt of the parent would provide an optimal target. After all, what could be more appealing than the parent's totality—a full, three-dimensional image with the right movements and odors. But consider the issue a bit more deeply: the hatchling has never seen a bird. Can the complexities of the entire parental form be engrafted innately upon its untested brain? Wouldn't it be more reasonable—easier to program if you will—for the hatchling to respond to one or a few abstract particulars, that is, to modules extracted from the total form?

In an exhaustive series of experiments, Tinbergen showed that hatchling gulls do respond to modules and abstractions. They peck preferentially at long and skinny things, red things, and regions of markedly contrasting colors. As an effect of this simplified modularity, they hit the red spot at the tip of the parental bill—the only red region at the end of a long object, in an area of contrasting color with surrounding yellow. Complex totality may be beyond the cognitive capacity of a hatchling gull, but any rich object can be broken down to simpler components, and then built up. Any developing complexity—whether in the cognitive growth of an individual or the evolution of a lineage—may require this principle of construction from modules.

If a hatchling gull favors abstraction (and doesn't perceive parental totality), then Tinbergen reasoned that he might construct a "super-gull"— a model exaggerating the key modules. This "improved" version might elicit more attention than the actual parents themselves. This idea bore fruit as hatchlings preferred several rather un-gull-like dummies to real birds. For example, narrow sticks longer than real bills, and color patches more starkly contrasted with surroundings than the red spot on an actual bill, elicited more pecks from hatchlings than did an accurately modeled head.

Tinbergen then generalized these observations to the important concept of a "super-normal stimulus"—an artificial exaggeration that elicits more favor or response than the feature itself. (In his book, Tinbergen includes an amusing discussion of his struggle to find a good name for this phenomenon. He first spoke of a "super-optimal" stimulus but finally rejected the term as oxymoronic—for, by definition, optima cannot be exceeded. He then remarks that "'supernatural' would be a good term, if it were not used already in another sense." Finally, he settled upon "super-normal.")

Many animals exploit this modular principle of supernormal stimuli to gain advantage over others. In the classical example, cuckoos subvert the propensities of their hosts to feed any chick in the nest that rises higher, squawks louder, or opens its beak wider. The mother cuckoo lays its egg in another bird's nest. The egg itself is an accurate mimic and often can't be distinguished from the host's own products. But the cuckoo hatchling quickly outstrips it nestmates in growth and may even toss them out to their death. The unwitting adult hosts, fooled by the supernormal stimuli arising from the large, loud cuckoo chick, continue to feed the usurper and murderer.

Obviously, if modularity didn't often rule over accurate perception of totalities, supernormal stimuli would not exist. Host parents would know their own children and reject the cuckoo. Hatchling gulls would peck at parental beaks (that might feed them), rather than at cardboard dummies with exaggerated features.

Modularity pervades all neurological organization, right up to what Darwin called "the citadel itself'"—human cognition. This principle of breaking complexity into dissociable units does not disappear the apex of known organization. We might not be fooled in toto by the analog of a cuckoo chick, but the fashion industry knows how well, and how sheepishly, we respond to a plethora of supernormal stimuli.

Interestingly, Darwin accompanied his M-notebook jottings on the modularity of emotional gestures with similar statements about cognitive items and units:

> People who can multiply large numbers in their head must have this high faculty, yet not clever people. ... The great calculators, from the confined nature of their associations (is it not so in punning) are people of very limited intellects, and in the same way are chess players. ... The son of a fruiterer in Bond St. was so great a fool that his father only left him a guinea a week, yet he was inimitable chess player.

The concept of modularity, explicitly so called, lies at the heart of much innovate research in cognitive science. The brain does a great deal of work by complex coordination among its parts, but we have also known for a long time that highly particular aptitudes and behaviors map to specific portions of the cerebral cortex. The modules are often stunningly precise and particular, as illustrated by unusual losses and misperceptions of people who have suffered damage to highly localized regions of cortex (*see* Oliver Sack's wonderful book *The Man Who Mistook His Wife for a Hat*). The September 19, 1991, issue of *Nature* tells the remarkable story of two men who suffered localized strokes that seriously impaired their ability to use and recognize vowels, but not consonants. Surely, we would have regarded our separation of sound into vowels and consonants as an artificial division of a totality—yet this distinction may record a deeper mapping of cerebral modules (*see* R. Cubelli, "A selective deficit for writing vowels in acquired dysgraphia," *Nature*, vol. 353, pp. 258–60).

Mozart was not yet Mozart when Daines Barrington witnessed his incredible performance. He was just a bratty kid at the acme of precocity. In fact, Barrington even speculated on his potential for future contributions. He spoke of another prodigy named John Barratier who knew Latin at four, Hebrew at six, and who translated the travels of Rabbi Benjamin, complete with learned notes and glosses, at eleven. But we know little of Barratier today because he died before the age of twenty.

Barrington notes the unhappy tendency of geniuses to die young, and he expresses his hope for Mozart by comparing him with England's greatest musical guest, the German emigré Handel. Young Handel may not have been quite so precocious as Mozart, but he did live a long and remarkably productive life, from 1685 to 1759, and Barrington took comfort:

> I am the more glad to state this short comparison between these two early prodigies in music, as it may be hoped that little Mozart may possibly attain to the same advanced years as Handel, contrary to the common observation that such *ingenia praecocia* are generally short lived.

Barrington got half his wish. Mozart lived long enough to become Mozart but died so young, at thirty-five, that his early demise has become the canonical example of a genre—the tragic and uncertain lives led by so many artists. (I learned of Barrington's article in an exhibit marking the bicentennial of Mozart's death. I write this essay during the month of the anniversary itself. I wish that I were composing this at the proper Handelian distance of forty years hence, which would be good for Mozart and good for me too.)

Daines Barrington thought that he was writing a scientific article about the modularity of human abilities. The later exaltation of Mozart makes us view his work in a more particular light—as a testimony about the early life of everyone's favorite musical prodigy. Is Barrington's article part of science or of art? Perhaps, for once, these are truly false modules, and our intellectual life would benefit by more integration. If Mozart had died before *Idomeneo* (his teen-aged opera), Barrington's article would endure as a respectable scientific account of a generic musical prodigy. I thank God for *Don Giovanni* (I even thank Him for every Musak rendition of *Eine Kleine Nachtmusik*). But even if Mozart had died in childhood, in the frosts of an English winter (in their damned buildings without central heating), his contribution to our understanding of the human mind would be no mean thing, no small potatoes.

Stephen Jay Gould teaches biology, geology, and the history of science at Harvard University.

17

The Return of Phineas Gage: Clues About the Brain from the Skull of a Famous Patient

Hanna Damasio, Thomas Grabowski, Randall Frank,
Albert M. Galaburda, Antonio R. Damasio

When the landmark patient Phineas Gage died in 1861, no autopsy was performed, but his skull was later recovered. The brain lesion that caused the profound personality changes for which his case became famous has been presumed to have involved the left frontal region, but questions have been raised about the involvement of other regions and about the exact placement of the lesion within the vast frontal territory. Measurements from Gage's skull and modern neuroimaging techniques were used to reconstitute the accident and determine the probable location of the lesion. The damage involved both left and right prefrontal cortices in a pattern that, as confirmed by Gage's modern counterparts, causes a defect in rational decision making and the processing of emotion.

On 13 September 1848, Phineas P. Gage, a 25-year-old construction foreman for the Rutland and Burlington Railroad in New England, became a victim of a bizarre accident. In order to lay new rail tracks across Vermont, it was necessary to level the uneven terrain by controlled blasting. Among other tasks, Gage was in charge of the detonations, which involved drilling holes in the stone, partially filling the holes with explosive powder, covering the powder with sand, and using a fuse and tamping iron to trigger an explosion into the rock. On the fateful day, a momentary distraction let Gage begin tamping directly over the powder before his assistant had had a chance to cover it with sand. The result was a powerful explosion away from the rock and toward Gage. The fine-pointed, 3-cm-thick, 109-cm-long tamping iron was hurled, rocket-like, through his face, skull, brain, and then into the sky. Gage was momentarily stunned but regained full consciousness immediately thereafter. He was able to talk and even walk with the help of his men. The iron landed many yards away (1).

Phineas Gage not only survived the momentous injury, in itself enough to earn him a place in the annals of medicine, but he survived as a different man, and therein lies the greater significance of this case. Gage had been a responsible, intelligent, and socially well-adapted individual, a favorite with peers and elders. He had made progress and showed promise. The signs of a profound change in personality were already evident during the convalescence under the care of his physician, John Harlow. But as the months passed it became apparent that the transformation was not only radical but difficult to comprehend. In some respects, Gage was fully recovered. He remained as able-bodied and appeared to be as intelligent as before the accident; he had no impairment of movement or speech; new learning was intact, and neither memory nor intelligence in the conventional sense had been affected. On the other hand, he had become irreverent and capricious. His respect for the social conventions by which he once abided had vanished. His abundant profanity offended those around him. Perhaps most troubling, he had taken leave of his sense of responsibility. He could not be trusted to honor his commitments. His employers had deemed him "the most efficient and capable" man in their "employ" but now had to dismiss him. In the words of his physician, "the equilibrium or balance, so to speak, between his intellectual faculty and animal propensities" had been destroyed. In the words of his friends and acquaintances, "Gage was no longer Gage" (1). Gage began a new life of wandering that ended a dozen years later, in San Francisco, under the custody of his family. Gage had never returned to a fully independent existence, never again held a job comparable to the one he once had. His accident had made headlines but his death went unnoticed. No autopsy was obtained.

Twenty years after the accident, John Harlow, unaided by the tools of experimental neuropsychology available today, perceptively correlated Gage's cognitive and behavioral changes with a presumed area of focal damage in the front region (1). Other cases of neurological damage were then revealing the brain's foundation for language, motor function, and perception and now Gage's case indicated something even more surprising: Perhaps there were structures in the human brain dedicated to the planning and execution of personal and socially suitable behavior, to the aspect of reasoning known as rationality.

Given the power of this insight, Harlow's observation should have made a scientific impact that the comparable suggestions based on the patients of Broca and Wernicke made (2). The suggestions, though surrounded by controversy, became the foundation of the understanding of the neural basis of language and were pursued actively, while Harlow's report on Gage did not inspire a search for the neural basis reasoning, decision-making, or social behavior. One factor likely to have contributed to the indifferent reception accorded to Harlow's work was that the intellectual atmosphere of the time made it somewhat more acceptable that there was a neural basis for processes such as movement or even language rather than for moral reasoning and social behavior (3). But the principal explanation must rest with the substance of Harlow's report. Broca and Wernicke had autopsy results, Harlow did not. Unsupported by anatomical evidence, Harlow's observation was the more easily dismissed. Because the exact position of the lesion was not known, some critics could claim that the damage actually involved Broca's so-called language "center," and perhaps would also have involved the nearby "motor centers." And because the patient showed neither paralysis nor aphasia, some critics reached the conclusion that there were no specialized regions at all (4). The British physiologist David Ferrier was a rare dissenting voice. He thoughtfully ventured, in 1878, that the lesion spared both motor and language centers, that it had damaged the left prefrontal cortex, and that such damage probably explained Gage's behavioral defects, which he aptly described as a "mental degradation" (5).

Harlow only learned of Gage's death about 5 years after its occurrence. He proceeded to ask Gage's family to have the body exhumed so that the skull could be recovered and kept as a medical record. The strange request was granted, and Phineas Gage was once again the protagonist of a grim event. As a result, the skull and the tamping iron, alongside which Gage had been buried, have been part of the Warren Anatomical Medical Museum at Harvard University.

As new cases of frontal damage were described in this century, some of which did resemble that of Gage, and as the enigmas of frontal lobe functions continued to resist elucidation, Gage gradually acquired landmark status. Our own interest in the case grew out of the idea that Gage exemplified a particular type of cognitive and behavioral defect caused by damage to ventral and medial sectors of prefrontal cortex, rather than to the left dorsolateral sector as implicit in the traditional view. It then occurred to us that some of the image processing techniques now used to investigate Gage's counterparts could be used to test this idea by going back in time, reconstituting the accident, and determining the probable placement of his lesion. The following is the result of our neuroanthropological effort.

We began by having one of us (A.M.G.) photograph Gage's skull inside and out and obtain a skull x-ray (Figure 1) as well as a set of precise measurements (6) relative to bone landmarks. Using these measurements, we proceeded to deform linearly the three-dimensional reconstruction of a standard human skull (7) so that its dimensions matched those of Phineas Gage's skull. We also constructed Talairach's stereotactic space for both his skull and Phineas Gage's real skull (8). On the basis of the skull photographs, the dimensions of the entry and exit holes were scaled and mapped into the deformed standard skull. Based on measurements of the iron rod and on the recorded descriptions of the accident, we determined the range of likely trajectories of the rod. Finally, we simulated those trajectories in three-dimensional space using Brainvox (9). We modeled the rod's trajectory as a straight line connecting the center of the entry hole at orbital level to the center of the exit hole. This line was then carried downward to the level of the mandibular ramus. The skull anatomy allowed us to consider entry points within a 1.5-cm radius of this point (20 points in all) (Figure 2).

Possible exit points were determined as follows: We decided to constrain the exit point to be at least 1.5 cm (half the diameter of the rod) from the lateral and posterior margins of the area of bone loss (Figure 3) because

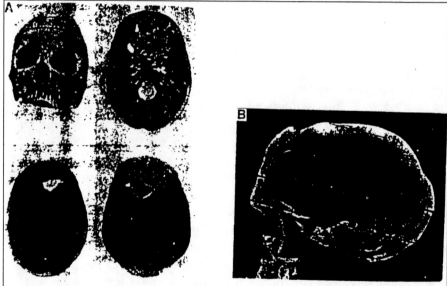

FIGURE 1. Photographs of (A) several views of the skull of Phineas Gage and (B) the skull x-ray.

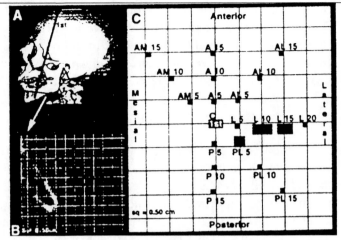

FIGURE 2. View of the entry-level area with the a priori most likely first trajectory. (A) Skull with this first vector and the level (red) at which entry points were marked. (B) View of a segment of section 1. On the left is the mandibular ramus, and on the right is the array of entry points. (C) Enlargement of the array of entry points. One additional point was added (L20) to ensure that every viable entry point was surrounded by nonviable points. Nonviable vectors are shown in red and viable vectors with labels identifying their exit points are shown in green. Abbreviations: A, anterior; L, lateral; P, posterior; AM, anteromesial; AL, anterolateral; PL, posterolateral; C, central.

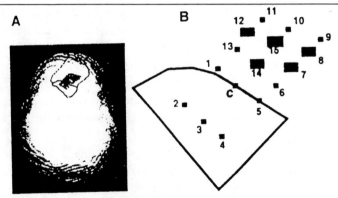

FIGURE 3. (A) View from above the deformed skull with the exit hole and the anterior bone flap traced in black. The blue circle represents the first sector tested, and the gray surface represents the area where exit points were tested. (B) Schematic enlargement of the exit hole and of the area tested for exit points. The letter C marks the first tested vector (blue). The numbers 1 through 15 mark the other exit points tested. Red indicates nonviable vectors, green indicates viable vectors, and the label identifies the entry point. Note that the priori best fit C was not viable.

there were no disruptions of the outer table of the calvarium in these directions (Figure 1, lower right panel). However, we accepted that the rod might have passed up to 1.5 cm anterior to the area of bone loss because inspection of the bone in this region revealed that it must have been separated completely from the rest of the calvarium (Figure 1). Furthermore, the wound was described as an inverted funnel (1). We tested 16 points within the rectangular-shaped exit area that we constructed (Figure 3).

The trajectory connecting each of the entry and exit points was tested at multiple anatomical levels. The three-dimensional skull was resampled in planes perpendicular to the best a priori trajectory (C in Figures 2 and 3). We were helped by several important anatomical constraints. We knew that the left mandible was intact; that the zygomatic arch was mostly intact but had a chipped area, at its medial and superior edge, that suggested the rod had grazed it; and that the last superior molar socket was intact although the tooth was missing. Acceptable trajectories were those which, at each level, did not violate the following rules: The vectors representing the trajectories could not be closer than 1.5 cm from the mid-thickness of the zygomatic arch, 1 cm from the last superior molar, and 0.5 cm from the coronoid process of the mandible (10). Only seven trajectories satisfied these conditions (Figure 4). Two of those seven invariably hit the anterior horn of the lateral ventricle and were therefore rejected as anatomically improbably because they would not have been compatible with survival (the resulting massive infection would not have been controllable in the preantibiotic era). When checked in our collection of normal brains, one of the remaining five trajectories behaved better than any others relative to the lower constraints and was thus chosen as the most likely trajectory. The final step was to model the five acceptable trajectories of the iron rod in a three-dimensional reconstruction of a human brain that closely fit Phineas Gage's assumed brain dimensions (11). Talairach's sterotactic warpings were used for this final step.

The modeling yielded the results shown in Figure 5. In the left hemisphere, the lesion involved the anterior half of the orbital frontal cortex (Broadmann's cytoarchitectonic fields 11 and 12), the polar and anterior mesial frontal cortices (fields 8 to 10 and 32), and the anterior-most sector of the anterior cingulate gyrus (field 24). However, the lesion did not involve the mesial aspect of field 6 [the supplementary motor area (SMA)]. The frontal operculum, which contains Broca's area and includes fields 44, 45, and 47, was also spared, both cortically and in the underlying white matter. In the right hemisphere, the lesion involved part of the anterior and mesial orbital region (field 12), the mesial and polar frontal cortices (fields

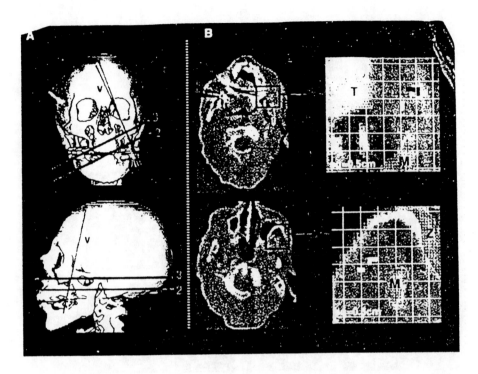

FIGURE 4. (A) Front and lateral skull views with the projection of the five final vectors (V). The two red lines show the position of the two sectors seen in (B). (B) Skull sections 2 and 3: examples of two bottleneck levels at which the viability of vectors was checked. Next to each section is an enlargement of the critical area. Abbreviations T, missing tooth; M, intact mandible; Z, intact zygoma with a chipped area (light blue).

8 to 10 and 32), and the anterior segment of the anterior cingulate gyrus (field 24). The SMA was spared. The white matter core of the frontal lobes was more extensively damaged in the left hemisphere than in the right. There was no damage outside of the frontal lobes.

Even allowing for error and taking into consideration that additional white matter damage likely occurred in the surround of the iron's trajectory, we can conclude that the lesion did not involve Broca's area or the motor cortices and that it favored the ventromedial region of both frontal lobes while sparing the dorsolateral. Thus, Ferrier was correct, and Gage fits a neuroanatomical pattern that we have identified to date in 12 patients within a group of 28 individuals with frontal damage (12). Their ability to make rational decisions in personal and social matters is invariable compromised and so is their processing of emotion. On the contrary, their ability to

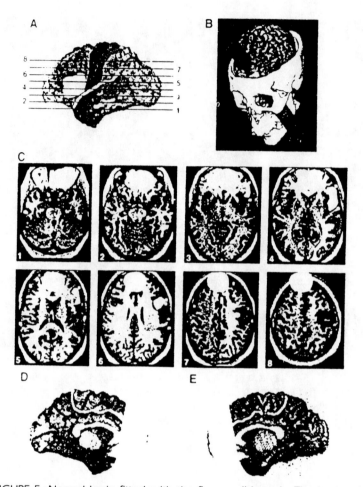

FIGURE 5. Normal brain fitted with the five possible rods. The best rod is highlighted in sold white [except for (B), where it is shown in red]. The areas spared by the iron are highlighted in color. Broca, yellow; motor, red; somatosensory, green; Wernicke, blue. (A) Lateral view of the brain. Numbered black lines correspond to levels of the brain section shown in (C). (D and E) Medical view of left and right hemispheres, respectively, with the rod shown in white.

tackle the logic of an abstract problem, to perform calculations, and to call up appropriate knowledge and attend to it remains intact. The establishment of such a pattern has led to the hypothesis that emotion and its underlying neural machinery participate in decision making within the social domain and has raised the possibility that the participation depends on the ventromedial frontal region (13). This region is reciprocally connected with subcortical nuclei that control basic biological regulation, emotional processing, and social cognition and behavior, for instance, in amygdala and hypothalamus (14). Moreover, this region shows a high concentration of serotonin S_2 receptors in monkeys whose behavior is socially adapted as well as a low concentration in aggressive, socially uncooperative animals (15). In contrast, structures in the dorsolateral region are involved in other domains of cognition concerning extrapersonal space, objects, language, and arithmetic (16). These structures are largely intact in Gage-like patients, thus accounting for the patients' normal performance in traditional neuropsychologic tests that are aimed at such domains.

The assignment of frontal regions to different cognitive domains is compatible with the idea that frontal neurons in any of those regions may be involved with attention, working memory, and the categorization of contingent relationships regardless of the domain (17). This assignment also agrees with the idea that in non-brain-damaged individuals the separate frontal regions are interconnected and act cooperatively to support reasoning and decision making. The mysteries of frontal lobe function are slowly being solved, and it is only fair to establish, on a more substantial footing, the roles that Gage and Harlow played in the solution.

ENDNOTES

1. J. M. Harlow, *Pub. Mass Med. Soc. 2, 327* (1868).

2. P. Broca, *Bull. Soc. Anthropol.* 6, 337 (1865); C. Wernicke, *Der apasische Symptomencomplex* (Cohn und Weigert, Breslau, Poland, 1874). A remarkable number of basic insights on the functional specialization of the human brain, from motor function to sensory perception and to spoken and written language, came from the description of such cases mostly during the second half of the 19th century. The cases usually acted as a springboard for further research, but on occasion their significance was overlooked, as in the case of Gage. Another such example is the description of color perception impairment (achromatopsia) caused by a ventral occipital lesion, by D. Verrey [*Arch. Opthalmol.* (Paris) 8, 289 (1888)]. His astonishing finding was the first denied and then ignored until the 1970s.

3. Reasoning and social behavior were deemed inextricable from ethics and religion and not amenable to biological explanation.

4. The reaction against claims for brain specialization was in fact a reaction against phrenological doctrines, the curious and often unacknowledged inspiration for many of the early case reports. The views of E. Dupuy exemplify the attitude [*Examen de Quelques Points de la Physiologie du Cerveau* (Delahaye, Paris, 1873); M. MacMillan, *Brain Cognit.* 5, 67 (1986)].

5. D. Ferrier, *Br. Med. J.* 1, 399 (1878).

6. The first measurements were those necessary to construct Gage's Talairach stereotactic space and deform a three-dimensional, computerized tomography skull: the maximum length of the skull, the maximum height of the skull above the inion-glabella line, the distance from this line to the floor of the middle fossa, the maximum width of the skull, and the position of the section contour of Gage's skull relative to the inion-glabella line. The second measurements were those necessary to construct the entry and exit areas: on the top external view, the measure of edges of the triangular exit hole; on the internal view the distances from its three corners to the mid-sagittal line and to the nasion; the distance from the borders of the hole to the fracture lines seen anteriorly and posteriorly to this hole; and the dimensions of the entry hole at the level of the orbit.

7. Thin-cut standard computerized tomography image of a cadaver head obtained at North Carolina Memorial Hospital.

8. We introduced the following changes to the method described by P. Fox, J. Perlmutter, and M. Raichle [*J. Comput. Assist. Tomgr.* 9, 141 (1985)]. We calculated the mean distance from the anterior commissure (AC) to the posterior commissure (PC) in a group of 27 normal brains and used that distance for Gage (26.0 mm). We also did not consider the AC-frontal pole and the PC-occipital pole distances as equal because our group of normals had a mean difference of 5 mm between the two measures, and Talairach himself did not give these two measurements as equal [J. Talairach and G. Szikla, *Atlas d'Anatomie Stereotaxique du Telencephale* (Masson, Paris, 1967); J. Talairach and P. Tournoux, *Co-Planar Stereotaxic Atlas of the Human Brain* (Thieme, New York, 1988)]. We introduced an anterior shift of 3% to the center of the AC-PC line and used that point as the center of the AC-PC segment. This shift meant that the anterior sector of Talairach's space was 47% of the total length and that the posterior was 53%. We had no means of calculating the difference between the right and left width of Gage's brain, therefore, we assumed them to be equal.

9. H. Damasio and R. Frank, *Arch. Neurol.* 49, 137 (1992).

10. There were two reasons to allow the vector this close to the mandible: (i) The zygomatic arch and coronoid process were never more than 2 cm apart; (ii) we assumed that, in reality, this distance might have been larger if the mouth were open or if the mandible, a movable structure, had been pushed by the impact of the iron rod.

11. The final dimensions of Phineas Gage's Talairach space were as follows: total length, 171.6 mm; total height, 111.1 mm; and total width, 126.5 mm. Comparing these dimensions to a group of 27 normal subjects, we found that in seven cases at least two of the dimensions were close to those of Phineas Gage [mean length, 169.9 mm (SD, 4.1); mean height, 113.6 (SD, 2.3); mean width, 125 (SD, 3.9). The seven brains were fitted with the possible trajectories to determine which brain areas were involved. There were no significant differences in the areas of damage. The modeling we present here was performed on subject 1600LL (length, 169 mm; height, 115.2 mm; width, 125.6 mm).

12. Data from the Lesion Registry of the University of Iowa's Division of Cognitive Neuroscience as of 1993.

13. P. Eslinger and A. R. Damasio, *Neurology* 35, 1731 (1985); J. L. Saver and A. R. Damasio, *Neuropsychologia* 29, 1241 (1991); A. R. Damasio, D. Tranel, H. Damasio, in *Frontal Lobe Function and Dysfunction,* H. S. Levin, H. M. Eisenberg, A. L. Benton, Eds. (Oxford Univ. Press, New York, 1991), pp. 217–229; S. Dehaene and J. P. Changeux, *Cereb. Cortex* 1, 62 (1991).

14. P. S. Goldman-Rakic, in *Handbook of Physiology: The Nervous System,* F. Plum, Ed. (American Physiological Society, Bethesda, MD, 1987), vol. 5, pp. 373–401; D. N. Pandya and E. H. Yeterian, in *The Prefrontal Cortex: Its Structure, Function and Pathology,* H. B. M. Uylings, Ed. (Elsevier, Amsterdam, 1990); H. Barbas and D. N. Pandya, *J. Comp. Neurol.* 286, 253 (1989).

15. M. J. Raleigh and G. L. Brammer, *Soc. Neurosci. Abstr.* 19, 529 (1993).

16. M. Petrides and B. Milner, *Neuropsychologia* 20, 249 (1982); J. M. Fuster, *The Prefrontal Cortex* (Raven, New York, ed. 2, 1989); M. I. Posner and S. E. Petersen, *Annu. Rev. Neurosci.* 13, 25 (1990).

17. P. S. Goldman-Rakic, *Sci. Am.* 267, 110 (September 1992): A. Bechara, A. R. Damasio, H. Damasio, S. Anderson, *Cognition* 50, 7 (1994); A. R. Damasio, *Descartes' Error: Emotion, Reason and the Human Brain* (Putnam, New York, in press).

18. We thank A. Paul of the Warren Anatomical Museum for giving us access to Gage's skull. Supported by National Institute of Neurological Diseases and Stroke grant PO1NS19632 and by the Mathers Foundation.

18

ORGANIZATION OF THE
HUMAN BRAIN

MICHAEL S. GAZZANIGA

Examination of structure-function correlates in the human brain reveals that there is a high degree of functional specificity in the information transmitted over neural systems. It also appears that the human brain has a modular organization consisting of identifiable component processes that participate in the generation of a cognitive state. The effects of isolating entire modular systems or of disconnecting the component parts can be observed. The features of a left hemisphere specialized capacity to interpret the actions of modules are discussed in terms of human consciousness.

The examination of neurologic patients with the use of experimental methods borrowed from psychology, neuroscience, and medicine yields insights into the cerebral organization of human cognition. An emerging view is that the brain is structurally and functionally organized into discrete units or "modules" and that these components interact to produce mental activities. The idea of modularity is used in several different contexts in the mind sciences. In this article I review the work from my laboratory on patients who have undergone partial or complete brain bisection and address the concept of modularity from three different perspectives.

First, structure-function correlations in the central nervous systems of animals have greatly advanced the understanding of cerebral organization in recent years and continue to represent one of the ways to think about modularity. The clearest instances are in the analysis of sensory systems and, in particular, vision (1). Over the past two decades, for example, several anatomically distinct cortical areas have been discovered that are preferentially but not inclusively or exclusively involved in the processing of various dimensions of visual information such as color, motion, and depth perception. Greater specificity in structure-function correlations has also been seen in the monkey for higher order processes such as memory and problem-solving capacity (2). Thus, research on animals has led to the belief that there are anatomic modules involved in information processing of all kinds and that they work in parallel and are distributed throughout the brain. Evidence for structure-function correlates in humans is presented.

Second, cognitive science has proved useful and diverse models of mental activity that are based on modular interactions. Particular mental capacities, such as the ability to form visual images, the ability to attend and to remember, the capacity for language, and a host of other cognitive skills, have been analyzed in terms of the "components" or modules that interact to produce what seems to be a unitary skill (3). As these models have developed, there have been continuing attempts to test their biologic validity by examining patients with brain damage, or with brain areas disconnected from one another in order to identify the specific structures involved in particular aspects of a mental activity. Models of human cognition (as opposed to animal cognition) allow for far more extensive examination of modular concepts because more complex mental activities can be studied.

Finally, the idea of modularity is considered at a more integrative level in which mechanism of consciousness such as human belief formation are investigated (4). Here the term modularity refers to the collective action of several subprocesses that produce either overt or covert actions and behaviors. Studies on split-brain patients have revealed the presence of a system in the left hemisphere that interprets these actions, moods, and thought processes that are generated by groups of modules that are acting outside the realm of our conscious awareness. The left-brain "interpreter" constructs theories about these actions and feelings and tries to bring order and unity to our conscious lives. It is a special system that works independently from language processes and appears to be unique to the human brain and related to the singular capacity of the brain to make casual inferences.

NEUROLOGIC CORRELATES OF FUNCTION

By combining in vivo anatomic data obtained by magnetic resonance (MR) imaging with neuropsychological data, investigators are able to determine some of the effects of brain lesions on human behavior and to evaluate the specificity of the correlations between structure and function. My colleagues and I have seen precise structure-function correlates when the corpus callosum (the structure connection the two halves of the brain) is surgically cut in an effort to control epilepsy.

In a patient whose corpus calosum is completely transected, there is little or no perceptual or cognitive interaction between the hemispheres (Figure 1A). Also, contrary to findings in primates and cats (5), there is no functional overlap at the visual midline after callosal section in humans (6). In a study of midline overlap, a double Purkinje image eye tracker was used that permitted the accurate presentation of visual information irrespective of subject's eye movements. This allowed stimuli to be presented to each hemisphere with a positional accuracy of 1 min of arc. Stimuli as close as 15 min of arc were presented to the left or right of the point of fixation. Under these conditions, visual information could be easily used by the hemisphere receiving the stimulus but was not available for the opposite hemisphere. If one assumes that these psychophysical data are a result of anatomical structure, these results emphasize the differences between the brain structures of animals and humans. We have also noted other structure-function differences for the anterior commissure and superior colliculus (7).

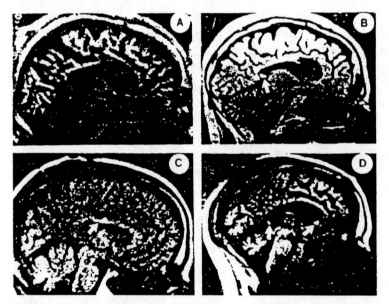

FIGURE 1. MR scans of four patents who have undergone callosal section. MR images of four normal intact callosa are shown in Figure 2. (A) Complete transection; (B) incomplete transection, splenium (arrow) intact; (C) incomplete transection, anterior half (arrow) intact; (D) incomplete transection, remnants in splenium and rostrum (arrows). The remaining fibers only transmit specific information from one half of the brain to the other.

There are, however, even more compelling examples of specificity of function in discrete callosal regions. The first example reveals the specificity in the domain of elementary cortical-cortical sensory-motor integration. Only the posterior half of the callosum was sectioned in the patient E. B. (Figure 1c). Although the designation "posterior half" is arbitrary, as the surgical section is only an estimate and the extent of the section varies from case to case, the general topology of the callosum would predict that information related to mechanisms of motor control would be affected by the transection.

This issue was examined by using a finger localization task devised for the first split-brain patients (8). In brief, a phalanx on one finger is stimulated out of view of the subject and the patient is required to indicate the point of stimulation with the thumb of the same hand. Both normal individuals and partial and complete split-brain patients can easily carry out this task for each hand as long as the stimulus and response are restricted to the same hand. In the second part of the task, after a phalanx is stimulated on one finger, the patient must find the corresponding point on the other hand. In this case a striking difference is seen for the fully split-brain patient. Although a normal individual finds this task easy, patients with a fully sectioned callosum can only perform this task at near chance proficiency.

The ability of E. B. to cross-integrate the needed information was impaired in only one direction. She had no problem integrating the information from right to left, but she failed to integrate information between the hands in the other direction. It would appear that her surgical section included fibers transmitting motor information in one direction but spared those transmitting it in the opposite direction. This condition persists years after the surgery (7).

The second example suggests that even a higher degree of specificity can be observed in these partially disconnected brains. In patient V. P. (Figure 1D), manipulation of the cognitive content of sensory information critically influenced whether or not spared fibers were activated (9). V. P. has been extensively studied and MR imaging revealed spared fibers in both the region of the splenium (posterior) and rostrum (anterior) portion of the callosum. On most tests of perceptual and cognitive functions, she showed little or no evidence of interaction between the hemispheres. Even though she had some spared fibers, informational interactions were not detected.

In the course of carrying out a series of electrophysiological studies on V. P., one highly specific stimulus condition that allowed information to pass between her hemispheres was observed. Printed words were presented, one to each half-field, and V. P. was asked to judge whether they rhymed. The word pairs varied along two dimensions. They either looked and sounded alike, looked alike but did not sound alike, sounded alike but did not look alike, or neither looked nor sounded alike. A fully split-brain patient performed at chance in all conditions. However, V. P. performed at chance in all conditions except for the case when the words both looked and sounded alike.

These data suggest there was something about the redundancy of the graphemic and phonemic elements of the stimulus that activated the remaining callosal fibers. It is not possible to say for sure if both remnant fiber groups participated in the communication. However, it is known that the posterior regions serve visual functions and the anterior regions interconnect frontal areas that might be involved in language processes.

The specificity of function indicated by these studies raises the question of how much genetic control there is of the development of a large brain structure such as the callosum. The callosum is far more similar in morphology and area in monozygotic twins than it is in pairs of unrelated controls (10) (Figure 2). Although the results strongly suggest there is a major genetic component of the formation of this structure, they also reveal there are major epigenetic influences as well because the callosa are not completely identical in monozygotic twins. In studies on the cat, such epigenetic factors influence the final formation of the callosum (11). Nonetheless, given the known anatomy of the callosum, these data suggest that a callosum of a particular shape and area would be more heavily

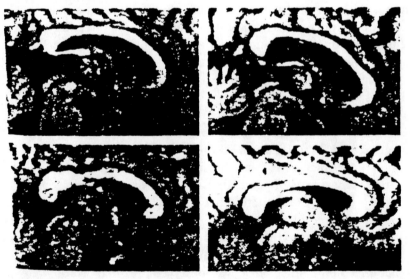

FIGURE 2. MR scans of the corpus collosa of monozygotic twins: (upper) one pair of twins; (bottom) another pair of twins. This great similarity of the twin pairs is seen by visual inspection (10).

involved in the projections to one cortical area than would a callosum of another shape and area.

An appreciation of the specificity of interhemispheric connections encourages one to consider a variety of neuropsychological data. Finding specific cognitive loss in a patient with intrahemispheric lesions requires careful interview and study. After left cerebral stroke, for example, patients can, on superficial examination, appear normal with respect to language function. Yet extended examination of such patients can reveal striking abnormalities that resemble the disconnection effects seen after commissurotomy. One patient, for example, was unable to name the color of fruits that were red. Thus, in response to the question, "What is the color of an apple?" there was a chance performance. Yet, the same patient was easily able to name the color of fire engines and school houses. It is conceivable that her incapacity to identify the color of red fruits was due to crucial fibers being interrupted within her left hemisphere that connected together the appropriate information sources. Revealing this sort of dissociation is only possible by carefully exploring each patient's psychological condition. Related observations have been made by others where specific categories have been lost after brain damage (12). Examination of a patient with a reading disorder revealed the presence of a functional intrahemispheric neural disconnection (13). Taken together, the partial disconnection studies argue for the view that specific neuronal systems are selective and specific in the types of information they process.

MODULAR COMPONENTS OF COGNITIVE PROCESSES

Disconnecting the cerebral hemisphere has allowed examination of the modular concept as it applies to the study of cognitive processes in two different ways. First, examples are given of the adverse effects of disconnecting processing subunits from one another; that is, disconnected modules cannot interact to produce a cognitive whole. Second, disconnection studies on complex processes such as language and facial recognition provide evidence for the existence of specific whole modular systems and reveal the consequences of their isolation from other cognitive systems.

Disconnecting cooperating modular subprocesses. Most studies on patients in whom the callosum has been sectioned have been carried out with the assumption that each half of the brain is a functioning, independent system that operates no differently when separated than when connected (14). New studies are beginning to challenge this original view and suggest a more intricate pattern of cerebral specialization (15). The new view is that such classical cognitive activities like those that are assessed by the Block

Design subtest of the Wechsler Audit Intelligence Scale are carried out through the interaction of several subprocesses that can be distributed either within or between the cerebral hemispheres.

The first reports on split-brain patients suggested that there were clear right-left dichotomies (16). However, in some more recent cases, right hemisphere performance after surgery was poor to nonexistent (15). This development raised the question of whether such patients possessed specialized right hemisphere skills at all. Alternatively, it was possible to view the specialized skills as simply "locked in" after disconnection from the dominant left half of the brain, which has verbal ability. That is, if such cerebral skills as performance on the Block Design test were dependent on a number of subprocesses, perhaps the surgery prevented key interactions. For example, before split-brain surgery, E. B. was tested on a number of tests including a nonsense wire figure test that is also believed to depend on right hemisphere specialized systems (15). In this test, an irregularly shaped wire figure is palpated out of view and must be subsequently selected from a group of four other wire figures. E. B. was able to perform the task with either hand. Her intact callosum, it would appear, assisted in distributing the information arriving in her left brain from the right hand over to the right hemisphere for specialized processing.

After the posterior half of the callosum was cut, E. B. was unable to name objects placed in the left hand in typical split-brain fashion. The fibers crucial for the interhemisphere transfer of stereognostic information had been severed, and as a result, the left hand-right hemisphere did not know what the right hand-left hemisphere knew. More importantly, however, E. B. could no longer perform the wire figure task with either hand.

Because E. B. could perform the task before surgery, the right hemisphere has the capacity to contribute to solving this kind of task when it is connected to the left. This observation suggests that the left hemisphere normally contributes certain functions to the right brain and vice versa. What was thought to be the producer of one integrated system with the capacity to carry out nonverbal tasks is actually the product of the interaction of at least two systems with discrete neural localization.

The same general finding was seen in the scores before and after on the Block Design test for E. B. and four other patients, D. R., L. L., E. S., and J. J. (Figure 3). This test is generally considered to be a right hemisphere task. Before the callosal surgery, performance on the Block Design test was fast and accurate with the right hand of these four patients. After surgery, neither the left nor right hand of any patient and could perform the task with ease. The time to solve the simplest patterns doubled, and completion of the more difficult patterns was usually not possible. Again, these data

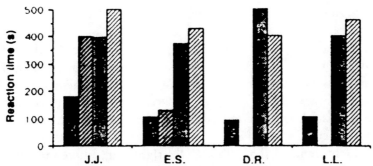

FIGURE 3. Comparison of patients in the Block Design test. When the preoperative performance J. S. and E. S. was compared with their interoperative performance, differences were seen. The surgical sections seemed to include fibers that were important for the proper execution of this task in J. J. but not E. S. However, on completion of full surgery, both patients showed impairments when either hand was tested. D. R. and L. L. were also affected after their callosal disconnection. Solid bars indicate preoperative performance, dark hatched bars, interoperative, shaded bars, postoperative, right hand; and light hatched bars, postoperative, left hand.

would suggest that before callosal section, both hemispheres participated in solving of the block design problem. Because the postoperative reaction times for the left hemisphere were also longer than the preoperative times, the left hemisphere must have benefited from processes located in the right half of the brain.

There are dissociable factors active in what appear to be unified mental activities. In the first patients tested (16), the right hemisphere seemed to possess all the subprocesses necessary to perform these visual-spatial tasks. When the early results are considered in light of the present results, it becomes clear that there is wide individual variation in what aspects of a neural system become lateralized in a particular brain. The developmental factors that govern this variation are not known. It also remains to be determined whether the variation seen in the pattern of cerebral specialization correlates with the vast individual differences seen in normal mental functions.

Disconnecting whole modules. When the brain is damaged or surgically disconnected, it is possible to observe other startling dissociations in cognitive function. When such dissociations are revealed, they suggest that the neural architecture honors these function distinctions and that different brain areas are involved in different aspects of a cognitive ability. Some general aspects of language organization manifested by those rare cases in which the right hemisphere is somewhat language competent should be considered. Additionally, the brain mechanisms involved with face perception can be examined.

1) Studies on language. After hemisphere disconnection the isolated right hemisphere in some patients possess limited language skills (17). In the few patients with right hemisphere language, all of them seem to have an extensive lexicon. Thus, for example, if the word apple is presented to the right hemisphere, the hand controlled by the right hemisphere can easily point to a picture of an apple. Results from various tests administered to these patients indicate that although the right hemisphere can possess an extensive auditory and visual lexicon that is almost equivalent to the left hemisphere's lexicon, it is severely limited in its capacity to use syntactic information in comprehension (18). For example, the right hemisphere has difficulty understanding semantically reversible active and passive sentences and recognizing the differences between phrases like "the flying planes" and "flying the planes."

However, these same right hemispheres are quite capable of judging whether a spoken sentence is grammatical. In short, the right hemisphere can judge the grammaticality of an utterance, but it cannot use syntactic information to place constraints on understanding word strings (19). It would be argued from this kind of observation that, not only are there dissociable processes involved in language in the right hemisphere, but that only the left hemisphere has the module for using syntax in a comprehension task.

The foregoing observation is consistent with other clinical studies that aim to determine the exact structures within the left hemisphere that are responsible for syntax. Until recently, accurately specifying the exact location and extent of a human cortical lesion that correlates with a functional disorder has been difficult. By using a new method of unfolding the cortex, the size and spatial relationship of specific cortical areas can be determined (20). When the cortex is "flat mapped" in two dimensions, there is what might be called a "language zone" that is contiguous (Figure 4). This observation contrasts with the traditional views (21) of how separate the language centers are from one another and allows for the determination of better structure-function correlates.

2) Studies on face perception. Clinical and split-brain studies suggest that the right hemisphere is specialized for facial recognition. Patients with local lesions in the right as opposed to the left hemisphere show impairments in recognizing unfamiliar faces (22). In split-brain patients, a right hemisphere superiority can also be elicited under special circumstances. Interpretations of the significance of these students have varied. Some investigators have suggested that the differences reflect differences in cog-

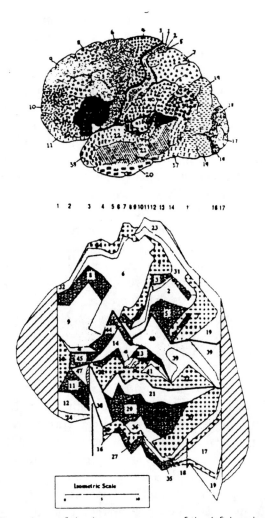

FIGURE 4. Two views of the language areas of the left hemisphere. (Top) Brodmann's cytoarchitectonic map, in which the shaded regions estimate the classical speech (Broca's) area anteriorly and the respective language (Wernicke's) area posteriorly on the visible left lateral surface. (Bottom) A cytoarchitectonic brainprint of the unfolded left hemisphere labeled in accordance with Brodmann's designations by Krieg (21). Those Brodmann's areas (13, 14, 15, 22, 41, 42, 39, 40, 44, 45) believed to subserve speech and auditory comprehension on clinical grounds are outlined to illustrate their spatial contiguity within a "language zone" (21). In the top illustration these areas appear noncontiguous and are separated by the pre- and post-central gyrus. With the brainprint, they are seen as contiguous.

nitive style, that is, processing strategies between the two hemispheres (23). Others have suggested that the apparent asymmetry is related to hemispheric differences in processing high- versus low-frequency spatial information (24).

My colleagues and I have shown that right hemisphere superiority in split-brain patients can be eliminated when familiar faces are used (25). These results suggested that if the stimulus was nameable, there was no apparent superiority. We proposed that the right hemisphere superiority for faces was due to the left hemisphere's tendency to engage in additional processing in the effort to distinguish (name) similar stimuli. Other studies have also shown that there is no consistent hemispheric difference in processing high and low spatial frequencies (26).

However, there has been a demonstration that split-brain monkeys are better able to distinguish monkey faces with the right hemisphere (27). This apparent specialization is complementary to a reported left hemisphere specialization for auditory processing in the monkey (28). Taken together, the evidence suggests that there are primitive mechanisms established early in primate evolution that are specialized for the important functions of face perception and language processing. Because of this finding and a variety of other specific physiological responses in animals, the issue of facial recognition mechanisms in the disconnected right and left hemisphere of J. W. was reexamined.

Tests examining recognition capacity in humans are easily confounded by intervening and ancillary cognitive and perceptual strategies that could mask underlying specialized systems. Therefore, each hemisphere was required to judge if a series of faces and objects were upside down or right side up. This approach was taken in part because of the apparent importance of viewing faces right side up (29). The faces used for this study were taken from the Benton Facial Recognition test. The subject was run on four 50-trial blocks on two separate occasions for a total of 400 trials. On each test day, the four blocks were counterbalanced for response hand. Each block of trials had eight stimulus conditions varying on field of presentation, type of stimuli (face versus non-face), and orientation (upside down versus right side up).

The results of J. W. were clear. For unfamiliar faces, the left hemisphere was significantly inferior to the right in judging whether an unfamiliar face was right side up or upside down [left visual field 0.91 versus right visual field 0.73 ($z = 3.2$, binomial $P < 0.01$)]. The left hemisphere was not significantly different from the right in judging the correct orientations of nonfacial stimuli. By asking the left and right hemisphere about the orientation of a face, a profound difference was revealed. It could be argued that through millions of years of selective pressures a neural circuit has evolved for the fast recognition of upright faces and that it is located in the right hemisphere. Disconnecting the module or circuit from the left hemisphere reveals the specialization. However, the left hemisphere with its vastly superior cognitive structure can also process such stimuli through alternative encoding mechanisms.

THE INTEGRATION OF MODULAR PROCESSES

In the atomization of cognitive and brain processes, there is a tendency to overlook possible mechanisms related to the truly psychological dimension of human life. In particular, although there is increasing evidence of the idea of modular processes, human beings enjoy what appears to be a unified and unitary experience of conscious awareness. Patients who have undergone brain bisection have the same basic experience of unity even though it is demonstrably the case that each disconnected half-brain can have separate and isolated experiences. Given all the evidence for specialization and specialized subsystems, how is their sense of conscious unity developed and maintained?

A number of yeas ago my colleagues and I began to make observations on how the left, dominant speaking hemisphere dealt with the behaviors we knew we had elicited from the disconnected right hemisphere (4). We revealed the existence of what we call the left brain "interpreter" by using a stimultaneous concept test. The patient was shown two pictures, one exclusively to the left hemisphere and one exclusively to the right, and was asked to choose (from an array of pictures placed in full view in front of him) the ones associated with the pictures lateralized to the left and right brain. In one example of this kind of test, a picture of a chicken claw was flashed to the left hemisphere and a picture of snow scene to the right hemisphere. Of the array of pictures placed in front of the subject, the obviously correct association is a chicken for the chicken claw and a shovel for the snow scene. P. S. responded by choosing the shovel with the left hand and the chicken with the right. When asked why he chose these items, his left hemisphere replied "Oh, that's simple. The chicken claw goes to the chicken, and you need a shovel to clean out the chicken shed." Here, the left brain, observing the response of the left hand, interprets that response into a context consistent with its sphere of knowledge—one that does not include information about the snow scene presented to the left hemifield.

Hundreds of such observations have now been documented in these cases over the years. When these results are compared to the poor performance the right hemisphere displays (as compared to the left hemisphere) in solving simple problems requiring making inferences and seeing causal relationships (30), it is concluded that the left brain interpreter evolved in association with the left hemisphere's specialized capacity in the human brain for such cognitive activities.

This same general result that has been observed when the left brain "interpreter" struggles to deal with overt behaviors has also been seen with more covert responses. Mood shifts, for example, can be produced in an experimental situation by manipulating the disconnected right hemisphere. A positive mood shift triggered by the right hemisphere finds the left interpreting its current experience in a positive way. Similarly, when the right triggers a negative mood state, the left interprets a previously neutral situation in negative terms.

These observations have led to insights into the nature of a variety of psychological disturbances that are initially produced by endogenous errors in cerebral metabolism, such as those known to be associated with panic attacks (31). Such biologically driven events produced a different felt state, which in turn must be interpreted (32). Each individual's interpretation, unique to their own past and present psychological history, is then stored in memory and becomes powerfully determinant in the content of an individual's ongoing consciousness. If the endogenous events mend through medication or natural events, the interpretations given to the brain's altered mood state remain. In extreme cases such as a panic attack, phobias can develop. The view here would be that the phobia is the interpretation of the altered felt state and can remain long after the precipitous panic attack problem has been medically resolved.

In conclusion, when considering the various observations reported here, it is important to keep in mind the evolutionary history of our species. Over the course of this evolution, efficient systems have been selected for handling critical environmental challenges. In this light, it is no wonder there are specialized systems (modules) that are active in carrying out specific and important assignments. What seems to be unique to the human brain, however, is the interpreter that allows the organisms to generate hypotheses about the nature of its responses, and, by doing so, not only presents the human species with a mechanism to both form and modify beliefs, but perhaps also frees the human agent from the shackles of environmental stimuli.

ENDNOTES

1. D. H. Hubel and T. N. Weisel, Proc. R. Soc. London Ser. B.198, 1 (1977); S. M. Zeki, Nature 274, 423 (1978); J. Kass, Annu. Rev. Psychol. 38, 129 (1987); M. Livingstone and D. Hubel, *Science* 240, 740 (1988).

2. M. Mishkin and T. Appenzeller, *Sci. Am.* 256, 80 (June 1987); P. S. Goldman-Rakic, in *Neurobiology of Neocortex,* P. Rakic and W. Singer, eds. (Wiley, New York, 1988), pp. 177–202.

3. S. M. Kosslyn, *Science* 240, 1621 (1988); D. Swinney, E. Zurif, J. Nicol, *J. Cog. Neurosci.* 1, 25 (1989); M. I. Posner, S. E. Petersen, P. T. Fox, M. E. Raichle, *Science* 240, 1627 (1988).

4. M. S. Gazzaniga and J. E. Ledoux, *The Integrated Mind* (Plenum, New York, 1978); M. S. Gazzaniga, *The Social Brain* (Basic Books, New York, 1985).

5. J. Stone, *J. Comp. Neurol.* 136, 585 (1966); _____, J. Leicester, S. M. Sherman, *ibid.* 150, 333 (1973); A. G. Leventhal, S. J. Ault, D. J. Vitek, *Science* 240, 66 (1988).

6. R. M. Fendrich and M. S. Gazzaniga, *Neuropsychologia* 27, 273 (1989). A detailed description of the eye tracker is in T. N. Cornsweet and H. D. Crane [*J. Opt. Soc. Am.* 63, 1192 (1973)].

7. J. D. Holtzman, *Vision Res.* 24, 801 (1984); M. S. Gazzaniga, in *Neurobiology of Neocortex,* P. Rakic and W. Singer, Eds. (Wiley, New York, 1988), p. 385–406; B. T. Foxman, J. Oppenheim, C. K. Petito, M. S. Gazzaniga, *Neurology* 36, 1513 (1986).

8. M. S. Gazzaniga, J. E. Bogen, R. W. Sperry, *Neuropsychologia* 1, 209 (1963).

9. M. S. Gazzaniga, M. Kutas, C. Van Patten, R. Fendrich, *Neurology* 39, 942 (1989).

10. J. S. Oppenheim, J. E. Skerry, M. J. Tramo, M. S. Gazzaniga, *Ann. Neurol.* 26, 100 (1989).

11. D. O. Frost and G. M. Innocenti, in *Two Hemispheres—One Brain,* F. Lepore, M. Tito, H. H. Jasper, Eds. (Liss, New York, 1986), pp. 255–266.

12. W. Warrington, *Br. J. Psychol.* 72, 175 (1981); _____ and T. Shallice, *Brain* 107, 829 (1984); J. Hart, Jr. R. S. Berndt, A. Caramazza, *Nature* 316, 439 (1985).

13. M. J. Tramo, P. Reuter-Lorenz, M. S. Gazzaniga, *Ann. Neurol.* 26, 126 (1989); P. Reuter-Lorenz and J. Brunn, *Cog. Neuropsychol.,* in press.

14. R. W. Sperry, M. S. Gazzaniga, J. E Bogen, in *Handbook of Clinical Neurology,* P. J. Vinken and G. W. Bruyn, Eds. (North-Holland, Amsterdam, 1969), vol. 4, pp. 273–290; M. S. Gazzaniga and J. E. Ledoux, *The Integrated Mind* (Plenum, New York, 1978).

15. M. S. Gazzaniga, in *Thought Without Language,* L. Weiskrantz, Ed. (Oxford Univ. Press, New York, 1988), pp. 430–450. For the test used, see B. Milner and L. Taylor [*Neuropsychologia* 10, 1 (1977)].

16. M. S. Gazzaniga, J. E. Bogen, R. W. Sperry, *Proc. Natl. Acad. Sci. U.S.A.* 48, 1765 (1962); *Brain* 88, 221 (1965).

17. M. S. Gazzaniga, *Am. Psychol.* 38, 525 (1983); M. Kutas, S. A. Hillyard, M. S. Gazzaniga, *Brain* 111, 553 (1988).

18. M. S. Gazzaniga, *The Bisected Brain* (Appleton Century Crofts, New York, 1970. _____, C. S. Smylie, K. M. Baynes, W. Hirst, C. McCleary, *Brain Lang.* 22. (1984); E. Zaidel, in *Cerebral Hemisphere Asymmetry: Method, Theory and App.,* J. B. Hellige, Ed. (Praeger, New York, 1953) pp. 95–151.

19. K. M. Baynes and M. S. Gazzaniga, in *Language Communications and the Brain.* E. Plum, Ed. (Raven, New York, 1987), pp. 117–126.

20. M. L. Jouander *et al., J. Cog. Neurosci* 1, 88 (1989).

21. K. Brodman, *Vergleichende Lokalisatonlehre der Grosshimrinde inihren Prinzipien telt auf Grund des Sellenvaues* (J. A. Barth, Leipzig, 1909); W. J. S. Krieg, *Connection of the Cerebral Cotex* (Brain Books, Evanston, IL, 1963).

22. E. K. Warrington and M. James, *Cortex* 3, 317 (1967); R. Yin, *Neuropsychology.* 395 (1970).

23. J. Levy, C. B. Trevarthen, R. W. Sperry, *Brain* 95, 61 (1972).

24. J. Sergent, *Psychol. Bull.* 93, 481 (1983).

25. M. S. Gazzaniga and C. S. Smylie, *Ann. Neurol.* 13, 536 (1983).

26. R. Fendrich and M. S. Gazzaniga, *Soc. Neurosci. Abstr.* 14, 2 (1988), *Neuropsychgia,* in press.

27. C. R. Hamilton and B. A. Vermeire, *Science* 242, 1691 (1988).

28. H. E. Heffner and R. S. Heffner, *ibid.* 226, 75 (1984).

29. P. Thompson, *Perception (London)* 9, 483 (1980).

30. M. S. Gazzaniga and C. S. Smylie, *Brain* 107, 145 (1984).

31. F. M. Reiman, M. E. Racihle, F. K. Butler, P. Herscovitch, E. Robins, *Nature,* 683 (1984).

32. M. S. Gazzaniga, *Mind Matters* (Houghton Mifflin, Boston, 1988).

33. I thank all of my colleagues who have made this work possible over the past years. Particular thanks for this article go to K. M. Baynes, R. Fendrich, M. L. Jounce, W. C. Loftus, P. Reuter-Lorenz, A. G. Reeves, D. W. Roberts, C. S. Smylie, M. J. Tramo. Supported in part by NIH grant 7P01–NS17778 and Javits Award. ROI–NS22626 and the James S. McDonnell Foundation.

19

The Communication Process

M.C. Howard and J. Dunaif-Hattis

The exchange of information is one of the most universal features of life, an essential part of the adaptation of any species to its environment. Organisms are almost constantly transmitting and receiving information. Without effective means of communication, an eagle cannot locate its prey, a flower cannot attract a bee, and a salmon cannot find its spawning site. Getting food, avoiding danger, and finding a mate all hinge on sending out the appropriate signals at the right time and on picking up essential information from the environment.

The hominid adaptation, made possible by the expansion and reorganization of the brain, includes increased intelligence and symbolic thought. These are the basis of much of human communication. Information exchange is a highly elaborated feature of the human adaptive strategy; without it, especially without language, culture as we know it would not exist.

How does human communication relate to culture, society, and the human adaptive strategy? This question and others are the focus of the anthropological subfield known as **linguistic anthropology**. In this chapter, we will explore aspects of communication that linguistic anthropologists study to further a holistic understanding of human life: general characteristics of communication, relationships between complexity in communication and complexity in group structure, the structure of human verbal and nonverbal communications, links between language and culture, variations within a single language, use of more than one language tradition, and the reconstruction of processes by which languages evolve.

THE COMMUNICATION PROCESS

Communication occurs whenever information is exchanged between a sender and a receiver. Information is transmitted by a sender via signals, such as a song, a sentence, a chest-thumping display, or a scent. At the other end, the information is received as a message.

Sending and Receiving Messages

As we all know from personal experience, what a signal means to the sender is not always what it means to the receiver. One person may smile at another to signal approval or friendship, for instance, but the message received may be quite different: You are making fun of me, or You think I am acting like a fool. The potential for misunderstanding exists in all communicative transactions.

Sending signals of one kind or another is inevitable. Simply by existing, any plant or animal betrays information as to its size, shape, and location. Even camouflaged organisms continue to emit signals. The flatfish, or sole, can alter its skin color to match the color and texture of the ocean floor. But it cannot camouflage its odor and electrical field, signals that mean "dinner" to a shark that swims close enough to detect them.

Since it is impossible to avoid sending signals entirely, the trick is to transmit appropriate information to appropriate receivers at appropriate times. From the point of view of the sender, the key to success lies in effective *impression management:* If signals must be transmitted, let them be to the advantage of the sender. In many instances, good impression management requires that signals be true. In other cases, it may benefit the sender to transmit purposely misleading signals.

Through impression management, the sender of signals in some way hopes to control the response of the receiver. However, there are limits to this power. Like the sole, an organism may be unable to control all the signals it emits. Another difficulty is that a sender cannot always determine who the receivers will be. A drug dealer needs to communicate his or her business to potential customers, but signals used also are likely to attract the police. A third problem is the one we mentioned earlier—the sender may intend one thing by a signal, but the receiver might get a message that means something else entirely.

Redundancy

For both senders and receivers, there is some uncertainty associated with all communication. Neither senders nor receivers have complete control over the meaning of the information they exchange. However, uncertainty can be reduced by **redundancy**—the repetition or reinforcement of a signal or message. An angry man, for example, may reinforce his verbal signal—"I'm mad as hell at you"—with other signals, such as a forceful tone of voice and aggressive gestures.

A receiver of contradictory or misleading messages also may be helped through redundancy. If we are not certain of someone's sincerity, for instance, we will watch carefully for consistency in the signals the other person emits. If what a person says is not reinforced by how he or she says it, we are likely to suspect him or her of a lack of truthfulness. Even with overlapping cues, clear mutual understanding is rare.

COMMUNICATION AND SOCIABILITY

Effective communication is basic to the survival of all organisms, but some require more complex systems of information exchange than others. An octopus does not require a very sophisticated system of communicating. Interactions with other octopi are rare and not particularly complex. Octopi that do meet attempt to drive each other away, retreat, or mate. The signals required for these simple interactions need not be elaborate.

Communication is far more complex among social animals. Ants, bees, penguins, elephants, and primates, such as baboons, gorillas, and humans, face their environments collectively rather than as individuals. Survival depends not just on the adaptive abilities of the individual but also on the ability of the members of a group to coordinate their behavior and integrate their activities in the pursuit of common objectives. This teamwork depends on efficient communication: members of a group have to know what each is up to in order to work together effectively.

Communication complexity increases not only with the importance of interactions, but also with the number of roles each actor plays. The repertory of roles that loners such as octopi play in their simple, brief encounters is very limited. The role relationships of social animals are considerably more complex. In a social setting, two individuals are likely to play a multitude of roles. At various times, they may be partners in sex, parenting, grooming, defense, and food procuring; the same individuals also may compete over resources. As they work together or compete in a diversity of contexts, their behaviors must vary with the situation. This complexity in role relationships requires a corresponding sophistication in communication.

While the communication systems of any social animals are always fairly well developed, some have more highly elaborated systems than others. Wolves, for example, have a more complex system of information exchange than ants. Most of the ant's behavior is genetically controlled, whereas wolves are much less the prisoners of their instincts. As we discussed earlier in the text, humans are virtually devoid of genetically determined instincts, depending instead primarily on culturally learned patterns of behavior.

The adaptive advantage of learned behavior is flexibility. Because of the human capacity for learning, we can alter our activities and procedures quickly to meet diverse and unstable environmental conditions. But it is not enough for individuals to be able to change their behavior. Rather, successful adaptation requires the maintenance of maximum behavioral flexibility at the group level. To alter their activities in coordinated group fashion, social animals need to have flexible systems of communication. Among ants, much of the information exchanged is in the form of information-bearing chemicals, called *pheromones*, each of which probably has only one meaning. This one-for-one correspondence places a significant limitation on the flexibility of any communication. In contrast, humans communicate mainly through symbols. As we will see, symbols represent the ultimate in communicational flexibility, for their meaning is not fixed or automatic.

COMMUNICATION AMONG HUMANS

Humans rely more on learning, engage in a greater variety of activities, and play more diversified roles than any other animal. Of all societies, those of humans are the most complex. It is no wonder, then, that human systems of communication are so flexible and highly developed. Humans exchange information through a wide variety of channels—sight, touch, sound, and smell—but the most important mode of human communication is verbal.

If anything can be considered the most basic element of culture, it is language. Language allows us to exchange detailed information about both interior and exterior conditions. Culture is transmitted from generation to generation primarily through language, and a person's language greatly influences how he or she perceives the world. It is difficult to imagine what human life would be like without it.

Signs and Symbols

All communication is based on signs. A **sign** is anything that can convey information, including physical objects, colors, sounds, movements, scents, and even silence. Among many animals, the meaning of a sign is *biologically* *determined.* A cricket does not need to learn how to chirp, nor does it need to learn what chirping by other crickets signifies: the meaning of chirping is part of its genetic makeup. In addition, the sign systems of most animals are *closed:* different signs cannot be combined to create new signs. Such animals cannot combine a sign that means "I want to mate" with one that means "danger," for example. For these animals, each sign functions independently. Such sign systems place considerable limitations on the flexibility and range of information exchanged.

Not all animals are limited to communicating through sign systems that are closed and determined; some primates have communications systems that are based on symbols. Human communication is based entirely on symbols. A **symbol** is a sign with a meaning that is *arbitrary.* Its significance is determined not by a genetic "program" but by social convention and learning. Words, whether written or spoken, are symbols, as is a crucifix, a coat of arms, or a flag.

Because the meaning of a symbol is arbitrary, different symbols may be used to mean the same thing. What English speakers call a *dog* is called *der Hund* by German speakers and *anjing* by speakers of Indonesian. Conversely, any particular symbol may have different meanings in different cultures. The swastika, for example, has highly negative connotations today in Western cultures because of its association with Nazis, but to Hindus it signifies good fortune, and to the Navajo, it is associated with the sun. The meaning of any symbol is determined by culture, not by biology.

The flexibility of human communication is increased further by another characteristic of symbols: they may be *multivocal;* that is, often they have multiple levels of meaning. To the Christian, a crucifix, for example, is a highly multivocal symbol. It may evoke hope for the hereafter, provide relief from suffering in this life, or signify the desirability of moral behavior. It may simply function as a decoration; and, in some Eastern European societies in the past, it was used as protection against vampires. By providing a single focal point to which a diversity of experiences may be related, such a symbol may help to integrate a variety of ideas.

A symbolic system of communication is also *open.* Unlike other signs, symbols can be combined with one another to produce entirely new meanings. Rather than being restricted to a limited set of signs, humans can invent new terms and concepts freely, as when the words *smoke* and *fog* are merged to form *smog*—a new symbol with a new meaning.

Symbols also are *abstract.* The term *book* refers not only to the object you are reading but to all other like objects. This aspect of symbol use enables humans to generalize about things and events to a degree far beyond the capacity of other animals.

Because human society involves such complex relationships and because human adaptation requires responding collectively to rapidly changing conditions, it is essential that human communication systems be equally complex and flexible. Symbols are the most complex and flexible devices for communication yet formed, allowing humans to adapt them to whatever purposes necessary.

Language and Speech

The terms *language* and *speech* often are used interchangeably, but there is a distinction between them. **Speech** consists of patterned oral behavior—a concrete, observable phenomenon. **Language**, however, is an abstraction—a set of rules for generating speech. Language exists only in people's minds; therefore, it is not observable. Just as the values, beliefs, and assumptions of culture guide and condition cultural behavior, so the code of a language generates speech behavior.

The capacity for language and speech is innate in all humans. All normal human beings are, in fact, programmed for linguistic interaction. Parents do not have to force their children to learn to talk in the same way that they enforce toilet training or table manners. Linguistic skills are something human children are motivated naturally to acquire. The human brain is organized in such a way that humans are programmed for "symboling," for communicating through signs that have arbitrarily assigned meanings. In addition, all normal human beings are endowed with a special kind of vocal apparatus that allows them to make the wide range of sounds required for speaking any language.

The configuration of the anatomical complex on which speech depends—the lips, teeth, palate, tongue, and larynx—occurs only in humans. But apparently humans are not the only animals with the capacity for language. Some other primates, especially chimpanzees, have demonstrated mastery of some rudimentary language skills (see, for example, Patterson and Linden 1981; Premack and Premack 1983; Fouts and Budd 1979).

Elements of Language

Human languages have two main levels of structure: sound and grammar. The analysis of a language's sounds is called **phonology**. Grammar has two dimensions: morphology and syntax. The **morphology** of a language determines how simple sounds are organized to form units of meaning; **syntax** determines how words are strung together to form statements.

Phonology

To describe a language, linguists must first determine what sounds it uses. Humans are capable of making a wide range of vocal sounds, but no one language makes use of them all. Some languages are based on a larger number of sounds than others. In English there are 45 distinct sounds, while in most Polynesian languages there are only about 15. Nor does English have the same sounds as other languages originating in Europe. The German "ch" sound in the words *Ich* and *Buch* and the Spanish trilled "r" as in *cerro* and *burro* do not occur in English.

The smallest linguistically significant units of sound—units that alter the meanings of the words in which they occur—are called **phonemes**. In English, {p} and {b} are considered separate phonemes because one cannot be substituted for the other without changing the meaning: *pat* and *bat* have distinctly different meanings.

A phoneme may consist of a single sound or a number of closely related sounds. For example, the {p^h} sound in *pike* and the {p} sound in *spike* are pronounced slightly differently: the {p^h} sound in *pike* is *aspirated* (that is, it is accompanied by expelling air), while in *spike* the {p} sound is unaspirated.[1] But in English, the difference is not given any meaning, so speakers are largely unaware of it. Such variations of a single phoneme that do not affect meaning in a language are called **allophones**. Sounds that are allophones in one language may be distinct phonemes in other languages. In Hindi, for example, {p} and {p^h} are not allophones, as they are in English, but separate phonemes. The difference between the two sounds is considered critical; it is as easily recognized by Hindi speakers as the difference between {p} and {b} is recognized by English speakers.

Morphology

Single sounds can be significant linguistically, but in most cases they do not have meaning in and of themselves. To create meaning, sounds are combined with one another to form morphemes. **Morphemes** are the smallest combinations of sound that convey meaning.

Leg, *store*, and *book*, all single morphemes in English, can each stand alone, so we call them *free morphemes*. Other morphemes, such as the suffix *-s*, which indicates plurality, cannot stand alone. Although *-s* adds new meaning and is thus considered a morpheme, it has no meaning except when attached to other morphemes; therefore, it is called a *bound morpheme*. Morphemes often are combined to form new concepts, such as *bookstores*, a word consisting of three morphemes.

We have seen that not all sound contrasts are recognized as linguistically significant in a particular language. Some contrasts are considered separate phonemes, while others are allophones of a single phoneme. Similarly, at the level of morphology, variations that have the same meaning will be considered **allomorphs** of a single morpheme. For example, the prefixes *in-, un-,* and *non-* all indicate negation of what follows; therefore, they are considered allomorphs and not distinct morphemes.

Syntax

All languages have standardized conventions for combining words to form statements that make sense to other speakers of the same language. These conventions are called the *rules* of *syntax*. The English sentence "If you use the light meter properly, you'll get a good picture" can be translated into German by substituting German words for English, but for a German speaker to make sense of the statement, the words would have to be rearranged as well. In German, the statement would be, "Wenn Sie den Belichtungsmesser richtig gebrauchen, dann muss es ein gutes Bild geben." Translated back into English, but keeping the German syntax, the statement reads, "If you the light meter properly use, then must it a good picture give."

The rules of syntax are not learned in a fully conscious manner. All native speakers of English "know" the rules of syntax in that language, yet few could say exactly what the rules are. But the fact that a 7-year-old child can talk and be understood by others is proof that the child has, somewhat subconsciously, acquired a basic knowledge of syntax.

Syntax is a more important indicator of meaning in some languages than in others. In English, for example, there is a significant difference between "dog bites man" and "man bites dog." In Latin, however, "dog bites man" can be stated as either "canis mordet hominem" or "hominem mordet canis" without any change in meaning. In Latin, word endings (which are bound morphemes) play a special role in constructing sentences. For example, the object of a verb will often have an *-em* ending. A person with knowledge of Latin will know who bit and who was bitten by noting the noun endings; the order in which the words occur is not important. Thus, one contrast a linguist would note between Latin and English is that English is more complex syntactically, while Latin is more complex morphologically.

Other Modes of Human Communication

Language is not the only means by which humans exchange information. In conversation, for example, humans communicate not only orally but also through facial expressions, voice tones, and gestures. Style of dress and grooming also may be interpreted as messages by others, and even the ways in which people organize the space around them can have communicative significance.

Kinesics is the study of gestural communication, or "body language" (Birdwhistell 1960). Since all humans are essentially alike physically, much of our body language has universal meaning. For example, a smile probably conveys roughly the same range of messages in any part of the world. But kinesic communication is influenced by culture, so some gestures or poses can mean one thing in one culture and something else in another (see Morris et al. 1979). In Western cultures, it makes no difference whether an individual uses the left hand or the right when he or she gives someone a piece of candy. In many Asian cultures, however, to offer anything with the left hand is considered an insult, or at least bad manners. Likewise, different gestures can convey the same meaning in different cultures. In northern Italy, as in the United States, a person shakes his or her head from side to side to mean "no," but in southern Italy and Greece the same meaning is communicated by an upward jerk of the chin.

While most of us are somewhat aware of how interaction is influenced by body language, we are probably less conscious of the ways in which information is exchanged through patterns of spacing. **Proxemics**, or the study of the cultural use of space, focuses on the "geometry of interaction" (Hall 1966). Spatial arrangements help to define interactions, such as the degree of formality or intimacy involved. In some interactions, such as a job interview, people are likely to maintain a considerable distance from one another. By contrast, the conversational distance between two good friends discussing a personal matter is more likely to be very close.

The "appropriate" use of space and the meaning of spatial arrangements are defined differently from culture to culture. For example, in a London post office, stamp buyers are expected to stand in a line without any physical contact with the others in line and patiently await their turn at the window. In Spain, however, people crowd up to the window; there may be considerable body contact, even some elbowing.

Another dimension of nonverbal communication involves bodily adornment. Everything about a person's appearance, such as clothing, hairstyle, jewelry, makeup, influences interaction with others. Conventions of dress and grooming serve as ready indicators of social status; moreover, they affect behavior, especially interactions between strangers. A person wearing a police uniform will elicit different behavior than someone in a clown suit. Bodily adornment thus helps to define situations within a cultural tradition.

Differences in dress and grooming often are important for cross-cultural interaction. In highland Guatemala, for instance, each Indian village traditionally had its own special customs of bodily adornment. But such styles of dress all fit within a general type identified cross-culturally as "Indian." Thus, dress also served to emphasize the cultural distinctiveness of all Indians in contrast to non-Indians. Scott Nind (1831), an early European resident of southwestern Australia, found that not knowing the language of bodily adornment in another culture can confound cross-cultural understanding. In his discussion of initial contact between Europeans and Aborigines, he noted that the Europeans' preconceived notions about native adornment and social organization led them to misinterpretation:

> We endeavored to discover whether they had any chiefs, and for a long time believed they had: indeed we had fixed upon two or three individuals to whom we supposed that rank belonged. The natives whom we selected were fine, tall active men, much painted and ornamented. ... We subsequently discovered that they were all single men, which accounted for their constantly ornamented appearance. (pp. 40–41)

LANGUAGE AND CULTURE

Culture cannot be understood without taking into account its language, probably its single most important element. It is also impossible to completely understand a language independent of its cultural context. As expressed by anthropologist John Beattie (1964), "A people's categories of thought and the forms of their language are inextricably bound together" (p. 31). But despite the many ways in which culture and language influence each other, their integration is not absolute. Each has many unique properties that are not directly, or even indirectly, influenced by the other. People with cultures that are otherwise very similar may speak different languages, and similar languages may be spoken by people with very different cultures.

Cultural Influence on Language

There has been little research into whether culture affects the grammatical structure of a language, but it is not difficult to show that social and cultural factors influence its vocabulary. Inuit (Eskimo), Saami (Lapps), and various other native groups who live in the far north, whose livelihoods and even lives may depend on snow, can distinguish many different types of snow conditions. By contrast, native Fijians traditionally had no word for snow until one was created in the nineteenth century, following the arrival of the Europeans. However, Fijians do have "distinct words for each species of coconut, and for each stage in the growth process of the coconut" (Clammer 1976, 31).

In any language, the elaboration of a category of words is related to the importance of the category to the society, to the real-world diversity of the category, and to the uses to which the vocabulary must be put. The Samal of the southern Philippines, for example, have words for more than 250 kinds of fish. This is partly because fish are a main source of food and cash for the Samal. It is also because many different types of fish are found in the waters off the coast where the Samal live.

All languages have both highly abstract and highly specific concepts. However, languages differ in this respect. Languages such as Mandarin and English, associated with societies having an extensive division of labor and spoken by large populations, tend to have elaborate general vocabularies. Such English words as *administrator, mammal, society*, and *rights* are not found in the vocabularies of many foraging societies, but they do have their counterparts in Mandarin.

Also, research indicates that vocabulary may be influenced by cultural, environmental, *and* physiological factors. This appears to be true, for example, of color terms. While all languages have highly specific words for colors (such as *peach*), not all have the same number of general color words. Some languages have as few as two general color words, *warm-light* and *cool-dark*; others, such as English and Hungarian, have as many as 11 or 12. Berlin and Kay (1969) found that the number of color terms in a language increases with increasing economic and technological complexity. Research conducted by Kay and McDaniel (1978) has shown that the order in which general color terms are added as societies develop reflects the physiology and neurology of the eye. "Orange," for example, is never found in a language without both "red" and "yellow," reflecting the neurological characteristics of the human eye. The appearance of "orange" is not merely a reflection of neurology, however, for it also tends to be associated with societies having standard dyes, pigments, and schools. The color vocabulary, then, reflects not only the pan-human exposure to color in the environment and the generally pan-human perception of color, but also the differential need of societies to talk about color.

Linguistic Influence on Culture

On the other side of the language/culture coin, language may determine or influence certain aspects of culture. In at least one way, language clearly helps shape our cultural practices: every language serves to organize our perceptions of the world. Language establishes categories by which things considered the same or similar can be distinguished from those considered different. The categories of one language will never be precisely identical to those of another. In American culture, a person's mother is called by one kinship term (*mother*) and the mother's sister by a different term (*aunt*). Iroquois children use the same term for both mother and mother's sister. Such linguistic differences influence cultural behavior. Anglo-American children relate to aunts differently than to mothers, but Iroquois are expected to relate to both in much the same way.

Some anthropologists have gone further and claimed that we are virtual prisoners of language. The classic expression of this is known as the **Sapir-Whorf hypothesis**, named for anthropological linguists Edward Sapir (1884–1939) and Benjamin Whorf (1897–1941). According to the Sapir-Whorf hypothesis, the structure of thought and that of language are closely related:

> Human beings do not live in the objective world alone, nor alone in the world of social activity as ordinarily understood, but are very much at the mercy of the particular language which has become the medium of expression for their society. ... The fact of the matter is that the real world is to a large extent unconsciously built up on the language habits of the group. No two languages are ever sufficiently similar to be considered as representing the same social reality. The worlds in which different societies live are distinct worlds, not merely the same world with different labels attached. (Sapir 1929, 209–214)

The Sapir-Whorf hypothesis maintains that the tyranny of language goes beyond mere influence on the way people relate to their experiences; it forces them to perceive the world in terms that are built into their language. If this view is correct, speakers of different languages will have correspondingly different conceptualizations of how "reality" is constructed.

Certainly language places some limitations on how a person can express his or her thoughts. For example, since verb tenses are a basic structural feature of the English language, almost any statement made by an English speaker must specify whether an event is happening now, has already happened, or will happen in the future. But a speaker of Indonesian, which has no verb tenses, is not forced to make the same kind of time specifications that are required in English. In Indonesian, one cannot say "I went to the store." Instead, one says, "I go to the store," whether that action is taking place in the present or has occurred in the past. According to the Sapir-Whorf hypothesis, the structural contrasts between the two languages give English speakers and Indonesian speakers very different views about the nature of time. The English language stresses periodicity by dividing time into distinct categories of past, present, and future; on the other hand, in Indonesia, time is seen as flowing and continuous. However, even though statements might be easier to make in one language than in the other, there are probably no thoughts or ideas that cannot be expressed in both languages. Indonesians can add a qualifier such as "yesterday" or "this morning" to their tenseless statements.

Although language and culture influence each other in many ways, both obvious and subtle, difficulties arise whenever one tries to show that culture *determines* language, or vice versa. The Sapir-Whorf hypothesis has generated interest in investigating connections between language and culture; it has also generated considerable controversy. As yet, the hypothesis remains unproved.

• • •

20

THE BRAIN AS "SEXUAL ORGAN"

ANN GIBBONS

When Oxford University anatomists Geoffrey Raisman and Pauline Field set out to study the differences between the brains of male and female rats in the late 1960s, most researchers were skeptical. The prevailing view was that male and female brains were alike. "People just didn't believe these significant structural differences existed," recalls Rockefeller University neuroscientist Bruce McEwen, who studies sex differences in rodent brains. But the pair forged ahead and, 20 years ago this month, published a study in *Science* that was the first to show conclusively a structural difference in the brains of male and female mammals: Male rats have fewer synapses connecting two parts of the hypothalamus than females do. McEwen says it's only since Raisman's and Field's study, which he calls "monumental," that researchers "have felt there could be structural sex differences in the brain."

Raisman and Field were quickly joined in these studies by an entire new generation of researchers who entered the field just in time to make use of high-tech tools that could show them the brain in minute detail. Electron microscopes gave a view of differences in autopsied brain structures the size of the period at the end of this sentence. Noninvasive imaging techniques, such as magnetic resonance imaging (MRI), helped show the interior of living heads for the first time. At the same time, rodent studies reached a new level of sophistication, allowing researchers to trace the way sex hormones work.

As a result of data gathered with these new tools during the 1970s and 1980s there is now a solid body of data indicating sex differences in the brains of almost every mammalian family examined so far: rodents, birds, monkeys, and—most recently and most intriguingly—human beings. "I see more and more studies involving different species and different parts of the brain," says McEwen. "Without question, these differences do exist, because they have been documented at the synaptic level and at the biochemical level." In the human brain, such differences have now been observed in three major structures—the hypothalamus, the anterior commissure, and the corpus callosum—as well as in lesser areas.

But if anatomical differences between male and female brains have been conclusively documented, their functional significance is far from clear. Indeed, attempts to explain differences in behavior between men and women in terms of their brain anatomy have ignited major controversies. Obviously, some of the anatomical differences have a role in controlling the reproductive functions of the two sexes. But some may not, prompting researchers to speculate that they have roots in strong evolutionary pressures on the sexes during prehistory when the brain was expanding rapidly. Such theories are, for the moment, mostly speculation. But what is not conjecture is the rapidly expanding body of evidence showing that the brain is a sexual organ.

The observed differences begin at the level of whole organ. "We should not forget that the entire brain *is* a sex difference," says Dick Swaab of the Netherlands Institute for Brain Research in Amsterdam. Men's brains are on average larger than women's by 15%—about twice the difference in average body size between men and women.

Male brains don't start out bigger, though: The brains of human babies are the same size until age 2 to 3. After that, male brains grow faster until age 6, when the full brain size is reached. Many researchers think this pattern reflects the fact that the basic structure of the brain is female and it is modified when male sex hormones kick in. "There is a large body of evidence, mainly in rodents, indicating that the default brain in mammals is female, and that androgens must be present very early in life to masculinize both genitalia and brain," writes University of Western Ontario neuropsychologist Doreen Kimura, in the *Encyclopedia of Neuroscience*.

Studies in rodents have shown that as male hormones surge through the growing brain, they apparently home in on a few key areas—such as the hypothalamus, which is the source of pituitary hormones and is responsible for sexual response and mating behavior. They effect their changes especially on a structure known as the sexually dimorphic nucleus (SDN), a cubic millimeter of tissue that is exquisitely sensitive to testosterone and estrogen. Gorski's UCLA team discovered the SDN in rats in 1977 and was rapidly "scooped" in its search for the same feature in humans by Swaab, says Gorski. Both groups found that the SDN is five times as large in normal male rats as in females, and Swaab has found in 100 human brain autopsies that it is 2.5 times larger in men than in women.

In a remarkable set of following studies, Gorski's group found that when testosterone is withheld by castrating rat pups, their brains look like those of females. Half their SDN neurons die within 24 hours. "It's very exciting," says Gorski. "But we can reverse this by giving a single injection of testosterone on day 1, or on days 2, 3, 4, or 5 after birth. But if we wait to day 6, we get nothing." By contrast, "by giving androgens to the female, we can make her SDN grow as big as the male's." Although the function of the SDN is unknown, Swaab speculates that it may play a role in male gender identity and in mounting behavior.

The body of data on the hypothalamus—from both animal and human studies—is larger than that for any other brain structure. But for humans alone, another brain region has so far been the most extensively studied. "The corpus callosum shows several sex differences," says Sandra J. Witelson, a behavioral neuroscientist at McMaster University, referring to the bundle of nerve fibers connecting the brain's right and left hemispheres. Yet although it is clear there are differences between males and females in the corpus callosum, researchers don't always agree on what those differences are. Early in the 1980s, one team that studied autopsied brains reported that the splenial portion of the corpus callosum is larger—or at least more bulbous—in women than in men.

But Witelson reviewed the 10 other studies done of the splenium since then and found that the majority find no sex difference in that part of the corpus callosum. Witelson has found, however, that a different region—the isthmus—is larger in women. "This is surprising because all other parts of the corpus callosum are larger in men," she says. While the corpus callosum starts out to be larger in men, it decreases in size with age, while in women it stays the same—at least until age 70, Witelson reported in the 18 July *New England Journal of Medicine*.

Sex differences in the anatomy of the corpus callosum likely reflect sex differences in cortical structure. This, in turn, could underlie the sex differences that have been documented in cognition and patterns of lateralization, such as women's greater use of both hemispheres for some language skills.

That interpretation dovetails nicely with observed differences in the anterior commissure, another band of fibers connecting the cerebral hemispheres, and in the massa intermedia, a band of gray matter and fiber that connects the right and left halves of the thalamus. While the data are sketchier for these areas than for the corpus callosum, Gorski's team found that the massa intermedia tends to be absent altogether in men more frequently than it is in women. While the function of the massa intermedia isn't known, some early NIH studies have found a correlation between the presence of it and I.Q. scores (with different patterns in men and women).

Says Witelson: "Obviously, intelligence isn't situated in the massa intermedia, but it could be correlated with other anatomical features that are relevant to some aspects of intelligence."

Although evidence of anatomical differences between male and female brains is accumulating fast, many researchers think the surface has barely been scratched. "People haven't [looked in other regions] so far," says Swaab. They should, he says, "because brain weight is already sexually dimorphic. That leads me to expect that differences will be found all over the brain."

One of the most promising regions for future study is the hippocampus, a temporal lobe structure that is thought to participate in memory and spatial processing. Studies of the hippocampus could go beyond documenting differences into the key puzzle of why male and female brains have evolved differently. That possibility is hinted at by intriguing studies of the hippocampus in wild rodents conducted by University of Pittsburgh anthropologist Steven J. C. Gaulin. "If the hippocampus was critically important in spatial processing, then I wondered if you could see something as gross as size differences in the hippocampus of males and females," says Gaulin.

Working with University of Utah animal behavioralist Lucia Jacobs, he studied the behavior of three species of voles; polygynous wild meadow voles, a species in which the males travel farther than females to find mates—an activity that requires considerable spatial processing—and prairie voles and pine voles that are monogamous and stayed by the sides of their mates. On autopsying the rodents, the pair found the polygynous males' hippocampi were 11% bigger on average than those of females. But the monogamous males' hippocampi were no bigger than the females'. Says Gaulin: "I think this is the only sex difference in the mammalian brain for which we have a plausible evolutionary function that has been tested."

Although it might seem that there's a huge evolutionary distance between a vole and a man, "the obvious next step is to use MRI to image the hippocampus in humans," says University of Arizona psychobiologist Lynn Nadel, a specialist in the hippocampus.

Whether ideas derived from work on voles can be applied directly to humans or not, the observed differences between men's and women's brains are no doubt there for solid evolutionary reasons. Says Gaulin: "If you look at the present-day organisms as bearing the stigmata of their polygynous past, such as higher male metabolism rates, larger male body size, and higher male aggressiveness, then it's not at all implausible for us to bear other marks of it in the brain." Now that anatomical differences are being established, surely one of the next key steps will be to understand why those differences came into being.

21

Is "Gender Gap" Narrowing?

Constance Holden

Do males and females have different kinds of intellectual abilities? That notion, which has probably prevailed through most of recorded history, has undergone sharp alterations as a result of both scientific and political developments in the last 3 decades. And particularly now, when "political correctness" has become a hot button, this area of research is something of a political minefield.

The starting point for this debate is a large body of evidence, accumulated over many decades, suggesting that there are some differences in cognition and perception between men and women. Generally speaking, test results show that females are somewhat better at verbal expression, while males have a persistent advantage in certain quantitative and spatial abilities. (These generalizations were the main ones that emerged from the first major attempt to synthesize the literature, *The Psychology of Sex Differences*, written in 1974 by Eleanor Maccoby and Carol Nagy Jacklin.)

But are these differences "real?" And are they diminishing? Both questions are currently being fiercely debated. Indeed, in the opinion of one researcher, psychologist Diane Halpern of the University of Southern California, "The hostile and politically charged climate surrounding sex differences research has called into question the possibility of ever obtaining bias-free research."

Within this supercharged atmosphere, there's something of a polarity between biologically and socially oriented researchers. Those at the biological end of the spectrum, such as behavioral neuroscientist Sandra Witelson of McMaster University in Ontario, think it's obvious that biology has a role in cognitive sex differences. "The neurobiological evidence is continuing to mount . . . there are too many incontestable findings—things that have to have consequences in behavior and thinking." In fact, she says, "if one didn't observe these sex differences, one would hypothesize that they must exist."

But more socially oriented investigators—such as psychologist Janet Hyde of the University of Wisconsin—flatly disagree. "We've constructed theories of sex differences in the brain to account for differences in abilities," says Hyde. But now, she argues, the gender gap in test scores is waning. "We've come to question the very existence of the phenomenon the brain theories were constituted to explain."

Getting a grip on the available data is not easy. Male-female differences in cognition are often subtle, they change according to age and ability level, and standardized tests are crude tools for resolving questions about sex differences they weren't designed to measure. As a result, even a slight change in a test question can result in a big change in "effect size"—the proportion of a standard deviation by which the sexes differ. Furthermore, generalizing about "verbal ability" obscures the fact that this category includes a variety of skills: verbal fluency (where females excel), analogies (where males do better), spelling, writing, and comprehension. Similarly, the typical male advantages in "visual-spatial ability" vary widely depending on test population and the subskill being measured.

But in spite of such subtleties and confusions, at least one general trend has become apparent in the past decade: increasing attention is being focused on the question of whether the "gender gap" is narrowing. Evidence to support a narrowing comes largely from the past decade's meta-analyses—studies of studies that crunch disparately gathered data into cumulative results. One such analysis, on "gender differences in verbal ability," published in the *Psychological Bulletin* in 1988 by Hyde and psychologist Marcia Linn of the University of California at Berkeley, proposed that, in fact, overall sex differences had almost disappeared. The effect size in favor of females from studies published before 1973 was .23, and it fell to .10 for those published after 1973. Since .80 is commonly regarded as a large effect size, this means the difference went from small to just about nothing.

In a companion meta-analysis on math performance, published in the *Psychological Bulletin* last year, Hyde and psychologists Elizabeth Fennema and Susan Lamon of the University of Wisconsin again found declines in the average effect size. In this case, it was presumed male advantages that were diminishing. The study covered scores on computation, concepts, problem-solving, arithmetic, algebra, geometry, and calculus. The overall effect size decreased from .31 before 1973 to .14 in the post-1973 period.

Other researchers have also found a narrowing of the disparity between males and females. And indeed, data from average test populations seem encouraging to those who say the gap is narrowing. But that hardly settles the question. Those who believe the gender gap still exists question the meta-analytical approach, saying that, by pooling data, meta-analysis blurs rather than clarifies differences. For example, Halpern argues that if statistically insignificant results were eliminated from Linn and Hyde's meta-analysis, the female advantage in verbal performance would have remained. In addition, says Halpern, SAT data (eliminated from Linn and Hyde's final estimates on the grounds that they would overwhelm the other results) show that the mathematical advantage of males—about half a standard deviation—has remained unchanged for 23 years.

Furthermore, critics such as Halpern say that results from high-ability test subjects don't indicate a narrowing of the gap at all. The most striking findings supporting this view come from the Study of Mathematically Precocious Youth (SMPY), initiated in 1970 by Julian Stanley of Johns Hopkins University, which administers the Scholastic Aptitude Test to high-ability seventh and eighth graders. According to his colleague Camilla Benbow, who is continuing the project at Iowa State University, the pattern has remained constant for 2 decades: among 12-year-olds who score 500 or higher on the math portion of the SAT, the male-female ratio is 2:1, rising to 4:1 at scores above 600, and 13:1 above 700.

A major reason for these surprising discrepancies is something cognitive researchers call "greater male variability," meaning that there are always more males than females at both the bottom and the top of score distributions. This is particularly evident in the lopsided SMPY results. Benbow argues that the intrinsic difference in math ability coupled with this greater variability means that in math "there are many more extremely talented males than females." Her colleague David Lubinsky adds that the greater variability also has the effect—at the top ability levels—of wiping out females' advantage in verbal tasks. In the top 1%, the sexes are equally represented.

But those who think the gender gap is mainly a function of social influences don't buy that argument. Linn, for example, contends instead that in highly achieving test populations, the males are even more highly selected than the females. Why? Smart males get more encouragement from parents and teachers than do smart females. They take more advanced courses in high school, and their spatial skills benefit from their greater athletic participation.

It's clear that the whole question of the gender gap in cognition is still a hotbed of dispute. Nonetheless, some investigators believe enough data have been gathered to start zeroing in on the essence of male-female differences—including the differences in spatial reasoning that seem to persist over time and across cultures. As stated by psychologist David Lohman of the University of Iowa, the hypothesis is that the core difference has to do with what he calls the "visual-spatial scratchpad"—the mental ability to retain and manipulate spatial and numeric data that cannot be solved verbally.

Lohman describes several tests that seem to rely on just such an internal scratchpad. One is "speed of closure"—a task involving the identification of a distorted or incomplete image. Another is a test of "horizontality," in which the subject must draw a line to show the water level in a tilted vessel. Males not only perform these tasks better than females, they do them more quickly. When females get a correct result, says Witelson, they seem to get it by reasoning. "Men just look at it and know that's the way it is ... it's almost as if they look at it without trying to analyze or process it."

Even those researchers who believe that intrinsic factors underlie sex differences in cognition don't believe that these differences alone are sufficient to make females less suited for scientific careers. Halpern, for example, says she believes that the reason for lower female achievement in science results "much more [from] psychosocial [factors] than [from] ability differences." But "psychosocial" covers a lot of ground. Benbow and Lubinsky report, for example, that although sexually stereotyped attitudes are much less prevalent among their precocious subjects than among students in general, few SMPY females are choosing careers in math, engineering, or the physical sciences. "It's a gender difference coupled with an interest/value difference," says Benbow.

Just as researchers differ on the causes of these discrepancies, so do they place different emphases on what to do about them. Researchers such as Hyde want more resources put into environmental interventions such as "girl-friendly science classrooms." Others, like Benbow, think it's necessary to do more fine-grained research on cognitive abilities.

But ultimately everyone agrees: The country should be doing whatever works to get more women into science.

22

HUMAN ADOLESCENCE AND REPRODUCTION: AN EVOLUTIONARY PERSPECTIVE

JANE B. LANCASTER

When the life cycle of the human female is viewed from the perspective of parenthood, its major features clearly support a uniquely human pattern of high levels of long-term parental investment and the dependency of multiple young of different ages. For a variety of reasons, most modern cultures present poor models for the female life cycle during most of human history because of their wide range of variation in women's activities, health, nutrition, numbers of children born and reared, and the use of artificial techniques to alter fertility. A real understanding of the evolutionary pressures lying behind women's reproductive biology must currently start with a reconstruction of how it unfolds in the hunting-gathering life style in which it evolved: a life style representing fully 99% of human history. Such a model, based on data drawn from the few remaining hunter-gatherers of today, is fraught with distortions and confounds but, nevertheless, has already provided us with some important insights into major evolutionary novelties in the reproductive lives of modern women. Short (1976), relying heavily on Howell's (1979) careful work on !Kung hunter-gatherer demography, sketches the most striking features of women's biological legacy from the hunter-gatherer era. They include a long period of adolescent subfertility following menarche, late age for first birth, a pattern of nearly continuous nursing during the day, many years of lactation, low frequency of menstrual cycling during the life course, and early menopause. Figure 2.1 illustrates the contrasting patterns of reproductive life found in hunter-gatherer and modern women. Whereas a hunter-gatherer woman can expect nearly 15 years of lactational amenorrhea and just under 4 years each of pregnancy and menstrual cycling, the modern woman experiencing two pregnancies with little or no breast feeding is likely to spend over 35 years in menstrual cycling—a ninefold increase. The generality of this worldwide shift from lactation amenorrhea to menstrual cycling has been confirmed in a recent review of data from preindustrial and industrial societies (Harrell, 1981).

A basic human pattern emerges from such a perspective which emphasizes low fertility and extremely restrained reproduction based on the postponed development of fertility in the life cycle, an extremely high rate of embryonic mortality, and long lactational amenorrhea (Short 1976,

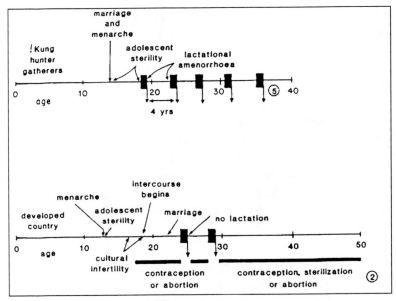

FIGURE 2.1. Changing patterns of human fertility. !Kung hunter-gatherers have a relatively late menarche and adolescent subfertility defers the birth of the first child until age 19. Lactational amenorrhea keeps births 4 years apart. Early menopause results in a completed family size of about 5 children, only 2 to 3 of whom will survive into adulthood.

In developed countries menarche occurs at 12 to 13, cultural infertility breaks down in the late teens, and intercourse before marriage requires the use of contraception or abortion. Lactation is so short that birth spacing is dependent on contraception. If the desired family size is 2, contraception, sterilization, or abortion are necessary for a further 20 years. The result of this imposed sterility is a ninefold increase in the number of menstrual cycles (after Short 1976:16).

1979b) supplemented by various cultural practices such as taboos on intercourse during lactation, infanticide, and birth control. In spite of what would seem to be an impressive array of biological and behavioral adaptations leading to late and low rates of fertility, the past 150 years has witnessed a period of radical population growth that appears to be associated with an increasingly earlier entrance into reproduction in the life cycle. Clearly, the presence of such evolutionary novelties in the modern human pattern of reproduction are important to provide insight into investigating the mechanisms involved and the search for possible remedies.

Following Short's lead, it is possible to gain major insights into the biology and behavior of modern adolescents by comparison with closely related species. Adolescence is a critical and expensive feature of the life cycle for any animal. Since its length postpones the adult phase of the life cycle but may also provide critical learning about the social and ecological setting of adult experience before undertaking reproduction, its course and duration must be shaped by conflicting evolutionary forces of intense measure. A cross-species perspective suggests that adolescence in the human species has its own unique set of characteristics—some of which are shared with our closest living relatives, the great apes, and others which may be found only in humans. Using an evolutionary cross-species, comparative perspective, the remainder of this chapter will explore these major features of human adolescence: the sequencing of human pubertal events, the low fertility once characteristic of adolescence, the relationship between body fat and fertility, and the relationship between pregnancy and lactation to the growth of the human brain. The goals of such an exploration include an alerting function in recognizing evolutionary novelties, the identification of appropriate animal models for research into mechanism, and the development of a general appreciation of the adaptive features of human biology and behavior shaped by millions of years of evolution.

THE SEQUENCING OF PUBERTAL EVENTS: A COMPARATIVE PERSPECTIVE

Short (1976) reviews the milestones in human pubertal events and notes the interesting fact that boys and girls have very different programs (Figure 2.2). For girls, the first external sign of puberty is the development of the breast bud. This is an odd and noteworthy feature of human development and one that is likely to go unnoticed without comparative mammalian data. The typical primate female will not begin to develop breasts until the later stages of pregnancy. The breasts of the human female are made conspicuous and stable with deposits of fat, in contrast to other primates whose breasts

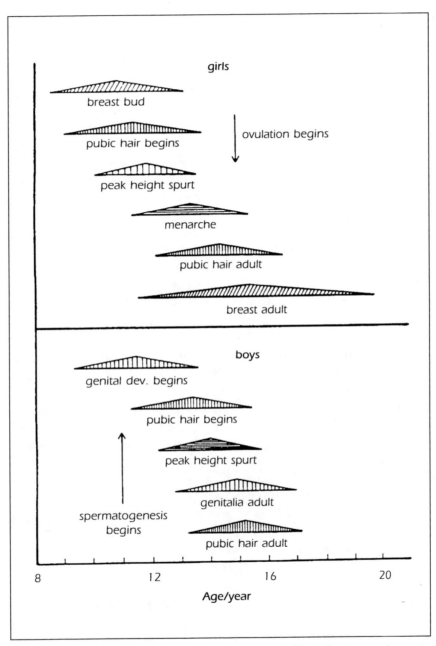

FIGURE 2.2. The sequence of pubertal events in boys and girls indicating a major contrast in the timing of fertility compared to other growth events (From Short 1976:7).

experience an increase in glandular tissue that resorbs again after weaning if another pregnancy does not ensue. The deposition of fat during human adolescence on the breasts and buttocks is a unique feature of human sexual dimorphism that constitutes a continuous advertisement of an ability to lactate rather than a cyclic fertility advertised by estrous swelling, as do so many other higher primates (Lancaster, 1984; J. B. Lancaster and C. S. Lancaster, 1982).

It is also worth noting that menarche is a relatively late event in the sequence of human pubertal changes, but that it still usually precedes the establishment of regular patterns of ovulation by several years. Menarche itself is preceded by most of the essential features of physical development indicating adult status: the adolescent growth spurt, the attainment of nearly adult values for weight and stature, and the growth of breasts and pubic hair. It is interesting that one of the most crucial features of reproductive success for women, adult capacity of the pelvic inlet and birth canal, is not attained until the very end of the sequence of pubertal events, years after menarche. Even among well-nourished, middle-class girls in a modern sample whose menarche was 12 to 13 years, adult pelvic dimensions were not attained until ages 17 to 18 (Moerman, 1982). The adolescent growth spurt which precedes menarche does not involve the growth of the female pelvis which, if anything, continues its unique, slow trajectory for several years after adult stature is reached. This late attainment of adult pelvic capacity gives indirect evidence for a very recent historical separation by as much as six years in the maturation of reproductive capacity and the completion of pelvic growth. Considering the heavy pressure by natural selection on cephalopelvic disproportion leading to infant deaths in time past, it is reasonable to surmise that our species has only recently been confronted with this problem on a regular basis.

Another contrast in pubertal sequencing can be found when comparing the production of sex cells in boys and girls. As Short has noted (1976, 1979a), the onset of spermatogenesis for boys precedes virtually all other pubertal changes, whereas in girls ovulation occurs very late in the sequence. As Richardson and Short (1978:21) state, the boy becomes potentially fertile at the very beginning of pubertal development, passing through a phase of being a "fertile eunuch" before acquiring his male secondary sex characteristics, whereas the girl develops nearly all her secondary sex characteristics to their fullest extent before acquiring her fertility. This fact suggests some special evolutionary pressure to delay fertility for the human female, giving her a time when she can function both socially and sexually as an adult but not assume a maternal role.

A delay in the establishment of fertility until after the attainment of adult stature is not universal to female primates, many of which continue to grow not only after menarche but even during their first pregnancy and lactation. Gavan and Swindler (1966) and Watts and Gavan (1982) note differences among the higher primates in the location of menarche in the growth period (see Figure 2.3). Rhesus monkey females have attained only 30% of their adult stature when they reach menarche in contrast to humans and chimpanzees who reached 70 and 80%, respectively. Altmann *et al.* (1981) note that female baboons in Kenya commence cycling at about $4\frac{1}{4}$ to 5 years of age, experience their first pregnancy at about 6 years, and give birth to their first infant at 6 1/2. Their attainment of full growth coincides with first pregnancy and birth, but not with menarche. Similarly, Froehlich *et al.* (1981) and Mori (1979) note a smoothly decelerating growth trajectory for wild monkeys in which females continue to gain weight for several years after their first pregnancy.

The adolescent growth spurt itself, so prominent in human development, may not be typical of other primates. In an early study, Gavan and Swindler (1966) concluded that while a growth spurt is so obvious for both human males and females, even on the basis of simple plots of annual increments in stature, nothing comparable could be demonstrated for nonhuman primates. However, in a follow-up study (Watts and Gavan, 1982) computer analysis of the same data base demonstrates that there is an adolescent growth spurt of much smaller magnitude than the human that can be discerned for the rhesus monkey and chimpanzee but only when compared to a predicted curve of growth. Such data suggest that an adolescent growth spurt comparable to the human may not occur at all in the monkey and ape females and whatever spurt that does occur is of minor magnitude. It is unlikely that this contrast is one that reflects dietary differences rather than species adaptation. Although Stini (1979) notes that humans growing under conditions of nutritional stress show an altered form of growth curve in both stature and weight which is more linear and has a more prolonged trajectory, the rhesus and chimpanzee data analyzed by Watts and Gavan came from well-fed laboratory populations. It is interesting that poor nutrition affects the growth patterns of a human male much more than it does a female. Frisch and Revalle (1969) found that in nutritionally growth-limited males there was a more rapid maturation, particularly in late growth, with a marked reduction in mature weight. For females, maturation rate was not particularly affected, and although there was a reduction in mature size, the growth pattern remained proportionate with adult size and weight 95% complete before menarche.

As noted in Figure 2.3, mean age of puberty closely coincides with that of the peak of the adolescent spurt in the female chimpanzee, but in the

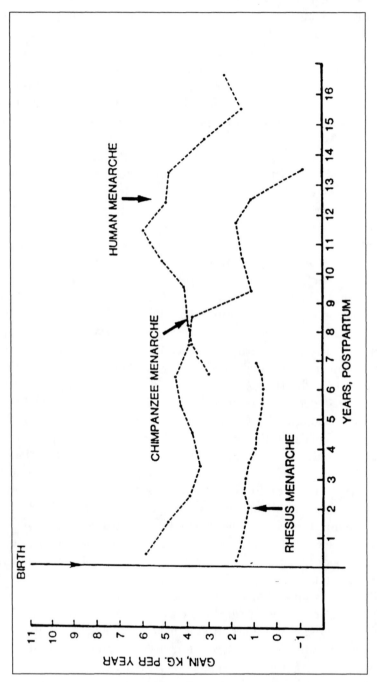

FIGURE 2.3. Comparative weight velocity curves for the rhesus monkey, chimpanzee, and humans. Major weight gain in the human and chimpanzee female occurs before menarche, whereas in the rhesus, it is nearly a year later (after Tanner, 1962).

female rhesus, menarche precedes the beginning of the adolescent acceleration and occurs, on the average, $1\frac{1}{2}$ years before the peak. Thus, sharp
contrasts exist between the human condition with a prominent growth
spurt in both height and weight preceding menarche and the nonhuman
primate pattern in which an adolescent growth spurt is minor and follows
(rhesus monkey) or is coincident with (chimpanzee) menarche.

It is possible that a pattern of female growth which allows for conflict
between maternal growth and weight gain and fetal growth and lactation
explains the poor figures for maternal success often reported for primiparous female monkeys and apes. For example, Drickamer (1974) for colony
rhesus, Nadler (1975) for captive gorillas, Dazey and Erwin (1976) for
colony pigtail macaques, Taub (1980) for colony squirrel monkeys,
Glander (1980) for wild howler monkeys, and Mori (1979) for provisioned
Japanese macaques, all report major contrasts in success in rearing infants
between primiparous and multiparous mothers. Generally, when statistics
are given, the mortality of infants born to primiparous primate mothers is
more than double that of experienced and fully matured females. To date,
only one study (Small and Rodman, 1981) reports no difference in reproductive success for first-time mothers observed in a laboratory colony of
bonnet macaques. Several of the authors point to differences in fatness,
body size, social rank, and food acquisition as keys to this differential in
reproductive performance. Both Mori (1979) and Drickamer (1974), re-
porting on free-ranging but provisioned macaque colonies, note that females from high-ranking matrilines begin reproduction as much as a year
earlier than other females, space their infants more closely, and are more
successful in rearing young. Mori (1979) suggests the same and finds the
maternal success is closely correlated with body weight and matrilineal
status. Small-for-age females have poor reproductive success indicating that
a reduction in body size in the face of restricted nutrition is a poor
reproductive strategy for female primates. As Ralls (1976) states, bigger
mothers are better mothers.

Finally, comparisons of life cycle events between wild and captive
primates must be tempered with the recognition that primates raised in
captivity show identical elements of a secular trend in growth described so
fully for human populations during the past 150 years and for modern
rural-urban comparisons. The major milestones of menarche, first birth,
and completed growth are advanced in the laboratory and completed adult
stature and weight are increased. According to Altmann *et al.* (1981),
virtually all primates reported so far, which are healthy and well-fed in the
laboratory or freely provisioned but free-ranging in the wild, show the
secular trend in growth. Altmann *et al.* demonstrate that the ages at which

developmental milestones for baboons occur in the field as compared to those in captivity were advanced by a ratio of approximately 5:3. Similarly, Coe et al. (1979), in reviewing similar data for captive and wild chimpanzees, reported advances in developmental milestones on the order of 5:4.2 and 7:5.25. In the laboratory, chimpanzee females reach menarche around 8.5 years and first give birth at age 10–11, whereas wild chimpanzees reach menarche at 11–13 and first birth is at 13–15 years. It would be interesting to investigate how the secular trend in development affects psychosocial and cognitive development in laboratory-reared primates. Certainly, the secular trend leading to more rapid psychosexual development in humans does not seem to correlate with an advance in cognitive maturation. Perhaps primates might serve as useful experimental models in which the effects of cultural values, education, and training could be ruled out.

THE PERIOD OF ADOLESCENT SUBFERTILITY

At least 40 years ago, there was a general recognition that adolescent female primates, whether rhesus monkey, chimpanzee or human, are not instantly fertile at the time of menarche (Montagu, 1979; Young and Yerkes, 1943). Data collected at that time suggested that a period of postmenarcheal subfertility lasted for about a year in the rhesus and up to two years for the chimpanzee and human. This information fits well with observations by anthropologists on tribal societies indicating that, although sexual activity almost invariably follows menarche, the likelihood of pregnancy is very low for the first few years. However, it is only very recently that the mechanism behind adolescent subfertility has been outlined (Lunenfeld et al., 1978; Reiter, this volume). It appears that rising ovarian estrogen secretion at puberty eventually triggers a reflex discharge of luteinizing hormone from the pituitary leading to ovulation. However, responsiveness of the pituitary and gonads is regulated by a progressive maturation of feedback regulatory centers in the hypothalamus. This positive feedback system takes time to mature: as Lunenfeld et al. noted, the ovary learns to ovulate. It appears that it takes nearly a year for this mechanism to develop in the rhesus monkey (Dierschke et al., 1974; Robinson and Goy, 1981). In a study of 8000 Finnish girls by Widholm and Kantero (1971: cited in Ryde-Blomqvist 1978:147) only 57% of the girls had established regular menstrual cycles by one year postmenarche and not until 6 years postmenarche were 80% cycling regularly. Similar data using basal body temperature changes to indicate ovulation suggest that not until age 18–20 are 75% of menstrual cycles ovulatory (Doring 1969). Short (1978) cites data on the sexual cycles of a wild female chimpanzee whose first estrous cycle began at age 11, followed 9 months later by menarche (a typical sequence for nonhuman primates). In spite of regular copulations, she did not conceive for nearly 3 more years. What is remarkable about this data is the extremely long time it takes in the higher primates for fertility to be established after regular sexual activity is assumed. According to Richardson and Short (1978), mammals such as sheep and rats have a first estrus associated with ovulation. For such species, the positive feedback mechanism regulating ovulation matures at birth, not years after menarche, so that for them, puberty equals instant fertility. One might speculate that the unusual demands placed on female primates for high levels of long-term parental investment based on experience in the social and physical environment has led to a delay in the maturation of the system regulating fertility but not in the one regulating the onset of sexual behavior.

The effect of the secular trend on the period of adolescent subfertility had not been fully explored. Papers by Lunenfeld *et al.* (1978) and Brown *et al.* (1978) make it clear that there is a wide range of variation in how soon after menarche an individual girl will establish regular ovulatory cycles. It is possible that not only is the mean age of menarche occurring earlier but that the timetable of developmental landmarks is collapsing; that is, fertility now follows menarche more rapidly in well-nourished, inactive girls.

FAT AND FERTILITY

A crucial factor in the fertility of human women relates to critical levels of fat shortage. First proposed by Frisch (1978) and recently reviewed by Cohen (1980) and Huss-Ashmore (1980), the critical fatness hypothesis suggests that human women will not ovulate unless adequate stores of fat have been deposited. These fat deposits represent enough stored energy (around 150,000 calories) to permit a woman to lactate for a year or more without having to increase her prepregnancy caloric intake. Frisch believes that not only birth-spacing but also the timing of the onsets of menarche and menopause may rest on the storage of energy fat. Cohen (1980) notes the appeal of this hypothesis for explaining the secular trend in both the earlier onset of menarche and also the loss of a long period of adolescent subfertility in modern society. Sedentism combined with high levels of caloric intake lead to early deposition of body fat in young girls and "fool" the body into early biological maturation long before cognitive and social maturity are reached.

Skeptics of the critical fatness hypothesis have tended to focus on its critical threshold aspect but do not really undercut the important relationship between fertility and fatness. Ellison (1981a, b) demonstrates that the completion of the adolescent growth spurt in stature is a much better predictor of impending menarche than is a weight gain based on fat storage. This is not surprising when it is remembered that, in terms of evolutionary priorities, human growth of stature is programmed to virtually stop at menarche, whereas there should still exist something on the order of two more years before fertility will be established during which fat can be stored. Perhaps the critical fatness hypothesis would be a better predictor of onset of fertility than of menarche.

A second line of criticism focuses on the fact that populations suffering from chronic malnutrition do not ordinarily cease reproduction and many such women will have children even though their ratio of fat to body weight is below the threshold proposed by Frisch (Bongaarts, 1980). Again, this is not an unexpected finding; an adaptive program for growth and reproduction would be one that hastens or slows growth and sexual maturation on the basis of food supply but only up to a point. The program should have limits on either end which prevent the establishment of reproduction in large juveniles or the indefinite delay of reproduction in the face of chronic food shortage. Evidence for just such a program in nonhuman primates is beginning to come from field studies. Mori (1979) investigated the relationship between population changes, food supply, body weight, and maturation in a group of Japanese macaques over a 25-year period. He found that daughters from high-ranking matrilines were larger in weight and stature than their peers and tended to give birth as soon as they had reached 6.5 kg, frequently a year before their peers and two years before the smallest and lowest-ranking females. Such females continued to gain weight during their early years of reproduction. Eventually, small females did become pregnant even if they weighted only 6 kg but their offspring showed a much higher mortality rate especially when the food supply was low. The relationship of rank to fat storage has been confirmed in the laboratory as well which suggests that even under conditions of ample food supply, low-status females may have problems of food access (Small, 1981).

In spite of the criticisms of Frisch's hypothesis, there is a growing body of evidence recently published by Garn (1980) demonstrating that early-maturing girls tend to be taller at puberty than their peers but ultimately shorter than the mean for adult women and fatter during their entire life course. Even at age 70, nearly 55 years after menarche, heavy rather than lean women report earlier menarcheal age. Both sons and daughters of such women tend to be faster growing; but reaching maturity earlier, they are ultimately shorter as well.

It is interesting that recent studies on the link between obesity and diabetes (Hartz et al., 1984; Kissebah et al., 1982) suggest that there may be two routes to fat deposition in the human. One route is influenced by androgens and tends to concentrate fat around the waist and upper body in fat cells that have the capacity to radically expand or shrink. The other route is via estrogens which concentrate fat that is very resistant to loss on the lower body. When obese women diet, there is a strong tendency for weight to be lost from the upper body but not from the lower. In fact, it appears to be much harder to shrink or kill normal-sized fat cells from the lower body, so that women who are fat only in these areas find it very hard to lose weight even if they diet faithfully. If concentrations of fat on the hips, buttocks, and thighs of women is "reproductive fat," it should not be surprising that these stores might be buffered against weight loss and accumulate under the influence of estrogens (Stini, 1979).

In spite of the fact that one of the most striking and uniquely developed features of human sexual dimorphism is fat deposition, very little significance has been attached to it. Reviews of sexual dimorphism in human and nonhuman primates (Alexander et al., 1979; Hamburg, 1978; Leutenegger, 1982; McCown, 1982) tend to focus on sex differences in body size and potential for aggression and do not note the extraordinary differences between men and women in fat storage or the lack of such conspicuous dimorphism in nonhumans primates. In fact, only Bailey (1982), Hall (1982), Huss-Ashmore (1980), and Stini (1979, 1982) give fat storage in women the emphasis it deserves. Sexual dimorphism in human body fat is much greater than in muscular tissue. Approximately 15% of body weight in the young adult male and about 27% of the female is adipose tissue, whereas muscle tissue represents an average of 52% for the male and 40% for the female (Bailey, 1982). When corrections are made for the smaller body size of the human female, women are indeed a great deal fatter than calculations of average sex differences would indicate. For instance, in comparing volume of body segments corrected for frame size, Bailey (1982) found that women are 40.2% larger than men for the gluteal (buttocks) segment. Huss-Ashmore (1980) argues that the distinctiveness of fat storage in women on breasts, buttocks, and thighs advertises healthy systemic function and the ability to reproduce and successfully rear children. As such, reproductive fat in women should be differentially located than fat in men, localized for more dramatic display and closely linked to the development of other secondary sex characteristics.

FAT RESERVES, LACTATION, AND GROWTH
OF THE HUMAN BRAIN

It is only very recently that evolutionary theorists have turned from such behavioral topics as aggression and sexual behavior to lactation as a key variable in understanding species' differences (Blurton-Jones, 1972; Daly, 1979; Pond, 1979). Perhaps one reason for this delayed interest was that few recognized the enormous interspecies variability in virtually all aspects of lactation: the constituents of milk, frequency of nursing, length of nursing bout, and duration of lactation. Blurton-Jones (1972) and more recently Anderson, (1983), Stini (1982), and Stini *et al.* (1980) profile the unusual features of human milk and lactation. One of the most striking of these is its exceedingly low protein content (46% that of the cow and 15% of the rabbit). At the same time, it is rich with lactose and lipids with values ranging 22 and 42% above those of the cow. The composition of human milk represents a balance of numerous other constituents as well, but it is clear from the ratios of protein, lactose, and lipids that it amply supplies the nutrients necessary for activity and growth of the brain and provides only low levels of nutrients necessary to develop lean muscle and tissue. This is not surprising when it is noted that even by age 10 a human reaches only 50% of adult body size but has reached virtually adult values for brain size by age 4 (Dobbing, 1974).

The peculiarities and uniqueness of human milk can be best understood if the unusual program for human brain growth is taken into account. At birth, the brains of rhesus monkey infants are approximately 68% of the adult size, chimpanzees 45%, and humans 23% (Kerr *et al.*, 1969; Passingham, 1975). The human infant's brain grows exceedingly rapidly after birth, but it does not reach 45% of the adult size until 6–7 months of age, and by the end of the first year, it has completed only 65% of its total growth (Figure 2.4). The human brain completes 93–95% of its growth in volume by the end of the fourth year, the usual age of weaning among human hunter-gatherers. There are other animal species which also have extensive postnatal growth of the brain but they are generally what zoologists have labeled as *r*-selected species; that is, they tend to rapidly produce litters of small embryonic young which grow very quickly after birth and are weaned within a few weeks or months (Dobbing and Sands, 1979). With the exception of the great apes and humans, most animals with single young and large adult body size produce precocial infants with well-developed brains, able to sense the world and locomote at birth. Figure 2.5 illustrates the extremely long duration of brain growth in the human, the nutrients for which cannot be ensured by the timing of births to an optimal season of the year.

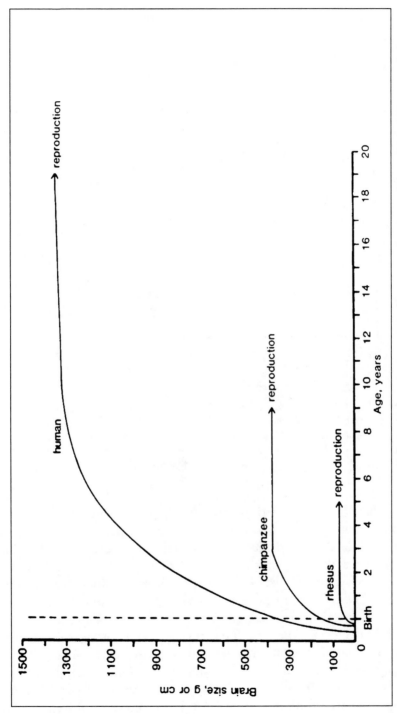

FIGURE 2.4. Growth of the brain in humans, chimpanzees, and the rhesus monkey (after Passingham, 1975; Kerr et al., 1969).

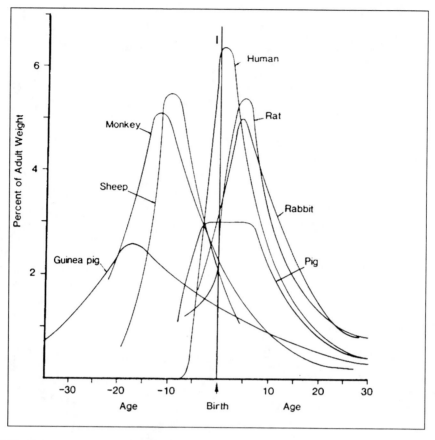

FIGURE 2.5. The brain growth spurts of 7 mammalian species expressed as first-order velocity curves of the increase in weight with age. The units of time for each species are: guinea pig, 1 day; rhesus monkey, 4 days; sheep, 5 days; pig, 1 week; human, 1 month; rabbit, 2 days; rat, 1 day. Rates are expressed as weight gain as a percentage of adult weight for each unit of time (from Dobbing and Sands, 1979).

Dobbing (1974) and Frisancho (1978), in reviewing the most critical and vulnerable periods of brain growth in humans, focus on the last trimester of fetal life and the first postnatal year as crucial. Although the adult number of nerve cells develops during the first trimester of pregnancy, the energetically demanding stages for the production of the brain's packing cells (oligodenroglia, glial cells) followed by synaptic aroborization of the nerve cells and by the production of insulating material (myelin) which coats the long fibers through which nerve cells send messages, occur in the three months just before birth and the subsequent year. The vulnerable nature of brain growth for such a long period postpartum may explain one recently described feature of maternal weight gain and fetal growth. According to Winick (1981), preparations for lactation are so important that, if the mother is inadequately nourished, they will take place at the expense of fetal growth. The pregnant woman will continue to deposit fat during pregnancy even it is means that fetal growth in body size will be reduced below optimal levels for neonate survival. Winick recommends that women should gain at last 25 pounds in pregnancy to ensure that the fetus will not have to compete for nutrients with maternal fat storage processes. The energetic greed of the human infant's brain is truly impressive. During the first year of life, up to 65% of its total metabolic rate is devoted to the brain and only 8% to muscle tissue (Holliday, 1978).

The question remains as to why human beings are committed to such a potentially vulnerable program of brain growth, one that is so dependent on maternal lactation over such a long time period. Schultz (1941) and, more recently, Lindburg (1982) have laid to rest what is known as the obstetrical dilemma theory which argues that, when humans evolved bipedal locomotion and a pelvis in the shape of a bony ring, the dual demands of efficient bipedalism and an intelligent, large brain were in direct conflict. The supposed solution to this conflict was the birth of an immature, helpless infant with major (75%) brain growth programmed for outside the womb. The only problem with this thesis is that it fails to explain the immaturity of the great ape infant whose brain grows 55 to 64% after birth even though maternal pelvic capacity is nearly one-third larger than needed. Lindburg turns to a work by Mason (1968) that suggests that the immaturity of great ape and human infants may best be understood as an adaptation for transition into a social, learning environment at an early stage of neural development. This might help to explain why we find similarities in the great ape and human pattern of slow growth in the juvenile period but the attainment of adult stature and weight before first pregnancy in contrast to the macaque mother whose infants brain grows little after birth but who still may be growing herself during her early reproductive years.

CONCLUSION

The timing of growth, development, and the onset of reproduction within the life cycle has always been under heavy selective pressure from natural selection. The result of this procedure is a special program for each species which provides a range of variation for each event which is appropriate to conditions ranging from optimal to suboptimal habitat. The basic evolutionary pattern for human females is one of slow growth during a prolonged period of juvenile dependency followed by a rapid completion of growth in stature, and sometimes body weight as well, before menarche. Menarche is followed by several years of sexual activity with very low probably of impregnation during which a young woman can gain experience about her social and physical environment before undertaking the demands of motherhood. During this period of adolescent subfertility, a substantial store of body fat will be deposited in the human female at the same time that her male peer is using energy surpluses to grow greater stature and lean muscle tissue. This differential in male and female growth patterns leads to the major element of human dimorphism in secondary sex characteristics: fat storage. The evolutionary pressure for the development of such an unusual degree of dimorphism in nutrient reserves is the unique demands of the developing human brain which grows 2/3 of its total size in the first four years postpartum. It is not noteworthy that the great ape pattern appears to be intermediate and foreshadows the human pattern. Great apes also have a long, 4-year period of lactation and bear relatively helpless infants with brains that will grow at least 55–64% between birth an the end of the second year.

The critical factor in adjusting this program to the environment, allowing it to take advantage of differences in habitat optimality, appears to be an interaction of diet and exercise, energy acquisition, and expense. Recent changes in human life styles including diets higher in simple carbohydrates and fats in combination with lowered energy demands appear to signal optimal habitat conditions, thereby speeding up sexual and physical maturation. Today, we may be witnessing a maximal lowering of the mean age for menarche and fertility to the lowest point within the range of variation established long ago by evolutionary processes. For most of human history, for most individuals, and under most conditions, the human pattern of growth and development was expressed in such a way as to allow social, physical, psychological, and sexual development to unfold at a more leisurely pace with first birth in the late teens preceded by several years of adolescent subfertility. Today, the earlier onset of adolescence and more rapid assumption of fertility by age 12–14 means that humans can no longer count on the evolved mechanisms of time past for appropriate timing of reproductive events. It is abundantly clear that only culturally based systems can ensure that a child will not become a mother.

ACKNOWLEDGMENTS

The stimulus for writing this article came from several years of planning and discussion with members of the Social Science Research Council's Committee for Biosocial Science Perspectives on Parent Behavior and Offspring Development. The support and encouragement of the Social Science Research Council is gratefully acknowledged. Partial funding of the activities of the committee was granted by the National Institute for Child Health and Human Development (Grant No. 5R13-HD11777-02) and by the William T. Grant Foundation. Data on reproduction, parental investment, and the human life cycle was developed during a Summer Research Fellowship awarded by the Faculty Research Council of the University of Oklahoma. Special thanks are due to LaDon Deatherage for her help in the collection of data and library references and to Carri Swope and Darlene Thornton for assistance in preparing the manuscript. The helpful comments on an earlier version of the manuscript are gratefully acknowledged to Judith K. Brown, Mildred Dickemann, Patty Gowati, James Gavin, Barbara King, Ron Nadler, and S. L. Washburn.

ENDNOTES

Alexander, R. D., Hoogland, J., Howard, R., Noonan, K., and Sherman P. Sexual dimorphisms and breeding systems in pinnipeds, ungulates, primates, and humands. *In* N. Chagnon and W. Irons (Eds.), *Evolutionary biology and human social behavior*. North Scituate, Mass.: Duxbury Press, 1979, pp. 402–435.

Altmann, J., Altmann, S., and Hausfater, G. Physical maturation and age estimates of yellow baboons, *Papio cynocephalus*, in Amboseli National Park, Kenya. *American Journal of Primatology*, 1981, 1389–399.

Anderson, P. The reproductive role of the human breast. *Current Anthropology*, 1983, 24, 25–46.

Bailey, Stephen M. Absolute and relative sex differences in body composition. *In* R. Hall (Ed.), *Sexual dimorphism in Homo sapiens*. New York: Praeger, 1982, pp. 363–390.

Blurton-Jones, Nicholas. Comparative aspects of mother-child contact. *In* N. Blurton-Jones (Ed.), *Ethological studies of child behaviour*. Cambridge: Cambridge University Press, 1972, pp. 305–329.

Bongaarts, John. Does malnutrition affect fecundity? *Science*, 1980, 208, 564–569.

Brown, J. B., Harrisson, Patricia, and Smith, Margery A. Oestrogen and pregnanediol excretion through childhood, menarche, and first ovulation. *Journal of Biosocial Science, Suppl.*, 1978, 5, 43–62.

Coe, C. L., Connolly, A. C., Kraemer, H. C., and Levine, S. Reproductive development and behavior of captive female chimpanzees. *Primates*, 1979, 2, 571–582.

Cohen, Mark N. Speculations on the evolution of density measurement and population in Homo sapiens. *In* M. N. Cohen, R. S. Malpass, and H. G. Klein (Eds.), *Biosocial mechanisms of population regulation.* New Haven: Yale University Press, 1980, pp. 275–304.

Daly, Martin. Why don't male mammals lactate? *Journal of Theoretical Biology,* 1979, 78, 325–345.

Dazey, J., and Erwin J. Infant mortality in *Macaca nemestrina. Theriogenology,* 1976, 5, 267–279.

Dierschke, D. J., Weiss, G., and Knobil, E. Sexual maturation in the female rhesus monkey and the development of estrogen-induced gonadotrophic hormone release. *Endocrinology,* 1974, 94, 198–206.

Dobbing, John. The later development of the brain and its vulnerability. *In* J. A. Davis, and J. Dobbing (Eds.), *Scientific foundations of paediatrics.* Philadelphia: W. B. Saunders, 1974, pp. 565–577.

Dobbing, J. and Sands, J. Comparative aspects of the brain spurt. *Early Human Development,* 1979, 3, 79–83.

Doring, G. K. The incidence of anovular cycles in women. *Journal of Reproductive Fertility, Suppl.,* 1969, 6, 77.

Drickamer, L. C. A ten-year summary of reproductive data for free-ranging *Macaca mulatta. Folia primatologica,* 1974, 21, 61–80.

Ellison, P. T. Prediction of age at menarche from annul height increments. *American Journal of Physical Anthropology,* 1981, 56, 71–75. (b)

Ellison, P. T. Threshold hypotheses, developmental age, and menstrual function. *American Journal of Physical Anthropology,* 1981, 54, 337–340. (a)

Frisancho, A. R. Nutritional influences on human growth and maturation. Yearbook *of Physical Anthropology,* 1978, 21, 174–191.

Frisch, Rose. Population, food intake, and fertility. *Science,* 1978, 199, 22–30.

Frisch, R., and Revelle, R. Variation in body weights and the age of the adolescent growth spurt among Latin American and Asian Populations, in relation to caloric supplies. *Human Biology,* 1969, 41, 185–212.

Froehlich, J. W., Thorington, R. W. Jr., and Otis. J. S. The demography of Howler monkeys (*Alouatta palliata*) on Barro Colorado Island, Panama. *International Journal of Primatology,* 1981, 2, 207–237.

Garn, S. M., Jr. Continuities and change in maturational timing. *In* O. Brim and J. Kagan (Eds.), *Constancy and change in human development.* Cambridge: Harvard University Press, 1980, pp. 113–162.

Gavan, J. A., and Swindler, D. R. Growth rates and phylogeny in primates. *American Journal of Physical Anthropology,* 1966, 24, 181–190.

Glander, K. Reproduction and population growth in free-ranging mantled howling monkeys. *American Journal of Physical Anthropology,* 1980, 53, 25–36.

Hall, R. L. (Ed). *Sexual dimorphism in Homo sapiens,* 1982. New York: Praeger.

Hamburg, B. A. The biosocial bases of sex difference. *In* S. L. Washburn and E. R. McCown (Eds.), *Human evolution: Biosocial perspectives.* Menlo Park, CA: Benjamin/Cummings, 1978, pp. 155–214.

Harrell, B. B. Lactation and menstruation in cultural perspective. *American Anthropologist,* 1981, 83, 796–823.

Hartz, A. J., Rupley, D. C., and Rimm, A. R. The association of girth measurements with disease in 32,856 women. *American Journal of Epidemiology,* 1984, 119, 71–80.

Holliday, M. A. Body composition and energy needs during growth. *In* F. Falker and J. M. Tanner (Eds.), *Human growth.* New York: Plenum, 1978, Vol. 2, pp. 117–139.

Howell, Nancy. *Demography of the Dobe !Kung,* 1979, New York: Academic Press.

Huss-Ashmore, R. Fat and fertility: Demographic implications of differential fat storage. *Yearbook of Physical Anthropology,* 1980, 23, 65–91.

Kerr, G. R., Kennan, A. L., Waisman, H A., and Allen, J. R. Growth and development of the fetal rhesus monkey. I. Physical growth. *Growth,* 1969, 33, 201–213.

Kissebah, A. H., Vydelingum, N., Murray, R., Evans, D. J., Hartz, A. J., Kalhoff, R. K., and Adams, P. W. Relation of body fat distribution of metabolic complications of obesity. *Journal of Clinical Endocrinology and Metabolism,* 1982, 54, 254–260.

Lancaster, Jane B. Evolutionary perspectives on sex difference in the higher primates. *In* A. S. Rossi (Ed.), *Gender and the life course.* New York: Aldine, 1984, pp. 3–27.

Lancaster, J. B. and Lancaster, Chet S. Parental investment: The hominid adaptation. *In* D. Ortner (Ed.), *How humans adapt: A biocultural odyssey.* Washington, D. C.: Smithsonian Institution Press, 1983, pp. 33–66.

Leutenegger, Walter. Sexual dimorphism in nonhuman primates. *In* R. Hall (Ed.), *Sexual dimorphism in Homo sapiens.* New York: Praeger, 1982, pp. 11–36.

Lindburg, D. G. Primate obstetrics: The biology of birth. *American Journal of Primatology, Suppl.,* 1982, 1, 193–199.

Lunenfeld, F., Kraiem, Z., Eshkol, A., and Werner-Zodrow, 1. The ovary learns to ovulate. *Journal of Biosocial Science, Suppl.*, 1978, 5, 43–62.

Marshall, W. A. and Tanner, J. M. Puberty. *In* A. Davis and J. Dobbing (Eds.). *Scientific foundations of paediatrics*. Philadelphia: W. B. Saunders, 1974, pp. 124–152.

Mason, W. A. Scope and potential of primate research. *Science and Psychoanalysis*, 1968, 12, 101–118.

McCown, E. R. Sex differences: The female as baseline for species description. In R. Hall (Ed.), *Sexual dimorphism in Homo sapiens*. New York: Praeger, 1982, pp. 37–84.

Moerman, Marquisa L. Growth of the birth canal in adolescent girls. *American Journal of Obstetrics and Gynecology*, 1982 143, 528–532.

Montagu, M. F. Ashley. *The reproductive development of the female: A study in the comparative physiology of the adolescent organism. 3rd ed.* Littleton, Mass.: Wright PSG, 1979.

Mori, Akio. Analysis of population changes by measurement of body weight in the Koshima troop of Japanese monkeys. *Primates*, 1979, 20, 371–399.

Nadler, R. D. Determinants of variability in maternal behavior of captive female gorillas. *In* S. Kondo, M. Kawai, A. Ehara, and S. Kawamura (Eds.), *Proceedings, Symposia of the 5th Congress of the International Primatological Society*. Tokyo: Japan Science Press, 1975, pp. 207–216.

Passingham, R. E. Changes in the size and organization of the brain in man and his ancestors. *Brain, Behavior and Evolution*, 1975, 11, 73–90.

Pond, Caroline M. The significance of lactation in the evolution of mammals. *Evolution*, 1977, 31, 177–199.

Ralls, Katherine. Mammals in which females are larger than males. *Quarterly Review of Biology*, 1976, 51, 245–276.

Richardson, D. W., and Short, R. V. Time of onset of sperm production in boys. *Journal of Biosocial Science Suppl.*, 1978, 5, 15–26.

Robinson, J. A., and Goy, R. W. The pubescent rhesus monkey: Characteristics of the menstrual cycle and effects of prenatal androgenization. *Biology of Reproduction*, 1981, 24 (Suppl. 1), abstract 90.

Ryde-Blomqvist, Elsa, Contraception in adolescence: A review of the literature. *Journal of Biosocial Science Suppl.*, 1978, 5, 129–158.

Schultz, A. H. The relative size of the cranial capacity in primates. *American Journal of Physical Anthropology*, 1941, 28, 273–287.

Short, R. V. The evolution of human reproduction. *Proceedings of Royal Society*, 1976, B195, 3–24.

Short, R. V. Discussion: Hormonal patterns in childhood and adolescence, *Journal of Biosocial Science, Suppl.,* 1978, 5, 58–61.

Short, R. V. Sexual selection and its component parts somatic and genital selection, as illustrated by man and the great apes. *Advances in the Study of Behavior,* 1979, 9, 131–158 (a).

Short, R. V. When a conception fails to become a pregnancy. *Maternal Recognition of Pregnancy, Ciba Foundation Series,* 1979, 54, 377–394. (b)

Small, Meredith F. Body, fat, rank, and nutritional status in a captive group of rhesus monkeys. *International Journal of Primatology,* 1981, 2, 91–95.

Small, Meredith F., and Rodman, Peter. Primigravidity and infant loss in bonnet macaques. *Journal of Medical Primatology,* 1981, 10, 164–169.

Stini, William A. Adaptive strategies of human populations under nutritional stress. *In* W. A. Stini (Ed.), *Physiological and morphological adaptation and evolution.* Mouton: The Hague, 1979, pp. 387–407.

Stini, William A. Sexual dimorphism and nutrient reserves. *In* R. Hall (Ed.), *Sexual dimorphism in Homo sapiens.* New York: Praeger, 1982, pp. 391–419.

Stini, W. A., Weber, C., Kemberling, S., and Vaughan, L. Lean tissue growth and disease susceptibility in bottle-fed versus breast-fed infants. *In* E. S. Green and F. E. Johnston (Eds.), *Social and biological predictors of nutritional status, physical growth, and neurological development.* New York: Academic Press, 1980, pp. 61–79.

Tanner, J. M. *Growth at adolescence,* 1962, London: Blackwell.

Taub, D. M. Age at first pregnancy and reproductive success among colony-born squirrel monkeys *(Samiri sciureus, Brazilian). Folia primatologica,* 1980, 33, 262–272.

Watts, E. S., and Gavan J. A. Postnatal growth of nonhuman primates: The problem of the adolescent spurt. *Human Biology,* 1982, 54, 53–70.

Winick, Myron. Food and the fetus. *Natural History,* 1981, 90, 76–81.

Young, W. C., and Yerkes, R. M. Factors influencing and reproductive cycle in the chimpanzee: The period of adolescent sterility and related problems. *Endocrinology,* 1943, 33, 121–154.

23

ADOLESCENCE IN EVOLUTIONARY PERSPECTIVE

B. BOGIN

This article reviews progress in the application of evolution theory to human growth and development, particularly adolescence. Evolution theory includes a variety of topics and only two of these are treated here: life history and biocultural modeling. "A broad definition of life history includes not only the traditional foci such as age-related fecundity and mortality rates, but also the entire sequence of behavioural, physiological, and morphological changes that an organism passes through during its development from conception to death" (1). This approach may be applied to both the study of the stages of life of modern people and to the evolution of the human pattern of growth.

The pattern of human development after birth is characterized by five stages; (i) infancy; (ii) childhood, (iii) juvenile; (iv) adolescence; (v) adulthood (2–4). Each of these stages can be defined by clear biological and behavioural characteristics. Infancy is the period when the mother provides all or some nourishment to her offspring via lactation. Infancy ends when the child is weaned, which in pre-industrialized societies occurs at a median age of 36 months (5). Childhood is defined as the period following weaning, when the youngster still depends on older people for feeding and protection. Childhood ends when growth of the brain (in weight) is complete. A recent morphological and mathematical investigation shows that this occurs at a mean age of 7 years (6) The child then progresses to the juvenile stage. Juveniles are defined as, "prepubertal individuals that are no longer dependent on their mothers (parents) for survival" (7). In girls, the juvenile period ends, on average, at about the age of 10 years, 2 years before it usually ends in boys, the difference reflecting the earlier onset of puberty in girls. The adolescent stage begins with puberty, marked by some visible sign of sexual maturation, such as pubic hair growth (indeed the term is derived from the Latin *pubescere*, to grow hairy). The adolescent stage (*adolescere*, to grow up) is marked by sexual maturation, development of the secondary sexual characteristics, a growth spurt in height and weight in both sexes, and the onset of adult patterns of sociosexual and economic behaviour. Adolescence ends with the attainment of adult stature which occurs, on average, at about age 18 years in women and 21 years in men.

Changes in the velocity of growth from birth to adulthood also signal the transitions between these five developmental stages. Idealized height velocity curves are presented in Figure 1. During infancy, height velocity plummets, followed by a period of slower decline in height velocity in childhood. The end of childhood is often marked by a small increase in height velocity, the mid-growth spurt (8). Height velocity declines further during the juvenile stage. The onset of adolescence is marked by a sudden and rapid increase in height velocity, which peaks at a level unequaled since early infancy. Adulthood begins when growth of the skeleton stops.

This pattern of growth and development is most unusual. Most mammals progress from infancy to adulthood seamlessly, without any intervening stages, and while their growth rates are in decline (9). Highly social

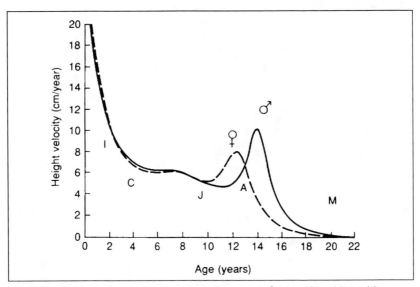

FIGURE 1. Idealized mean height velocity curves for healthy girls and boys. I, infancy; C, childhood; J, juvenile; A, adolescence; M, mature adult. Modified from Prader (24) and other sources.

mammals, such as wolves, wild dogs, lions, elephants and the primates, postpone puberty by inserting a period of juvenile growth and behaviour between infancy and adulthood. In these animals puberty occurs while the rate of growth is still decelerating and there is no readily detectable growth spurt in skeletal dimensions. Only the human species has childhood and adolescence as stages in the life cycle.

WHEN DID ADOLESCENCE EVOLVE?

Figure 2 represents a summary of the evolution of the human pattern of growth and development. This figure must be considered as 'a work in progress,' as only the data for the first and last species (*Pan* and *Homo sapiens*) are known with some certainty. The patterns of growth of the fossil hominid species are reconstructions based on the traditional methods of human paleontology; comparative anatomy, comparative physiology, comparative ethnology, archaeology and speculation! In particular, the work of Martin *et al.* (10, 11) on comparative patterns of a growth in apes and humans is utilized. Martin shows that apes have a pattern of brain growth that is rapid before birth and slower after birth. In contrast, people have rapid brain growth both before and after birth. Martin also notes that from the neonatal to adult stage, apes slightly more than double their brain size— a multiplier of 2.3—whereas humans more than triple their brain size— a multiplier of 3.5. Finally, Martin argues that an adult brain size of 873 ml

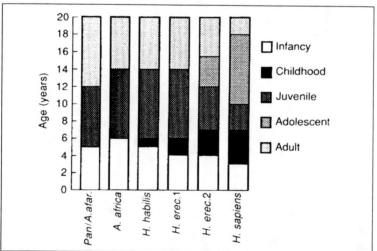

FIGURE 2. The evolution of hominid life history during the first 20 years of life. Abbreviated nomenclature is as follows: A. afar, Australopithecus afarensis; A. africa, Australopithecus africanus; H. habilis, Homo habilis; H. erec. 1, early Homo erectus; H. erec. 2. late Homo erectus; H. sapiens, Homo sapiens.

or larger represents a 'cerebral rubicon.' The 873 ml value calculated by multiplying the mean human infant brain size of 384 ml by the ape multiplier of 2.3. The value of the 'cerebral rubicon' is, therefore, a biological marker, separating ape-like and human-like patterns of brain growth.

Although *Australopithecus afarensis* was a hominid, it shared many anatomical features with non-hominid species, including an adult brain size of about 400 ml (12). Analysis of its dentition indicates a rate of dental development indistinguishable from extant apes (13). Therefore, the chimpanzee and *A. afarensis* are depicted as sharing infancy, juvenile and adult periods, the typical stages of postnatal growth of social mammals. To achieve the larger adult brain size of *A. africanus* (442 ml) may have required an addition to the length of infancy. The rapid expansion of adult brain size during the time of *Homo habilis* (650 ml to 800, ml) might have been achieved with the insertion of a brief childhood stage into hominid life history. Discussion of the evolution of human childhood lies outside the scope of this article (2, 3, 14).

Further increases in brain size occurred during the time of *H. erectus*. The earliest adult specimens have brain sizes of 850-900 ml, placing *H. erectus* at or above Martin's 'cerebral rubicon'. Smith (15) analysed the skeleton and dentition of the fossil specimen KMN-WT 15000, or the 'Turkana boy', a 1.6 million-year-old (early) *H. erectus* skeleton. She concluded that, "His dental age, skeletal age and body size are quite consistent with the idea that the adolescent growth spurt had not yet evolved in *Homo erectus.*" But, "the unique skeleton of KMN-WT 15000 stands at a point near the very beginning . . . of the evolution of human life history." Thus, later *H. erectus,* with adult brain sizes up to 1100 ml, is depicted with further expansion of childhood and the insertion of the adolescent stage. Along with bigger brains, later *H. erectus* showed increased complexity of technology (tools, fire and shelter) and social organization that were likely to require an adolescent stage of development in order to become a successful adult member of society. The transition to archaic and finally modern *H. sapiens* expanded the childhood and adolescent stages to their current dimensions.

WHY DID THE HUMAN PATTERN OF GROWTH EVOLVE?

In the book *Size and Cycle,* Bonner (16) develops the idea that the stages of the life cycle of an individual organism, a colony, or a society is, ". . . the basic unit of natural selection." Bonner shows that the duration of each stage relates to such basic adaptations as locomotion, reproductive rates and food acquisition. To make sense out of the pattern of human growth one must look for the 'basic adaptations' that Bonner describes. The most basic of these adaptations are those that relate to evolutionary success, which is traditionally measured in terms of the number of offspring that survive and reproduce.

Human beings are the most reproductively successful of mammals. Even people without the benefits of modern medicine raise about 50% of their infants to adulthood, while our closest relative, the chimpanzee, rears fewer that 35% to adulthood, and social carnivores, such as lions, rear about 12% (17). An essential part of the human success comes from learning and practising adult behaviours related to sex and child-rearing, particularly provisioning children with food. Parents in all human societies help to ensure survival of their offspring by providing all their children, not just their current infant with food for a decade or longer. The mother, father and other kin all participate in provisioning the child with food. Lancaster and Lancaster (17) call this type of parental investment "the hominid adaptation", for no other primate or mammal does this.

In the traditional human societies of hunters and gatherers, horticulturalists, pastoralists and agriculturalists, the adolescent stage of life is the time when parental skills are learned and practised before actual reproduction occurs. Children and juveniles also learn many skills related to food production and may even contribute significant amounts to their families (18). There are limits to the amount of work these preadolescents can do, however, as they do not have the muscular development and aerobic capacity of adults. Moreover, preadolescents do not have the capacity nor the motivation to learn about the intricacies of adult sexual, economic and political life, due to their very low levels of sex hormones. These hormones are known to prime the young person's interest in adult sexual, social and economic behaviour. Furthermore, preadolescent boys and girls look child-like and are very similar in terms of size and body composition (amount of muscle and fat). Because they do not have the sexual dimorphism of reproductively mature individuals, they are unlikely to be treated as such by adults. Together, child-like appearance and low sex hormone levels limit learning about how to be reproductively successful.

The hallmarks of human adolescence are the development of dimorphism in the secondary sexual characteristics, such as muscularity, fatness, body hair distribution, and the rapid acceleration in growth of the skeleton that accompanies the onset of sexual maturation. This growth spurt occurs in all clinically normal and healthy people and, at its peak, height velocity averages 9.0–10.3 cm/year in boys and 7.1–9.0 cm/year in girls (19, 20). This type of skeletal growth spurt does not occur in any other primate species so far investigated (2, 4). As a species-specific characteristic, the evolution of the human adolescent growth spurt is likely to have a significant role in the story of our species' reproductive success.

WHY DID THE GROWTH SPURT EVOLVE?

One often-cited reason for the adolescent growth spurt is the prolonged time required to learn technology, social organization, language and other aspects of culture during the infant, child and juvenile stages of growth. At the end of this period, so the argument goes, our ancestors were left with proportionately less time for procreation than most mammals, and therefore needed to attain adult size and sexual maturity quickly (21, 22), but surely this cannot be the whole story. Consider first that there is no need to experience an adolescent growth spurt to reach adult height or fertility. Historical sources describe the *castrati*, male opera singers of the 17th and 18th centuries who were castrated as boys to preserve their soprano voices, as being unusually tall for men (23). Also, children who are born without gonads or have them removed surgically before puberty (due to diseases such as cancer) do not experience an adolescent growth spurt, but do reach their normal expected adult height (24). Of course, *castrati*, whether or not they are opera singers, do not become reproductively successful. There are normal individuals, however, for the most part late-maturing boys and many girls, who have virtually no growth spurt. Nevertheless, these individuals do grow to be normal-sized adults and the late maturers become fertile by their early 20's—not significantly later than individuals who experience a growth spurt.

Another problem with the 'lost time' argument for the adolescent growth spurt is that it does not explain the timing of the spurt. Girls experience the growth spurt before becoming fertile, but for boys the reverse is true. Why the difference? Sexual dimorphism in adult height is one obvious consequence of the timing difference, and hence a possible positive value for the growth spurt itself. Largo *et al.* (20) reported that Swiss adult men are 12.6 cm taller than Swiss adult women due to: (i) boys growing 1.6 cm more before the onset of the girls' adolescence (ii) the delay in the onset of adolescence in boys adding 6.4 cm; (iii) the greater intensity of the spurt in boys adding 6.0 cm; (iv) the longer duration of growth following the spurt in girls subtracting 1.4 cm from the final difference.

ADOLESCENCE AS A HUMAN ADAPTIVE CHARACTERISTIC

Dimorphism in stature is only one of a series of sex-based differences in development that take place during adolescence. In girls, the first outward sign of puberty is the development of the breast bud and wisps of pubic hair. This is followed by the laying down of fat on the hips, buttocks and thighs, the intensified growth of body hair, the adolescent growth spurt and, finally, menarche. The path of development in boys starts with enlargement of the testes and then penis. This genital maturation begins, on average, only 6 months after that of girls; however, the developmental order of other secondary sexual characteristics—deepening of the voice, growth of facial and body hair, the growth spurt and muscular development—do not manifest themselves until genital maturity is nearly complete. The sex-specific order of pubertal events tends not to vary between early or late maturers, between well-nourished girls and boys and those who suffered from severe malnutrition in early life, between rural and urban dwellers, or between European and African ethnic groups (25–29) Given this, the sexual dimorphism expressed in this sequence of epigenetic events may be considered a species-specific characteristic. Evolutionary biologists usually find that species-specific traits evolve to enhance survival and reproductive success, Thus, the human adolescent growth spurt must have its own intrinsic evolutionary value and is not just a byproduct of slow prepubertal development.

WHY DO GIRLS HAVE ADOLESCENCE OR WAIT SO LONG TO HAVE A BABY?

Differences between boys and girls in the timing, duration and intensity of the adolescent growth spurt require that each sex be analysed individually, if we are to understand how the separate paths of development that each takes through adolescence promotes their reproductive success as adults. Moreover, the value of adolescence becomes apparent only when we consider human biology and behaviour cross culturally and historically, including contemporary Western society. Taking this approach from the female perspective, the human mother-to-be must acquire knowledge of pregnancy, adult sociosexual relations and child care. The dramatic physical changes that girls experience during adolescence serve as efficient advertisements of their sexual and social maturation. So efficient, in fact, that they stimulate adults to include adolescent girls in their social circles and encourage the girls themselves to initiate adult social interactions, such as male-female bonding and sexual intercourse. The hormonal changes taking place in the girl are also known to stimulate interest in the economic behaviour of adult women. Psychologists call this the intensification of gender-related roles (30). Ethnographic research shows that gender role intensification during adolescence is a universal feature of human cultures (31).

Menarche, which occurs at a median age of 12.5 years in healthy populations, is the most overt and unambiguous signal of a girl's sexual maturation. Many cultures define the transition from girlhood to woman-hood by this signal. Yet menarche is usually followed by a period of 1–3 years of adolescent sterility in which menstrual cycles occur but without ovulation. So, on average, it is not until age 15 years, or older, that young women become fertile. Fertility, however, does not equal reproductive maturity. Becoming pregnant is only a part of the business of reproduction. Maintaining the pregnancy to term and raising offspring to adulthood are equally important. The 15-year-old woman has difficulty with both of these, because the risks of spontaneous abortions, complications of preg-nancy, and low birthweight babies are more than twice as high as those for women 20–24 years old. A unique study by Moerman (32) clarified the relationship of mother's age, growth in size and health of the baby. She found that the crucial variable is size of the pelvic inlet, the bony opening of the birth canal. Moerman measured pelvic radiographs from a sample of healthy, well-nourished girls who achieved menarche between 12 and 13 years of age. These girls did not attain adult pelvic inlet size until 17–18 years of age. Quite unexpectedly, the adolescent growth spurt, which occurs before menarche, does not influence the size of the pelvis. Rather, the female pelvis has its own unique slow and continuous pattern of growth, which continues for several years even after adult stature is achieved. For this very fundamental biological reason girls should wait up to a decade from the time of menarche to reach full reproductive maturity. Cross-cultural behaviour verifies this conclusion, as age at first marriage and childbirth clusters around 19 years for women from such diverse cultures as the Kikuyu of Kenya, Mayans of Guatemala, Copper Eskimo of Canada, and both the Colonial period and contemporary USA.

From these bioanthropological studies it seems that female adolescence evolved because it enabled girls to learn how to be more reproductively and productively successful as young women. There is direct evidence for the reproductive value of human adolescence when the data from non-human primates are examined. The first-born infants of monkeys and apes are more likely to die than those of humans. Studies of yellow baboons, toque macaques and chimpanzees show that between 50% and 60% of their first-born offspring die in infancy, whereas in hunter-gatherer human societies of Africa, only about 44% of !Kung infants and 30% of Hadza infants die.

Studies of wild baboons by Altmann (33) show that while the infant mortality rate for the first-born is 50%, mortality for the second-born drops to 38% and for the third- and fourth-born is only 25%. The difference in infant survival is in part due to the experience and knowledge gained by the mother with each subsequent birth. Such maternal information is mastered by women during adolescence, which gives them a reproductive advantage.

The initial human advantage may seem small, but it means that up to 21 more people than baboons or chimpanzees survive out of every 100 first-born—more than enough over the vast course of evolutionary time to make the evolution of human adolescence an overwhelmingly beneficial adaptation.

WHY DO BOYS HAVE ADOLESCENCE?

The most important difference in the pattern of adolescent development for girls and boys is that boys become fertile well before they assume adult size and the physical characteristics of men. Analysis of urine samples from boys aged 11–16 years show that they begin producing sperm at a median age of 13.4 years (34). Yet the cross-cultural evidence is that few boys successfully father children until they are into their third decade of life. Traditional Kikuyu men do not marry and become fathers until about age 25 years, though they become sexually active following their own circumcision rite at around age 18 years (35). The National Center for Health Statistics of the United States reports that only 4% of all births are fathered by men under 20 years old, while another nationally representative longitudinal survey shows that only 7% of young men 20–27 years old fathered a child while they were teenagers (36) One explanation for the lag between sperm production and fatherhood may be that the sperm of younger adolescents are not motile or do not have the endurance to swim to an egg cell in the woman's fallopian tubes. A more probable reason, however, is that the average boy at 13.4 years is only beginning his adolescent growth spurt. In terms of physical appearance, physiological status and psychosocial development he is still more of a child than an adult.

The reason for the delay between sperm production and reproductive maturity may lie in the subtle psychophysiological effects of testosterone and other androgen hormones that are released following gonadal maturation and during early adolescence—effects that may 'prime' boys to be receptive to their future roles as men. Studies on a cross-section of youths in Europe, North America, Japan and Africa established that as blood levels of testosterone begin to increase, but before the growth spurt reaches its peak, there is an increase in psychosexual activity. Nocturnal emissions begin (37) and there is an increase in the frequency of masturbation. In more recent research with longitudinally measured samples, it has been found that it is the social stimulus of early puberty, more than the testosterone levels *per se* that initiates these changes in sexual behaviour (38). Whether due to hormones or social context, sociosexual feelings, such as infatuations and dating, intensify, as do other feelings, such as guilt, anxiety, pleasure and pride (39, 40). At the same time, boys become more interested in adult activities, adjust their attitude to parental figures, and think and act more independently. In short, they begin to behave like men.

However—and this is where the survival advantage may lie—they still look like boys. Because their adolescent growth spurt occurs late in sexual development, young males can practise behaving like adults before they are actually perceived as adults. The sociosexual antics of young adolescent boys are often considered to be more humorous than serious, yet they provide the experience to fine tune their sexual and social roles before either their lives, or those of their offspring, depend on them. For example, competition between men for women favours the older, more experienced man. As such competition may be fatal, the childlike appearance of the immature, but hormonally-primed, adolescent male may be life-saving as well as educational.

In summary, the argument for the evolution and value of human adolescence is this. Girls best learn their adult social roles while they are infertile but perceived by adults as mature, whereas boys best learn their adult social roles while they are sexually mature but not yet perceived as such by adults. Without the adolescent growth spurt this unique style of social and cultural learning could not occur.

ADOLESCENCE IN CONTEMPORARY POPULATIONS: BIOCULTURAL MODELLING

Each generation of people follows a cycle of reproduction, growth and maturation that has evolved over several millions of years. Adolescence, particularly the growth spurt, is a unique part of this human cycle. Most societies have accommodated the biology of adolescence into their cultural behaviour. "In many societies around the world training for parenthood is an apprenticeship experience learned along with the performance of domestic and subsistence tasks within shared-function family systems. In such shared caretaking families, child-care skills are acquired first, followed only gradually by autonomy from parents and siblings, and then by full managerial control of a household" (41). This behavioural sequence is in harmony with the normal succession of stages in human biological development and is, therefore, a biocultural process that promotes good physical growth, health and reproductive success.

In the industrialized/Westernized nations, adolescents are not able to follow the developmental sequence of traditional societies due to smaller family sizes, nuclear families (rather than extended families), age group segregation in formal schools, and employment that separates family members for much of the day. The social isolation caused by these factors may delay the acquisition of parental skills and knowledge until after the adolescent matures and reproduces. The consequences of these changes in social learning for the physical growth and development of the next generation have not been well studied.

A provocative hypothesis of the possible consequences of delays and deficiencies in learning parenting skills was proposed by Belsky *et al.* (42). In an attempt to develop a biocultural model of early socialization and later reproductive strategy, they described two alternative developmental pathways. "One is characterized, in childhood, by a stressful rearing environment and the development of insecure attachments to parents and subsequent behaviour problems; in adolescence by early pubertal development and precocious sexuality; and, in adulthood by unstable pair bonds and limited investment in child rearing". The other pathway "is characterized by the opposite". Presumably, this means that childhood is non-stressful with secure attachments and few behaviour problems, pubertal development and adolescent sexual behaviour occur at average or late ages, and in adulthood, stable pair bonds and intensive investment in child rearing occur. Moffitt *et al.* (43) tested this hypothesis using data from a longitudinal study of 16-year-old girls in New Zealand. Among these girls, results indicated that the incidence of behavioural problems did not predict either earlier or later menarche—the measure of sexual development used in this study. An earlier age of menarche was associated with family conflict and absence of the father from the family during a girl's childhood. The age of menarche was better predicted, however, by a genetic inheritance model; that is, mother's age at menarche, than by any of the behavioural data.

Although the original hypothesis is not supported by this empirical study, the biocultural approach taken may still offer valuable insights into social regulators of sexual maturation. For example, a study by Herman-Giddens *et al.* (44) found a 1 in 15 prevalence of early pubertal development in a group of 105 girls, aged 10 years or younger, who were victims of confirmed or suspected sexual abuse. Based on these results the authors propose two hypotheses to guide further research. First, a genetic tendency toward early expression of secondary sexual characteristics could lead to sexual abuse by stimulating inappropriate behaviour by the perpetrators. Secondly, sexual abuse is, "a stressor that in some way stimulates adrenal androgen secretion or early activation of the hypothalamic-pituitary-ovarian axis". Either hypothesis calls for an interactive biocultural model of sexual maturation and sexual abuse.

CONCLUSIONS

Adolescence became part of human life history because it conferred significant reproductive advantages to our species, in part by allowing the adolescent to learn and practise adult economic, social and sexual behaviours before reproducing. Over the course of time and space, the styles of learning these behaviours have come to vary considerably in different cultures. The evolution of human adolescence, therefore, has to be modeled in terms of both its biological and cultural ramifications.

Viewing human adolescence in this life history and biocultural perspective has significant implications. Some of these may pertain to medical treatment of growth disorders, for example the effects of early or delayed puberty on the physical and psychological well-being of the adolescent. Other implications relate more to economic, social and legal policies that impact on the lives of adolescents. Biological anthropology, paediatrics and the other disciplines devoted to the study and welfare of adolescents have the intellectual resources, and perhaps the moral obligation, to promote policies that are in accord with human evolutionary biology.

ACKNOWLEDGMENTS

Sincere thanks are due to Mary Ann Wnetrzak for editorial assistance and critical discussion of the ideas presented in this article.

B. Bogin, Professor of Anthropology, Department of Behavioral Sciences, University of Michigan-Dearborn, Dearborn, MI 48128, USA

ENDNOTES

1. Shea, BT. *Dynamic morphology: growth, life history, and ecology in primate evolution.* In: DeRousseau CJ, ed. Primate life history and evolution. New York: Wiley-Liss, 1990:325–52.

2. Bogin B. *Patterns of human growth.* New York: Cambridge University Press, 1988.

3. Bogin B. *The evolution of human childhood.* Bioscience 1990; 40:16–25.

4. Bogin B. *Why must I be a teenager at all?* New Scientist 1993; 137 (March 6): 34–38.

5. Detwyller KA. *A time to wean: the hominid blueprint for the natural age of weaning in modern human populations.* Am J Phys Anthropol 1994; Suppl 18:80.

6. Cabana T, Jolicoeur P, Michaud J. *Prenatal and postnatal growth and allometry of stature, head circumference, and brain weight in Québec children.* Am J Hum Biol 1993; 5:93–9.

7. Pereira ME, Altmann J. *Development of social behaviour in free-living nonhuman primates.* In Watts ES, ed. *Nonhuman primate models for human growth and development.* New York: Alan R Liss, 1985:217–309.

8. Tanner JM. *The morphological level of personality.* Proc R Soc Med 1947; 40:301–3.

9. Von Bertalanffy L. *Principles and theory of growth.* In Nowinski NW, ed. *Fundamental aspects of normal and malignant growth*, Amsterdam: Elsevier, 1960:137-259.

10. Martin RD. *Human brain evolution in an ecological context.* Fifty-second James Arthur Lecture, American Museum of Natural History, New York, 1983.

11. Harvey PH, Martin RD, Clutton-Brock TH. *Life histories in comparative perspective.* In Smuts BB, Cheney DL, Seyfarth RM, Wrangham KW, Struhsaker TT, eds. *Primate societies.* Chicago: University of Chicago Press, 1987; 181–96.

12. Simons, E.L. *Human origins.* Science 1989; 245:1343-50.

13. Smith BH. *Dental development and the evolution of life history in Hominidae.* Am J Phys Anthropol 1991; 85:157–74.

14. Bogin B. *The evolution of learning.* In Husen T, Postlethwaite TN, eds. *The international encyclopedia of education*, 2nd edn, volume 5. Oxford: Pergamon Press, 1994:2681–5.

15. Smith BH, *Physiological age of KMN-WT 15000 and its significance for growth and development of early Homo.* In Walker AC, Leakey RF, eds. *The Nariokotme Homo erectus skeleton.* Cambridge, Massachusetts: Belknap Press, 1993:195–220.

16. Bonner JT. *Size and cycle.* Princeton, New Jersey; Princeton University Press, 1965.

17. Lancaster JB, Lancaster CS. *Parental investment: the hominid adaptation.* In Ortner DJ, ed. *How humans adapt.* Washington, DC: Smithsonian Institution Press, 1983:33–65.

18. Blurton Jones NG. *The lives of hunter-gatherer children: effects of parental behavior and parental reproductive strategy.* In Pereira ME, Fairbanks LA, eds. *Juvenile primates.* Oxford: Oxford University Press, 1993:309–26.

19. Tanner JM, Whitehouse RH, Marubiri E, Resele F. *The adolescent growth spurt of boys and girls of the Harpenden Growth Study.* Ann Hum Biol 1976; 3:109–26.

20. Largo RH, Gasser T, Prader A, Stutzle W, Huber PJ. *Analysis of the adolescent growth spurt using smoothing spline functions.* Ann Hum Biol 1978; 5:421–34.

21. Watts ES. *Evolution of the human growth curve.* In Falkner F, Tanner JM, eds. *Human growth: a comprehensive treatise,* 2nd edn, volume 1. New York: Plenum Press, 1986:153–65.

22. Watts ES. *Evolutionary trends in primate growth and development.* In DeRousseau CJ, ed. *Primate life history and evolution.* New York: Wiley-Liss, 1990:89–104.

23. Peschel RE, Reschel ER. *Medical insights into the castrati of opera.* Am Sci 1987; 75:578–83.

24. Prader A. *Biomedical and endocrinological aspects of normal growth and development.* In Borms J, Hauspie R, Sand A, Susanne C, Hebbelinck M, eds. *Human growth and development.* New York: Plenum, 1984; 1–22.

25. Marshall WA. Tanner JM. *Puberty.* In Falkner F, Tanner JM, eds. *Human growth,* 2nd edn, volume 2. New York: Plenum, 1986:171–209.

26. Cameron N, Mitchell J, Meyer D et al. *Secondary sexual development of Cape 'Coloured' girls following kwashiorkor.* Ann Hum Biol 1988; 15: 65–76.

27. Cameron N, Mitchell J, Meyer D et al. *Secondary sexual development of 'Cape Coloured' boys following kwashiorkor.* Ann Hum Biol 1990; 17:217–28.

28. Cameron N, Grieve CA, Kruger A, Leschner KF. *Secondary sexual development in rural and urban South African black children.* Ann Hum Biol 1993; 20:583–93.

29. Bogin B, Wall M, MacVean RD. *Longitudinal analysis of adolescent growth of ladino and Mayan school children in Guatemala: effects of environment and sex.* Am J Phys Anthropol 1992; 89:447–57.

30. Hill JP, Lynch ME. *The intensification of gender-related role expectations during early adolescence.* In Brooks-Gunn J, Petersen AC. eds. *Girls at puberty.* New York: Plenum Press, 1983:201–28.

31. Whiting BB, Edwards CP. *Children of different worlds.* Cambridge, Massachusetts: Harvard University Press, 1988.

32. Moerman ML. *Growth of the birth canal in adolescent girls.* Am J Obstet Gynecol 1982; 143:528–32.

33. Altmann J. *Baboon mothers and infants.* Cambridge, Massachusetts: Harvard University Press, 1980.

34. Muller J, Nielsen CT, Skakkebaek NE. *Testicular maturation and pubertal growth and development in normal boys*. In Tanner JM, Preece MA, eds. *The physiology of human growth*. Cambridge: Cambridge University Press, 1989: 201–7.

35. Worthman C. *Developmental dyssynchrony as normative experience: Kikuyu adolescents*. In Lancaster J, Hamburg BA eds. *School-age pregnancy and parenthood: biosocial dimensions*. New York: Aldine de Gruyter, 1986:95–112.

36. Marsiglio W. *Adolescent fathers in the United States: their initial living arrangements, marital experience and educational outcomes*. Fam Plann Perspect 1987; 19:240–51.

37. Laron Z, Arad J, Gurewitz R, Grunebaum M, Dickerman Z. *Age at first conscious ejaculation—a milestone in male puberty*. Helv Paediatr Acta 1980; 35:13–20.

38. Halpern CT. Udry RJ, Campbell B, Suchindran C. *Testosterone and pubertal development as predictors of sexual activity: A panel assessment of adolescent males*. Psychosom Med 1993; 55:436–47.

39. Higham E. *Variations in adolescent psychohormonal development*. In Adelson J, ed. *Handbook of adolescent psychology*. New York: Wiley, 1980; 472–94.

40. Petersen AC, Taylor B. *The biological approach to adolescence: biological change and psychological adaption*. In Adelson J, ed. *Handbook of adolescent psychology*. New York: Wiley, 1980:117–55.

41. Weisner TS. *Socialization for parenthood in sibling caretaking societies*. In Lancaster JB, Altmann J, Rossi AS, Sherrod LR, eds. *Parenting across the life span: biosocial dimensions*. New York: Aldine de Gruyter, 1987: 237–70.

42. Belsky J, Steinberg L, Draper P. *Childhood experience, interpersonal development, and reproductive strategy: an evolutionary theory of socialization*. Child Dev 1991; 62:647–70.

43. Moffitt TE, Caspi A, Belsky J, Silva PA. *Childhood experience and the onset of menarche: a test of a sociobiological model*. Child Dev 1992; 63:47–58.

44. Herman-Giddens ME, Sandler AD, Friedman NE. *Sexual precocity in girls. An association with sexual abuse?* Am J Dis Child 1988; 142:431–3.

DISCUSSION

M Ritzén (Stockholm, Sweden): How do you include in your model the changes that have occurred in the age at onset of puberty, at least in western Europe and the USA, within the last one-hundred years?

B Bogin (Michigan, USA): The age at onset of puberty can vary markedly between different cultures. For example, in healthy, well-nourished European girls, age at menarche is about 12.5 to 13 years, whereas it is as late as 18 years in highland New Guinea. Despite this tremendous variation in timing, the events of puberty are similar in both populations, and in boys and girls throughout the world.

M Ritzén: There has been some speculation that the uniquely long prepubertal period in humans is one of the major reasons why we have advanced so far. There is a long time for learning before men have to go out and fight for a woman. Would you agree?

B Bogin: Yes, it is certainly part of my argument, that juvenile stages and adolescence are good for the young to learn, but such stages of growth would not evolve unless they are also beneficial for the parents, or for the juveniles when they become parents. From the parents' point of view these stages are advantageous because juveniles and adolescents provide a considerable amount of labour in many human societies, particularly child care. If the mother can release her current infant to a juvenile or an adolescent daughter, then she can more easily have a second baby, thus increasing her reproductive potential.

24

HUMAN AXILLARY SECRETIONS INFLUENCE WOMEN'S MENSTRUAL CYCLES: THE ROLE OF DONOR EXTRACT OF FEMALES

GEORGE PRETI, WINNIFRED BERG CUTLER, CELSO RAMON GARCIA, GEORGE R. HUGGINS, AND HENRY J. LAWLEY

The Monell Chemical Senses Center, 3500 Market Street, Philadelphia, Pennsylvania 19104, Athena Institute for Women's Wellness Research, 30 Coopertown Rd., Haverford, Pennsylvania 19041, and Department of Obstetrics and Gynecology, School of Medicine, Hospital of the University of Pennsylvania, Philadelphia, Pennsylvania 19104

Menstrual synchrony in human females has previously been demonstrated among women attending a predominantly female university as well as among women attending coeducational universities. In each of these studies, women who spent the most time together were mostly likely to show the menstrual synchrony. In this experiment, the possibility that substances in axillary secretions might mediate this effect was tested using a prospective, double-blind research design and a combined axillary extract from a group of female donors. Female subjects who reported themselves to have normal (29.5 ± 3 day) cycles were exposed to the axillary extracts or blank/ethanol for 10 to 13 weeks. Recipients of the axillary extracts showed a significant reduction in "days' difference in menses onset" relative to the donor cycle, no change was evident for recipients of blank/ethanol. These results demonstrate that constituents from the axillary region of donor females can shift the time of menstrual onset of another group to conform with the donors' cycle and that this effect can occur even in the absence of social contact. © 1986 Academic Press, Inc.

A number of exogenous influences have been shown to influence the length and timing of reproductive cycles in mammals (McClintock, 1983; Vanderbergh, 1983; Cutler and Garcia, 1980). Germane to the research reported here is the influence of females or their odors on the estrous cycle of other female conspecifics as this has been documented in recent studies employing nonhuman mammals (Izard and Vandenbergh, 1982; McClintock, 1978). For example, the estrous cycle of rats can be manipulated through the use of odors generated from females during specific phases of the estrous cycle (McClintock, 1983, 1984). In addition preovulatory cervical mucus mixed with water and sprayed into the noses of a group of female Holstein cows advanced the time of estrous (Izard and Vandenbergh, 1982). Particularly intriguing has been the demonstration of menstrual synchrony in women; first, women attending a predominately female university (McClintock, 1971), and subsequently among women attending coeducational universities (Graham and McGrew, 1980; Quadagno, Shubeita, Deck, and Francoeur, 1981). In each of these studies, women who spent the most time together were most likely to show the menstrual synchrony.

The possibility that odors emanating from the axillary region might mediate these effects has been recently examined (Russell *et al.*, 1980). Axillary secretions from a single female donor rubbed onto the upper lip of subjects caused the recipients to show a tendency toward menstrual synchrony with the donor cycle. In the pretreatment month recipients were, on average 9.3 days apart in menses onset from the donor's menstrual onset; after 4 months of treatment this difference was reduced to 3.4 days. However, this preliminary report has been criticized for lacking a double-blind research design (Doty, 1981); the technician who applied the odors was the same person who supplied the secretion.

The study reported here employed a double-blind research design and a combined axillary extract from one group of female donors. When this extract was applied to a separate group of females, the recipients' cycles approached menstrual synchrony with the donor females.

METHODS

Donor secretions: Female extracts. Axillary secretions were collected from four female volunteer donors (ages 25, 26, 29, and 35) recruited from among co-workers and members of the community. All had the following characteristics: they were engaged in a heterosexual relationship; they had large numbers of lipophilic diptheroids in their axillary region, and for the duration of the experiment they did not shave; they did not use deodorant, deodorant soaps, or perfumes in the axillary region; and they washed each morning with only Ivory soap. The odor which develops in the axillae has been shown to be a function of the resident microorganism present there (Labows, McGinley, and Kligman, 1982; Leyden, McGinley, Hoelzle, Labows, and Kligman, 1981). Correlations of odor quality and bacterial populations have been found in recent studies; these results show that when a faint or acid odor was present micrococcasceae were present in 100% of subjects. A more pungent odor similar to that of $C_{19} \Delta^{16}$ androgen steroids is produced by the lipophilic diphtheroids, a different species of bacteria. These more pungent substances were found in 85% of males and 66% of females examined (Leyden *et al.*, 1981). Our odor donors were picked for their ability to produce the complete spectrum of axillary odorants having both the lipophilic diphtheroids and the micrococcaceae as their resident microorganisms. The dominant constituents of both of these are currently though to be both volatile acids and steroids.

Secretions were collected on 4 x 4 in. cotton pads which had been previously extracted, autoclaved, dried, and wrapped in solvent extracted aluminum foil (Preti and Huggins, 1975). Each donor wore a pad in each axillae three times a week during a convenient 6- to 9-hr period. After removal, pads were immediately frozen in acid/solvent cleaned glass jars and stored at -60°C until extraction, approximately 1 year later. Each donor collected secretions for three complete menstrual cycles. However, the axillary pads included in the preparation of the stimulus came from only five of the donated cycles and represented all four donors which met the following more rigorous criteria: each was 29 ± 2 days in length; the basal body temperature charts were clearly biphasic and presumably ovulatory with basal body thermal rises which lasted 12 or more days (Cutler, Garcia, and Krieger, 1979; Cutler, Preti, Erikson, Huggins, and Garcia, 1985; Treloar, Boynton, Behn and Brown, 1967; Vollman, 1977); and menstruation occurred within 7 days of a full moon (Cutler, 1980; Friedman, 1981; Cutler, Schleidt, Friedman, Garcia, Preti, and Stine, 1987).

Because of the similarity in cycle lengths employed we made the assumption that each of the 3-day sequences from each donor (i.e., cycle Days 1, 2, and 3) would be endocrinologically similar and consequently combined the pads. To prepare the stimuli, pads were grouped in 3-day segments: e.g., all pads from cycle Days 1-3 were combined, and called "combined donor Day 2" (the first day of menstruation = Day 1 of a menstrual cycle); all pads in Days 4-6 were combined and called "combined donor day 5"; all pads in Days 7-9 were combined to form "combined donor Day 8", and so on. In this fashion, 10 separate extracts were prepared, each containing odors from different portions of the menstrual cycle to form the "donor cycle" of combined donor days 2, 5, 8, 11, 14, 17, 20, 23, 26, and 29. All pads from each 3-day group were placed in a glass column and allowed to soak in doubly distilled EtOH for 1 hr at room temperature. Fifteen milliliters of ethanol were used for each pad in the column. After 1 hr the ethanol extracted materials were allowed to run out the bottom of the column through a Teflon stopcock as the pads were squeezed with a Teflon disc. Approximately two-thirds of all ethanol put on the pads was recovered. The ethanol extracted stimuli were subsequently frozen at -60°C until needed.

SUBJECT SELECTION

Female subjects who were to receive the axillary extracts were recruited from among the members of the university community. The 19 subjects who completed the study ranged in age from 19 to 32. All met the following criteria: "gynecological maturity" (as defined by Treloar et al. (1967) as menstruating for at least 7 years), nulliparous, not currently (nor within the last 3 months) using oral contraceptives nor an I.U.D., and a willingness to make a daily entry of basal body temperature (BBT), sexual behavior, and menstrual occurrence. Each potential subject who met the criteria and indicated her interest in participating was asked whether her menstrual cycle was normal (29.5 ± 3) or aberrant (<26 or >33 days) in length (Cutler et al., 1979, 1985; Vollman, 1977). Those who indicted a normal-type cycle length were included in this study; the women with aberrant cycle lengths were diverted to the "male axillary extract" experiment (Cutler, Preti, Huggins, Garcia, and Lawley, 1986). All subjects also agreed to provide blood samples for steroid analysis during 3 days of one week in the luteal phase of the last menstrual cycle studied.

Seasonal constraints. This experimental protocol was designed to accommodate to the potential for a seasonal fluctuation in sexual cycles. Two relevant seasonal influences are the lunar and the annual geophysical cycles (for a brief review see Cutler, 1980). It has been shown that lunar and menstrual phase locking occurs (Cutler, 1980; Friedman, 1981). In the autumn, a maximum number of menses occurs concomitantly with the full moon (Cutler, 1980; Cutler et al., in preparation). For this reason we designed the experimental protocols in an attempt to minimize the potential influences of either of these geophysical effects on the experiment by (1) collecting extracts in the autumn of one year, storing them at -60°C, and applying them (after thawing) in the autumn of the following year, and (2) selecting those autumn donors whose menses onset occurred within 1 week of the full moon.

Experimental protocol. Each subject was provided with BBT charts, BBT thermometers and a calendar card to record sexual behavior. Instructions for their use were given by a female technician who was blind to the purpose of the study. Subjects were unaware of the true nature of the stimuli; they were told that they were receiving "natural fragrance" extracted into ethanol. The informed consent form had two paragraphs pertaining to this.[2] Thus, the study was double-blind. Subjects were randomly assigned to group C, female axillary extract/ethanol or group D, blank/ethanol. The average age of the C group ($n = 10$) receiving female extract was 25.5 years while the average age of the D group ($n = 9$) receiving blank/ethanol was 21.5 years.

Because of individual variation in menstrual patterns, a woman could enter the study at any point within her cycle. Consequently if a women entered the study on Day 10 of her cycle, she was scored as 9 days out of phase with the first application of the donor extract. If she entered the study on Day 20 of a 29 day cycle she was also scored as 9 days out of phase with the first application of the donor extract. Upon entry to the study, women received female extract from "combined donor Days 2" (i.e., pooled sample from cycle Days 1, 2, and 3). Sequential presentations of the remaining extracts were applied during subjects' subsequent visits to the laboratory (e.g., on her next visit "combined donor Days 5" was applied; on her next visit "combined donor days 8" extract and so on until her 11th visit to the laboratory, when the sequential process began again and she received combined donor Day 2 once again. Consequently, the 11th application (i.e., combined donor Day 2 extract for subjects or ethanol for controls) was given to women in groups C and D, respectively every 22–25 days.

Subjects came into the laboratory three times each week for 10 to 13 weeks. Subjects in group C received an application of the timed female extract, subjects in group D received extract (or blank/ethanol). Substance was applied in the following manner.

Each morning the stimuli to be used that day were removed from the freezer and allowed to warm to room temperature for 30 min. Individual 5-ml samples of stimuli and blank (ethanol) were then removed via pipet and placed in separate vials labeled C and D, respectively, and transported to the Ivy Research Laboratory where the stimuli were applied. The technician was instructed which subject was to receive vial contents. The Ivy Laboratory is in a building some distance from the Monell Center; consequently, neither the technician nor the subjects came to the Monell Center. The technician pipetted 0.5 ml of the stimuli onto a clean 4 x 4 in. cotton pad and rubbed the contents of pad onto the upper lip of the subject and instructed her not to wash the area for at least 6 hr. She then recorded the blood pressure and pulse of the subject in an attempt to dilute the focus of the study. Neither of the experimenters handling the extracts on a routine basis (G.P.; H.J.L.) could distinguish a difference in odor between the blank and female extracts. Following completion of the experiment, the technician said she could not tell the difference between C and D samples, nor had any of the subjects commented on an odor from either sample.

RESULTS

Figure 1 shows the average number of days difference between the menstrual bleeding onset of members of group C and of group D and the "menses" (combined donor Day 1) of the "donor cycle" during each of the 3 months of the study. Table 1 lists each woman's data for each of the three menses occurring during participation in the study. For subjects receiving extract application the differences in days of menstrual bleeding onset from the combined donor Day 2 extract is listed. For controls the difference between menses onset and the start of each series of 10 blank/ethanol applications is listed. In the first cycle, the mean difference in group C menses onset to the "donor cycle" menses onset (i.e., combined donor Day

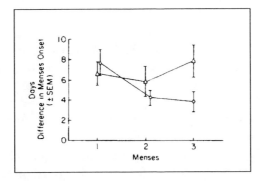

FIGURE 1. Each symbol shows the mean number of days difference in menstrual cycle onset of one group compared to combined donor Day 1. The circle represents treatment with female extract; the triangle represents treatment with blank/ethanol.

2) was 8.3 days. For group D this was 6.2 days, both near the expected difference of 7.38.

The expected difference of 7.38 days is calculated as follows: since a criterion for inclusion in the study was a cycle length of 29.5 ± 3 days, any two menses onsets will average somewhere between 0 and 14.75 days apart (half of 29.5). As a consequence, the theoretical average difference is 7.38 days (half of 14.75). Group C at 8.3 days and Group D at 6.2 days reflect this tendency. After 2 more months of female extract application the number of day's difference in menses onset relative to the "donor cycle" was significantly reduced (by about 50%) for group C from 8.3 to 3.9 days while no change was evident for group D (Figure 1). An analysis of variance with repeated measures showed a significant month x group interaction $F(2, 34) = 5.09$; $P < 0.05$. No other term was significant in the analysis. Post hoc tests were used to explore the source of interaction more fully. F tests were run separately for the experimental and control groups. Only the experimental group showed the significant shift in menses onset during the periods monitored [$F(2, 18) = 7.53$; $P < 0.01$]; the control group showed no such effect [$F(2, 18) = 1.82$; $P = 0.20$]. Thus, only the experimental group showed a change in cycle timing reflective of synchrony. Post hoc t tests were also performed; they revealed that the control and experimental groups differed only in the third menses period ($t_{17} = 2.04$; $P < 0.05$).

Blood samples drawn during the last cycle of participation, showed no apparent difference in the levels of estradiol, testosterone or progesterone between groups C and D when controlled for time of cycle.

DISCUSSION

This study represents the first systematically designed, prospectively conducted, double-blind research in humans to attempt to manipulate the menstrual cycle with female-derived secretions. In this experiment naturally occurring 29.5 ± 3 day cycles could be modulated with repeated applications of extract at a 22 to 25 day interval. This study establishes phenomena in humans which are analogous to previously demonstrated olfactory/reproductive relationships in nonhuman mammals. These data also demonstrate that constituents from the axillary region of a group of women can be frozen for 1 year and combined in pooled batches that can alter the menstrual cycles in another group of women after thawing 1 year later. We note that this occurs in the absence of social contact between the

Table 1

Number of Days by Which a Given Cycle Onset Varied from Donor Menses

Subject	Menses 1	Cycle length (1 -> 2)	Menses 2	Cycle length (2 -> 3)	Menses 3
		Subjects receiving female axillary extract[a]			
1	-12	30	-6	30	-11
2	-11	30	-5	28	-7
3	+10	30	+5	28	+2
4	-13	24	-2	27	-5
5	-8	30	-2	26	-4
6	-1	29	+3	30	-1
7	+6	26	+10	26	+5
8	+8	28	+4	28	-1
9	+3	26	+1	28	-3
10	+11	28	+5	34	0
Absolute mean					
Difference	8.30		4.30		3.90
SEM	1.32		1.43		1.10
		Subjects receiving blank/ethanol			
1	+1	26	+2	31	-9
2	+6	32	-2	32	-9
3	-4	26	-8	30	+9
4	+1	20	+3	24	0
5	+4	26	+1	28	-1
6	+10	21	+10	22	+12
7	-12	24	-9	25	-6
8	+8	33	-2	28	-9
9	+10	24	+9	25	+13
Absolute mean					
Difference	6.22		5.11		7.56
SEM	1.42		1.33		1.58

[a]Minuses and plusses are used to show where in the menstrual cycle the subject was as she began receiving each sequence of donor or blank extract. The minus reflects days before next menses indicating ovulation has already occurred, i.e., luteal phase. The plus reflects days since onset of menses for women in the follicular (preovulatory) stage of the cycle.

donors and the recipients. The donor constituents do not have to be from either the same cycle or same female.

Although experiments with rodents (McClintock, 1983, 1984) have shown that airborne odors can produce estrous synchrony, the design of this study does not permit conclusions about whether the synchrony effect is mediated by olfaction or by absorption of the correct constituents. However, the subjects in this study worked and/or attended classes in a heterosexual environment. All were either engaged in or were "in-between" a heterosexual relationship and presumably had a close circle of female friends which could influence cyclicity. Despite this, the cyclicity of subjects receiving combined female extract was rapidly altered well within the 3–4 months discussed by McClintock (McClintock, 1984) or the 4–5 months shown by Russell's subjects (Russell, Switz, and Thompson, 1980). It is of interest to note that an ovarian follicle requires approximately 85 days for maturation (Gougeon, 1982), which parallels the time needed to see a significant trend toward synchrony in this study.

The short time required to demonstrate synchrony with the donor cycle suggests that using a stimulus from a group of donors may provide a stronger stimulus than using the stimulation of a single donor (Russell *et al.*, 1980). Thus, in the strength and frequency used here, application of a combined female axillary extract can alter the menstrual cycles of normal cycling women.

ACKNOWLEDGMENTS

This study was supported in part by a grant from the National Science Foundation, BNS 82-03018. The authors thank Gary K. Beauchamp and Carol Christensen for their constructive comments concerning the manuscript, Mrs. Helen Liebich for her technical assistance, and Mrs. Janice Blescia for processing the manuscript. Dr. James Leyden, Dr. Ken McGinley, and Dr. Joseph Nicholson of the Duhring Laboratories are thanked for their screening of potential subjects for the correct axillary microflora and odor production.

REFERENCES

Cutler, W. B. (1980). Lunar and menstrual phase locking. *Amer. J. Obstet. Gynecol.* 137, 834–839.

Cutler, W. B., and Garcia, C. R. (1980). The psychoneuroendocrinology of the ovulatory cycle of women. *Psychoneuroendocrinology.* 5(2), 89–111.

Cutler, W. B., Garcia, C. R., and Kreiger, A. M. (1979). Sexual behavior frequency and menstrual cycle length in mature premenopausal women. *Psychoneuroendocrinology.* 4, 297–309.

Cutler, W. B., Preti, G., Erikson, B., Huggins, G., and Garcia, C. R. (1985). Sexual behavior frequency and biphasic ovulatory type menstrual cycles. *Physiol. Behav.* 34, 805–810.

Cutler, W. B., Preti, G., Huggins, G. R. Garcia, C. R., and Lawley, H. J. (1986). Human axillary secretions influence women's menstrual cycles: The role of donor extract of men. *Hormon. and Behav.*

Cutler, W. B., Schleidt, W. M., Friedman, E., Preti, G., Garcia, C. R., and Stine, R. (1987). Lunar influences on the reproductive cycle in women. Submitted for publication.

Doty, R. L. (1981). Olfactory communication in humans—a review. *Chem. Senses* 6(4), 351–376.

Friedman, E. (1981). Menstrual and lunar cycles. *Amer. J. Obstet. Gynecol.* 140, 350.

Gougeon, A. (1982). Rate of Follicular Growth in the Human Ovary. In R. Rolland, E. van Hall, S. G. Hillier, K. P. McNatty, and J. Schoemaker (Eds.), *Follicular Maturation and Ovulation,* pp. 155–163 Excerpta Medica, Princeton.

Graham, C. A., and McGrew, W. C. (1980). Menstrual synchrony in female undergraduates living on a co-educational campus. *Psychoneuroendocrinology.* 5, 245–252.

Izard, M. K., and Vandenbergh, J. G. (1982). Priming pheromones from estrous cows increase synchronization of estrous in dairy heifers after PGF-2 injection. *J. Reprod. Fertil.* 66, 189–196.

Labows, J. N., McGinley, K. J., and Kligman, A. M. (1982). Perspectives on axillary odor *J. Soc. Cosmet. Chem.* 34, 193–202.

Leyden, J. J., McGinley, K. J., Hoelzle, E., Labows, J. N., and Kligman, A. M. (1981). The microbiology of the human axillae and its relation to axillary odors. *J. Invest. Dermatol.* 77, 413–416.

McClintock, M. K. (1971). Menstrual synchrony and suppression. *Nature (London)* 229, 244–245.

McClintock, M. K. (1978). Estrous synchrony and its mediation by airborne chemical communication (*Rattus norvegicus*). *Horm. Behav.* 10, 264–276.

McClintock, M. K. (1983). Pheromonal regulation of the ovarian cycle: Enhancement, suppression and synchrony. In J. G. Vandenbergh, (Ed.),

Pheromones and Reproduction in Mammals, pp. 113–149. Academic Press, New York.

McClintock, M. K. (1984). Estrous synchrony: Modulation of ovarian cycle length by female pheromones. *Physiol. Behav.* 32, 701–705.

Preti, G., and Huggins, G. R. (1975). Cyclic changes in volatile acidic metabolites of human vaginal secretions and their relation to ovulation. *J. Chem. Ecol.* 1, 361–376.

Quadagno, D. M., Shubeita, H. E., Deck, J., and Francoeur, D. (1981). Influence of male social contacts, exercise and all female living conditions on the menstrual cycle. *Psychoneuroendocrinology.* 6, 239–244.

Russell, M. J., Switz, G. M., and Thompson, K. (1980). Olfactory influences on the human menstrual cycle. *Pharmacol. Biochem. Behav.* 13, 737–738.

Treloar, A. E., Boynton, R. E., Behn, D. G., and Brown B. W. (1967). Variation of the human menstrual cycle through reproductive life. *Int. J. Fertil.* 12, 77–126.

Vandenbergh, J. G. (Ed.) (1983). Pheromonal regulation of puberty. In *Pheromones and Reproduction in Mammals,* pp. 113–149. Academic Press, New York.

Vollman, R. F. (Ed.) (1977). The menstrual cycle. In *Major Problems: Obstetrics and Gynecology,* Vol. 7. Saunders, Philadelphia.

ENDNOTES

1. This work was conducted at The Monell Chemical Senses Center, Philadelphia, in conjunction with the Department of Obstetrics and Gynecology, School of Medicine, Hospital of the University of Pennsylvania.

2. Information given to subjects as part of informed consent:

> *I understand that these odor preparations will be applied to the skin region between my nose and upper lip or the skin area behind my knee. My blood pressure, pulse and respiration rate will be measured following this to determine if the preparation affects any of these parameters although no changes are expected. I will be asked not to wash these areas for 6 hrs. following the application. I understand that my menstrual cycle may be altered or changed by the study procedures.*

> *I understand that I will be asked to keep a basal body temperature chart to monitor the time in my menstrual cycle. Since some absorption of the preparation may occur in the second half of my cycle, I will be asked to donate 3 samples of blood within one week, each 5 ml. The blood will be drawn from one of my arm veins.*

25

HUMAN AXILLARY SECRETIONS INFLUENCE WOMEN'S MENSTRUAL CYCLES: THE ROLE OF DONOR EXTRACT FROM MEN

WINNIFRED BERG CUTLER, GEORGE PRETI,
ABBA KRIEGER, GEORGE R. HUGGINS,
CELSO RAMON GARCIA, AND HENRY J. LAWLEY

Menstrual cycle lengths of 29.5 ± 3 days ("normal cycles") are more frequent in women who have weekly coital activity than in women who do not. In order to investigate potential mechanisms controlling the association between heterosexual activity and menstrual cycle length, and in light of the nonhuman literature suggesting that a chemical signal from males could be involved, menstrual cycle lengths of nulliparous women were evaluated following regular application of axillary extract from donor males. Compared to controls receiving only blank/ethanol applications, women receiving axillary extracts for 12.5 to 14.5 weeks showed the following changes: (1) a reduced incidence in variability of cycle lengths; and (2) a reduced proportion of aberrant length cycles. © 1986 Academic Press, Inc.

Studies in several mammals have shown that the presence of a male or his odors influences the reproductive physiology of the female (Izard, 1983; McClintock, 1983; Richmond and Conoway, 1969). For example, in several rodent species, exposure to the odors of urine or cage bedding of males can promote estrus or stimulate ovulation (Marsden and Bronson, 1964; Whitten, Bronson, and Greenstein, 1968). In some infrahuman primates, males can influence cycle length. Female baboons denied mating show significantly longer cycles (Howard-Tipp and Bielert, 1978) and rhesus monkeys show a summer amenorrhea 2 to 4 months after a male decrease in sexual potency (Michael and Zumpe, 1976).

In humans, studies by several investigators (McClintock, 1971; Cutler, Garcia, and Kreiger, 1979; Cutler, Preti, Erickson, Huggins, and Garcia, 1985; Veith, Buck, Getzlaf, Van Dolfsen, and Slade, 1983) have shown that women who spend more time with men have a greater probability of having regular (29.5 ± 3 day) menstrual cycles. Cycle lengths of 29.5 ± 3 days have the highest likelihood of normal biphasic basal body temperature rhythms (Treloar, Boynton, Behn, and Brown, 1967; Vollman, 1977). A recent study demonstrated that sex with men, when it occurs in a consistent and regular pattern increases, or is associated with an increased incidence of, normal biphasic type basal body temperature rhythms (Cutler et al., 1985). In contrast, consistent masturbation (i.e., weekly or more) was not associated with an increased incidence of 29.5 ± 3 days cycles. In combination, these studies show that women who have regular (at least weekly) sexual activity with males are more likely to show presumptively biphasic ovulatory type patterns of menstrual cyclicity than women whose sexual activity with males is either infrequent or nonexistent.

Regular sexual behavior and normal biphasic menstrual cycle patterns occur together (Cutler et al., 1985). That regular sexual behavior leads to regular cycle lengths can be inferred from published data by noting that (1) women with a pattern of *weekly* heterosexual behavior consistently showed a high incidence of "normal" (29.5 ± 3 day) cycles, fertile-type basal body temperature rhythm, and higher postovulatory estrogen levels, but (2) the reverse situation—the presence of a normal cycle length, a normal biphasic basal body temperature rhythm, or higher postovulatory estrogen levels did not necessarily suggest which pattern of sexual behavior would exist (Cutler, Davidson, and McCoy, 1983; Cutler, Garcia, and Kreiger, 1979a; Cutler et al., 1985; Cutler, Garcia, Huggins, and Preti, 1986). Therefore, we have previously suggested that the pattern of weekly sex may have some actual influence on the underlying endocrine milieu of women (Cutler et al., 1985, 1986). Moreover, the physical presence of a man appears to be necessary, but the actual act of coitus may not be, provided there is genital stimulation; since masturbation is not, while genital stimulation (short of coitus) by a male is, effective as an associate of biphasic ovulatory type cycles. In order to investigate potential mechanisms controlling the association between heterosexual activity and menstrual cycle length, and in light of the nonhuman literature suggesting that a chemical signal from males could be involved, we investigated whether an extract from the male axillary region would be a sufficient stimulus to induce these presumptively biphasic ovulatory type cycles. We now report evidence indicating that it can.

METHODS

Seasonal constraints. This experimental protocol was designed to accommodate to the potential for a seasonal fluctuation in sexual cycles. Two relevant seasonal influences are the lunar and the annual geophysical cycles. In women, it has recently been shown that lunar and menstrual phase locking occurs. A maximum in number of menses occurred within a week of the full moon in the autumn in 3 separate years (Cutler, 1980; Friedman, 1981; Cutler, Garcia, Preti, and Stine, in preparation). In men, an annual variation in testosterone rhythms was reported with peak levels in autumn (Baker, 1975; Doering et al., 1975). Therefore, in order to minimize the potential influences of either of these geophysical effects on the experiment, male extracts were collected in the autumn of one year, frozen, and applied (after thawing) in the autumn of the following year.

Donor secretions. Male extract. Axillary secretions were collected from three male volunteers (ages 41, 35, and 32). Each was engaged in a heterosexual relationship and had large numbers of lipophilic diptheroids in his axillary region (Labows, McKinley, and Kligman, 1982). The quality of the odor which develops in the axillae has been shown to be a function of the resident microorganisms present there. Correlations of odor quality and bacterial populations how that micrococcaceae were present in 100% of subjects when a faint or acid odor was present (Leyden, McGinley, Hoelzle, Labows, and Kligman, 1981). In comparison, the lipophilic diptheroids were associated with a more pungent odor. These were found in 85% of the males and 66% of the females examined. This pungent odor is similar to that of C_{19}-Δ^{16}-androgen steroids such as androstenone. Consequently, our extract donors, who had lipophilic diphtheroids and micrococcaceae as their resident microorganisms were selected for their ability to produce the complete spectrum of axillary odorants, the dominant constituents of which are currently thought to be volatile acids and volatile steroids. Secretions were collected in the autumn of 1982 and applied in the autumn of 1983.

During the 3 months in which donors collected secretions they were required to (1) not use deodorant, deodorant soap, or perfumes in the axillary region and (2) wash once in the morning with Ivory soap. Secretions were collected on 4 x 4 in. cotton pads which had been previously extracted, autoclaved, dried, and wrapped in solvent extracted foil (Preti and Huggins, 1975). Each donor wore a pad in each axillae three times a week during a 6- to 9-hr period which was most convenient for him. Each day after removal, the pads from any one donor were placed in an individual acid-cleaned glass jar and frozen at -60°C until extraction. Secretions were collected 3 times a week from each donor for a 12-week period.

Preparation of extracts were conducted after all pads had been collected and frozen. Batches of glass jars were grouped consecutively according to the date received. Six to eight jars containing pads from all three individuals were used to prepare each batch of pooled extract. A total of 14 separate batches were prepared in this manner. All pads from each batch were placed in a glass column and allowed to soak in doubly distilled ethanol (15 ml/pad) for 1 hr. The ethanol was allowed to drain from the column through a Teflon stopcock and the pads were squeezed with a Teflon disk. Recovery approached 66% of the ethanol added to the pads. Presumably the remaining 34% remained within the pads. The ethanol extracted stimulus batches were then stored at -60°C.

Subject selection. Assignment of subjects to the Female Extract Experiment (Preti, Cutler, Huggins, Garcia, and Lawley, 1986) or the Male Extract Experiment was made after asking each potential subject to estimate her previous cycling pattern. Women who believed themselves to cycle within the 26 to 32 day range were assigned to the Female Extract Experiment (Preti *et al.*, 1986); women who believed themselves to have aberrant length menstrual cycles (<26 or >32 days) were assigned to the Male Extract Experiment reported here. Subsequently 15 women, varying in age from 19 to 22 and one aged 30 were enrolled in and completed the male extract study. All met the following criteria: "gynecological maturity" (as defined by Treloar *et al.*, 1967, as menstruating for at least 7 years), nulliparous, unmarried, not currently (nor within the last 3 months) using oral contraceptives nor an I.U.D. and a willingness to make daily entry of basal body temperature (BBT) and sexual behavior. In addition, all subjects agreed to provide blood samples for steroid analysis during 3 days of 1 week in the luteal phase of the last menstrual cycle studied. A complete history and physical exam was performed on each subject by one of us (G.R.H.). This screening process for possible pathologies which might influence the length of the menstrual cycle failed to find any.

The experimental protocol. Each subject was provided with BBT charts. BBT thermometers, and a calendar card to record sexual behavior, cycle length, and menstruation. Instructions for their use were given by a technician who was blind to the purpose of the study. Subjects were unaware of the true nature of the stimuli, and were only told that they were receiving a "natural fragrance" extracted into ethanol. Thus the study was double-blind. Subjects were randomly assigned to group A (axillary extract/ethanol) or group B (blank/ethanol). The average of the A group was 20 while the average age of the B group was 22. Application of the stimuli began in September, 1983, but because of individual variation in menstrual patterns, any particular woman could enter the study at any point within her cycle.

The technician was housed in an office in the Ivy Research Laboratories which is several buildings removed from the Monell Center. A blind test at the end of the experiment revealed that personnel at the Monell Chemical Senses Center as well as the technician working at Ivy Labs were unable to distinguish fresh samples "A" from "B" when tested. The technician also noted that none of the subjects in the study had commented on either A or B having an odor. Subjects came to this laboratory three times each week for 12.5 to 14.5 weeks for application of the stimuli (male extract or placebo). Each morning the previously frozen stimuli were removed and allowed to warm to room temperature for 30 min. Individual 5-ml samples were removed via pipet and placed in separate vials (labeled A and B) for transport to the laboratory where the stimuli were applied. One-half milliliter of the stimuli (axillary extract or blank/ethanol) was pipetted onto a clean 4 x 4 in. cotton pad. The technician rubbed the contents of the pad on the upper lip of the subject and instructed her not to wash the area for at least 6 hours. She then recorded the blood pressure and pulse of the subjects in an attempt to dilute the focus of the study.

Treatment began in the third week of September as subjects were enrolled into the study. The first menses thereafter and the one which followed this formed the boundaries of "first cycle" of the experimental period. A typical example then, is represented as follows ... 9/22 (enter study, treatment begins) ... 10/4 (first menses onset) ... 11/8 (second menses onset) ... 12/4 (third menses onset) ... 12/12 (treatment ends). In this case, two cycles of 35 and 26 days would form the first and the last cycle length of this subject.

RESULTS

Figure 1 shows the last cycle length of all subjects receiving stimulus or placebo. The last cycle of each subject was selected for data presentation and analysis since this would allow the maximum time to test for an effect during this 14-week experiment. One-tailed tests define all probability

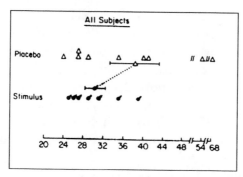

FIGURE 1. Each symbol ($\male$, Δ) shows one menstrual cycle length of one subject dichotomized according to treatment (placebo Δ vs male extract $\male$). The screened region arrays (presumptively fertile) range (29 ± 3 days). Placebo group (Δ mean cycle length was 38.33 ± 5.15 (SE); male extract group ($\male$) mean cycle length was 30.29 ± 2.07 (SE). One notes that four of the women receiving placebo had cycles more aberrant than any of the women receiving male extract (i.e., cycle lengths of 24, 41, 53, and 68 days).

levels because a prediction—that male extracts will reduce the incidence of aberrant length menstrual cycles—is fundamental to this experiment. The mean cycle length of the two groups were not significantly different ($T = 1.45$, $p < 0.10$).

An initial glance at Figure 1 seems to suggest that stimulus recipients have less variance in their cycle length about their own means and a greater incidence of cycle lengths that occur within the screened area. i.e., 29.5 ± 3 days. In order to test these observations, it is useful to distinguish (1) decreased variability in cycle length from (2) increased incidence of normal (29.5 ± 3 day) length menstrual cycles.

We ran the Mann-Whitney U test (Dixon and Massey, 1969) on the absolute deviations from the mean of each group. This was done to test whether the placebo population had greater variability in cycle length. The results were significant $U = 15$; ($P < 0.05$). When the Mann-Whitney U test is run on the absolute deviations from the grand mean, including women with weekly sexual activity, the results fail to achieve significance ($U = 21$, $P < 0.05$).

Because weekly coital behavior and 29 day cycles are associated (Cutler et al., 1979a, b, 1985; McCoy et al., 1985) we removed the data of those women who were having weekly coital activity with men from the data set and reanalyzed the data (see Figure 2). The mean cycle lengths again were not significantly different ($t = 1.645$, $0.05 < P < 0.10$). The Mann-Whitney U test was again applied to the absolute deviations from the mean of each group. This showed significantly less variability in cycle length for stimulus recipient ($U = 5, P < 0.02$). When the Mann-Whitney U test was rerun with the more conservative method using the absolute deviations from the grand mean, the results again achieved significantly less variance among extract recipients ($U = 6, P < 0.03$). The analysis of these data which evaluate data variance relationships suggests that variance in cycle length is reduced by male extract treatment, when no regular heterosexual behavior is occurring. Analysis of the biologically more relevant question: Does male extract reduce the proportion of aberrant length cycles?, suggests that it does this as well. Table 1 shows the incidence of aberrant length cycles (<26 or >32 days) to vary as a function of treatment in all women (left) and when controlled for sexual activity (right). In studying either all the subjects, or only those subjects who were not having weekly sexual activity, exposure to male axillary secretions yielded a greater proportion of "normal" (29.5 ± 3 day) cycle lengths than exposure to the blank (Test of Proportions, $Z = 1.512. P < 0.066$ all subjects and $Z = 1.754, P < 0.04$ subjects who are not sexually active weekly).[2] There were no apparent differences in testosterone, progesterone, or estradiol levels among women who received different treatments.

TABLE 1

Incidence of Aberrant Cycle Lengths Varies as a Function of Treatment and Sexual Activity

	Treatment (all subjects)			Treatment (subjects not experiencing weekly heterosexual contact)	
	Male extract	Blank		Male extract	Blank
Aberrant cycle length	2	6	Aberrant cycle length	2	5
Normal cycle	5	3	Normal cycle	4	1
	$Z = 1.512$[a]			$Z = 1.754$[a]	
	$P < 0.066$			$P < 0.04$	

Note. One notes that most of the women whose cycles remained aberrant were recipients of the placebo, while most of the women whose cycles became normal (29.5 ± 3) in length were recipients of the male extract.

[a]The Test of Proportions was used to obtain Z scores.

DISCUSSION

This study represents the first systematic, prospective, double-blind research in humans to attempt manipulation of the menstrual cycle with male derived secretions. The constraint of college calendars and budgetary restrictions limited the experimental period to a 14-week span. Inspection of the raw data did show a very high incidence of aberrant length cycles in both experimental subgroups for the first cycle (bounded by menses 1 and menses 2) suggesting that the women in the sample were indeed having aberrant length cycles at the onset of the experiment.

The data in Table 1 which show significant differences in the menstrual cycle, as a function of axillary extract, conform to sample-size constraints of other recent reports of manipulations of the menstrual cycle. For example, a recent study successfully altered menstrual cycles with GnRH-agonist in a group of subjects half the size of the samples presented here (Muse, Cetel, Futterman, and Yen, 1984). In that study, data from the first cycle were also omitted from both the statistical analysis and the graphic presentation under the same assumption that we have made—that the first cycle is too early to analyze for effects.

Figure 1 contains data from women potentially receiving two weekly influences: male extract and/or heterosexual behavior in weekly frequencies. Heterosexual behavior (see studies cited in Introduction), *or* male extract for those women not experiencing weekly sex (see Figure 2 and Table 1, right column) appear adequate to limit the incidence of aberrant menstrual cycle lengths. Therefore, the data in Figure 1 may contain the influence of weekly heterosexual contact which masks the influence of male extract. Figure 2 therefore, shows the potential for male extract effects without the confounding variable of weekly heterosexual exposure. One should note that while "mean cycle length" is an insensitive indicator of the effect under consideration, the variance about the mean is quite sensitive to the question of fertility potential (Cutler *et al.*, 1979a, 1976; Cutler and Garcia, 1980; McCoy *et al.*, 1985). A group of women with aberrant cycle lengths can share a mean cycle length in the normal (29.5 ± 3 day) range while every individual comprising the data base shows an aberrant length. If one were to focus on difference between the mean cycle length of the experimental and control groups, one might overlook this essential point. The results of this initial experiment have shown that although male extracts do not change the *mean* cycle lengths, they do reduce the proportion of aberrant length cycles within 14 weeks of treatment.

The possible role that odors plays in human reproductive biology has received considerable attention particularly with respect to the extent to

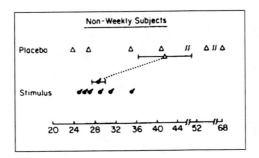

FIGURE 2. As in Figure 1 except that those subjects in Figure 1 who were having regular weekly heterosexual activity were deleted from this analysis. Placebo group (Δ) mean cycle length was 41.50 ± 7.53 (SE); male extract group ($\male$) mean cycle length was 28.83 ± 1.36 (SE). One notes that four of the women receiving pla-cebo had cycles more aberrant than any of the women receiving male extract (i.e., cycle lengths of 24, 41, 53, and 68 days).

which menstrual synchrony may occur in females who live together. Dis-cussions of male-female effects have often centered on the possibility that odors act to attract, or sexually arouse, the male. The data presented here suggest that prolonged exposure to one or more constituents from the male axillae may alter the female endocrine system. Since both the experimental and the control subjects in this study spent a considerable portion of their day in a heterosexual environment, the usual social distance appears inad-equate to transmit the active constituent. Therefore, the causative factor in male axillary extract is likely to have a low vapor pressure at body tempera-ture (or none at all) and critical concentrations may be transferred only during intimate contact. The experimental protocol did not allow us to determine whether the effect is mediated by olfactory stimuli or if the constituents causing the effect are absorbed through the skin and thus through a less direct (endocrine) route. Nonetheless, male extract does appear able to affect female menstrual pattern; but the effect may require some "priming time" since 14 weeks were required to reveal the effect. It is of interest that ovarian follicular development needs about 85 days for completion (Gougeon, 1982), a timing which corresponds nicely with the results discussed here. We find an effect by completion of the third cycle (Gougeon, 1982). In addition, this time requirement supports earlier tenta-tive conclusions that stability in exposure to males affects menstrual cycles (Cutler *et al.*, 1979a, b) and that a "feast and famine" approach to coital exposure may disrupt the menstrual cycle (Cutler *et al.*, 1980, 1986).

This is the first double-blind perspective investigation of the potential for male extract to manipulate women's menstrual cycles. Because human experiments are extremely costly in both time and money it is appropriate that these initial results be recorded in the hope that these studies will stimulate further research by other groups. Future efforts to replicate these findings should employ a control cycle with placebo before the experimental procedure begins in order to confirm that all participants have aberrant length cycles before they begin the treatment protocols.

ACKNOWLEDGMENTS

This study was supported in part by a grant from the National Science Foundation, BNS 82-02018. We thank Dr. Gary K. Beauchamp and Dr. Charles Wysocki for their constructive comments concerning the manuscript, Mrs. Helen Liebich for her technical assistance and Mrs. Janice Blescia for processing the manuscript. Dr. James Leyden, Ken McGinley and Joseph Nicolson of the Duhring Laboratories are thanked for their screening of potential subjects for the correct anxillary microflora and odor production.

REFERENCES

Abrahamson G. E., Maroulis, G. B., and Marshall, J. K. (1974). Evaluation of ovulation and corpus luteum function using measurements of plasma progesterone. *Obstet. Gynecol.* 44, 522–525.

Baker H. W. G., *et al.* (1975). Changes in the pituitary testicular system with age. *Clin. Endocrinol.* 5, 349–372.

Cutler, W. B. (1980). Lunar and menstrual phase locking. *Amer. J. Obstet Gynecol.* 834–839.

Cutler, W. B., Davidson, J. M., and McCoy, N. (1983). Relationships between estrus level, hot flashes and sexual behavior in perimenopausal women. *Neuroendrocrinol. Lett.* 5(3), 185.

Cutler, W. B. and Garcia, C. R. (1980). The psychoneuroendocrinology of the ovulatory cycle of women. *Psychoneuroendocrinology* 5(2), 89–111.

Cutler, W. B., Garcia, C. R., and Kreiger, A. M. (1979a). Sexual behavior frequency and menstrual cycle length in mature premenopausal women. *Psychoneuroendocrinology* 4, 297–309.

Cutler, W. B., Garcia, C. R., and Kreiger, A. M. (1979b). Luteal phase defects: A possible relationship between short hyperthermic phase and sporadic sexual behavior in women. *Horm. Behav.* 13, 214–218.

Cutler, W. B., Garcia, C. R., and Kreiger, A. M. (1980). Sporadic sexual behavior and menstrual cycle length in women. *Horm. Behav.* 14, 163–172.

Cutler, W. B., Garcia, C. R., Huggins, G. R., and Preti, G. (1986). Sexual behavior and steroid levels among gynecologically mature premenopausal women. *Fertil. Steril.* 45, 496–502.

Cutler, W. B., Preti, G., Erickson, B., Huggins, G. R., and Garcia, C. R. (1985). Sexual behavior frequency and ovulatory biphasic menstrual cycle patterns. *Physiol. Behav.* 34, 805–810.

Dixon, W. J., and Massey, S. J., Jr. (1969). *Introduction to Statistical Analysis,* 3rd ed., pp. 249–250. McGraw-Hill, New York.

Doering, C. *et al.* (1975). A cycle of plasma testosterone in the human male. *J. Clin. Endocrinol. Metab.* 40, 497.

Friedmann, E. (1981). Menstrual and lunar cycles. *Amer. J. Obstet. Gynecol.* 140, 350.

Gougeon, A. (1982). Rate of Follicular Growth in the Human Ovary. In R. Rolland, E. V. van Hall, S. G. Hillier, K. P. McNatty, and J. Schoemaker (Eds.), Follicular Maturation and Ovulation, pp. 155–163. Excerpta Medica, Princeton.

Howard-Tipp, M. E., and Bielert, C. (1978). Social contact influences on the menstrual cycle of the female chacma baboon *(Papio ursinus). J. S. Afr Assoc.* 49, 191–192.

Izard, M. K. (1983). Pheromones and Reproduction in Domestic Animals. In J. G. Vandenbergh (Ed.), *Pheromones and Reproduction in Mammals,* pp. 253–281. Academic Press, New York.

Labows, J. N., McKinley, K. J., and Kligman, A. M. (1982). Perspectives on axillary odor. *J. Soc. Cosmet. Chem.* 34, 193–202.

Leyden, J. J., McGinley, K. J., Hoelzle, E., Labows, J. N., and Kligman, A. M. (1981). The microbiology of the human axillae and its relation to axillary odors. *J. Invest. Dermatol.* 77, 413–416.

Marsden, H. M., and Bronson, F. H. (1964). Estrous synchrony in mice: Alteration by exposure to male urine. *Science* 144, 1469.

McClintock, M. K. (1971). Menstrual synchrony and suppression. *Nature (London)* 229, 244–245.

McClintock, M. K. (1983). Pheromonal Regulation of the Ovarian Cycle: Enhancement, Suppression and Synchrony. *In* J. G. Vandenbergh (Ed.), *Pheromones and Reproduction in Mammals,* pp. 113–149. Academic Press, New York.

McCoy, N., Cutler, W., and Dawson, J. M. (1985). Relationships among sexual behavior, hot flashes and hormone levels in perimenopausal women. *Arch. Sex. Behav.* 14, 385–394.

Michael, R. P., and Zumpe, D. (1976). Environmental and endocrine factors influencing annual changes in sexual potency in primates. *Psychoneuroendocrinology,* 1, 303–313.

Muse, K. N., Cetel, N. S., Futterman, L. A., and Yen, S. S. C. (1984). The premenstrual syndrome: Effects of "medical ovariectomy." *N. Engl. J. Med.* 311, 1345–1349.

Preti, G., Cutler, W. B., Huggins, G. R., Garcia, C. R., and Lawley, H. J. (1986). Human axillary secretions influence women's menstrual cycles: The role of donor extract from women. *Horm. Behav.* 20.

Preti, G., and Huggins, G. R. (1975). Cyclic changes in volatile acidic metabolites of human vaginal secretions and their relation to ovulation. *J. Chem. Ecol.* 1, 361–376.

Richmond, M., and Conoway, C. H. (1969). Induced ovulation and oestrus in *Microtus ochrogashi. J. Reprod. Fertil. Suppl.* 6, 357–376.

Siegel, S. (1956). *Non-Parametric Statistics for the Behavioral Sciences,* McGraw-Hill, New York.

Treloar, A. E., Boynton, R. E., Behn, D. G., and Brown, B. W. (1967). Variation of the luman menstrual cycle through reproductive life. *Int. J. Fertil.* 12, 77–126.

Veith, J., Buck, M., Gertzlaf, S., Van Dolfsen, P. and Slade, A. (1983). Exposure to men influences the occurrence of ovulation in women. *Physiol. Behav.* 31, 313–315.

Vollman, R. F. (ed.). (1977). The Menstrual Cycle. *Major Problems: Obstetrics and Gynecology,* Vol. 7. Saunders, Philadelphia.

Whitten, W. K., Bronson, F. H., and Greenstein, J. A. (1968). Estrus-inducing pheromone of mice: Transport by movement of air. *Science,* 161, 584–585.

ENDNOTES

1. This work was conducted at the Monell Chemical Senses Center, Philadelphia, in conjunction with the Department of Obstetrics and Gynecology, Hospital of the University of Pennsylvania, and the Department of Statistics, Wharton School, Philadelphia.

2. In order to apply appropriate statistical tests to these data, several considerations are relevant. While at first glance, one might consider Fisher's Exact Probability test (Siegel, 1956) the appropriate one, this is not so for several reasons. Fisher's Exact Probability test is a finite population test which means in this context, that two prerequisites hold; (A) the number of individuals receiving the stimulus and placebo is prefixed by the research design (true of this experiment), and (B) the number of individuals with aberrant and normal length cycles are prefixed by the design (a condition which is not true of this experiment). In contrast, the Test of Proportions (Dixon and Massey, 1969) only assumes condition A, that the experimental design predetermines the number of women assigned to each stimulus or placebo group. Condition B, the number of aberrant cycles might very well vary in a replication of this experiment. For this reason, Fisher's Exact Test is inappropriate and the Test of Proportions (Dixon and Massey, 1969) was applied.

26

RACE WITHOUT COLOR

JARED DIAMOND

Science often violates simple common sense. Our eyes tell us that the Earth is flat, that the sun revolves around the Earth, and that we humans are not animals. But we now ignore that evidence of our senses. We have learned that our planet is in fact round and revolves around the sun, and that humans are slightly modified chimpanzees. The reality of human races is another common sense "truth" destined to follow the flat Earth into oblivion. The common sense view of races goes somewhat as follows. All native Swedes differ from all native Nigerians in appearance: there is no Swede whom you would mistake for a Nigerian, and vice versa. Swedes have lighter skin than Nigerians do. They also generally have blond or light brown hair, while Nigerians have very dark hair. Nigerians usually have more tightly coiled hair than Swedes do, dark eyes as opposed to eyes that are blue or gray, and fuller lips and broader noses.

In addition, other Europeans look much more like Swedes than like Nigerians, while other peoples of sub-Saharan Africa—except perhaps the Khoisan peoples of southern Africa—look much more like Nigerians than like Swedes. Yes, skin color does get darker in Europe toward the Mediterranean, but it is still lighter than the skin of sub-Saharan Africans. In Europe, very dark or curly hair becomes more common outside Scandinavia, but European hair is still not as tightly coiled as in Africa. Since it's easy then to distinguish almost any native European from any native sub-Saharan African, we recognize Europeans and sub-Saharan Africans as distinct races, which we name for their skin colors: whites and blacks, respectively.

What could be more objective?

As it turns out, this seemingly unassailable reasoning is not objective. There are many different, equally valid procedures for defining races, and those different procedures yield very different classifications. One such procedure would group Italians and Greeks with most African blacks. It would classify Xhosas—the South African "black" group to which President Nelson Mandela belongs—with Swedes rather than Nigerians. Another equally valid procedure would place Swedes with Fulani (a Nigerian "black" group) and not with Italians who would again be grouped with most other African blacks. Still another procedure would keep Swedes and Italians separate from all African blacks but would throw the Swedes and Italians into the same race as New Guineans and American Indians. Faced with such differing classifications, many anthropologists today conclude that one cannot recognize any human races at all.

If we were just arguing about races of nonhuman animals, essentially the same uncertainties of classification would arise. But the debates would remain polite and would never get attention outside the halls of academia. Classification of humans is different "only" in that it shapes our views of other peoples, fosters our subconscious differentiation between "us" and "them," and is invoked to justify political and socioeconomic discrimination. On this basis, many anthropologists therefore argue that even if one *could* classify humans into races, one should not.

To understand how such uncertainties in classification arise, let's steer clear of humans for a moment and instead focus on warblers and lions, about which we can easily remain dispassionate. Biologists begin by classifying living creatures into species. A species is a group of populations whose individual members would, if given the opportunity, interbreed with individuals of other populations of that group. But they would not interbreed with individuals of other species that are similarly defined. Thus all human populations, no matter how different they look, belong to the same species because they do interbreed, and have interbred whenever they have encountered each other. Gorillas and humans, however, belong to two different species because—to the best of our knowledge—they have never interbred despite the coexisting in close proximity for millions of years.

We know that different populations classified together in the human species are visibly different. The same proves true for most other animal and plant species as well, whenever biologists look carefully. For example, consider one, the most familiar species of bird in North America, the yellow-rumped warbler. Breeding males of eastern and western North America can be distinguished at a glance by their throat color: white in the east, yellow in the west. Hence they are classified into two different races, or subspecies (alternative words with identical meanings), termed the myrtle and Audubon races, respectively. The white-throated eastern birds differ from the yellow-throated western birds in other characteristics as well, such as in voice and habitat preference. But where the two races meet, in western Canada, white throated birds do indeed interbreed with yellow throated birds. That's why we consider myrtle warblers and Audubon warblers as races of the same species rather than different species.

Racial classification of these birds is easy. Throat color, voice, and habitat preference all vary geographically in yellow-rumped warblers, but the variation of those three traits is "concordant"—that is, voice differences or habitat differences lead to the same racial classification as differences in throat color because the same populations that differ in throat color also differ in voice and habitat.

Racial classification of many other species, though, presents problems of concordance. For instance, a Pacific island bird species called the golden whistler varies from one island to the next. Some populations consist of big birds, some of small birds; some have black-winged males, others green-winged males; some have yellow-breasted females, others gray-breasted females; many other characteristics vary as well. But, unfortunately for humans like me who study these birds, those characteristics don't vary concordantly. Islands with green-winged males can have either yellow-breasted or gray-breasted females, and green-winged males are big on some islands but small on other islands. As a result, if you classified golden whistlers into races based on single traits, you would get entirely different classifications depending on which trait you chose.

Classification of these birds also presents problems of "hierarchy." Some of the golden whistler races recognized by ornithologists are wildly different from all the other races, but some are very similar to one another. They can therefore be grouped into a hierarchy of distinctness. You start by establishing the most distinct population as a race separate from all other populations. You then separate the most distinct of the remaining populations. You continue by grouping similar populations, and separating distinct populations or groups of populations as races or groups of races. The problem is that the extent to which you continue the racial classification is arbitrary, and it's a decision about which taxonomists disagree passionately. Some taxonomists, the "splitters," like to recognize many different races, partly for the egotistical motive of getting credit for having named a race. Other taxonomists, the "lumpers" prefer to recognize few races. Which type of taxonomist you are is a matter of personal preference.

How does that variability of traits by which we classify races come about in the first place? Some traits vary because of natural selection: that is, one form of the trait is advantageous for survival in one area, another form in a different area. For example, northern hares and weasels develop white fur in the winter, but southern ones retain brown fur year-round. The white winter fur is selected in the north for camouflage against the snow, while any animal unfortunate enough to turn white in the snowless southern states would stand out from afar against the brown ground and would be picked off by predators.

Other traits vary geographically because of *sexual* selection, meaning that those traits serve as arbitrary signals by which individuals of one sex attracts mates of the opposite sex while intimidating rivals. Adult male lions, for instance, have a mane, but lionesses and young males don't. The adult male's mane signals to lionesses that he is sexually mature, and signals to young male rivals that he is a dangerous and experienced adversary. The length and color of a lion's mane vary among populations, being shorter and blacker in Indian lions than in African lions. Indian lions and lionesses evidently find short black manes sexy or intimidating; African lions don't.

Finally, some geographically variable traits have *no* known effect on survival and are invisible to rivals and to prospective sex partners. They merely reflect mutations that happened to arise and spread in one area. They could equally well have arisen and spread elsewhere—they just didn't.

Nothing that I've said about geographic variation in animals is likely to get me branded a racist. We don't attribute higher IQ or social status to black-winged whistlers than to green-winged whistlers. But now let's consider geographic variation in humans. We'll start with invisible traits, about which it's easy to remain dispassionate.

Many geographically variable human traits evolved by natural selection to adapt humans to particular climates or environments—just as the winter color of a hare or weasel did. Good examples are the mutations that people in tropical parts of the Old World evolved to help them survive malaria, the leading infectious disease of the old-world tropics. One such mutation is the sickle-cell gene, so-called because the red blood cells of people with that mutation tend to assume a sickle shape. People bearing the gene are more resistant to malaria than people without it. Not surprisingly, the gene is absent from northern Europe, where malaria is nonexistent, but it's common in tropical Africa, where malaria is widespread. Up to 40 percent of Africans in such areas carry the sickle-cell gene. It's also common in the malaria-ridden Arabian Peninsula and southern India, and rare or absent in the southernmost parts of South Africa, among the Xhosas, who live mostly beyond the tropical geographic range of malaria.

The geographic range of human malaria is much wider than the range of the sickle-cell gene. As it happens, other anti-malarial genes take over the protective function of the sickle-cell gene in malarial Southeast Asia and

New Guinea and in Italy, Greece, and other warm parts of the Mediterranean basin. Thus human races, if defined by anti-malarial genes, would be very different from human races as traditionally defined by traits such as skin color. As classified by anti-malarial genes (or their absence), Swedes are grouped with Xhosas but not with Italians or Greeks. Most other people usually viewed as African blacks are grouped with Arabia's "whites" and are kept separate from the "black" Xhosas.

Antimalarial genes exemplify the many features of our body chemistry that vary geographically under the influence of natural selection. Another such feature is the enzyme lactase, which enables us to digest the milk sugar lactose. Infant humans, like infants of almost all other mammal species, possess lactase and drink milk. Until about 6,000 years ago most humans, like other mammal species, lost the lactase enzyme on reaching the age of weaning. The obvious reason is that it was unnecessary—no human or other mammal drank milk as an adult. Beginning around 4000 B.C., however, fresh milk obtained from domestic mammals became a major food for adults of a few human populations. Natural selection caused individuals in these populations to retain lactase in adulthood. Among such peoples are northern and central Europeans, Arabians, north Indians, and several milk-drinking black African peoples, such as the Fulani of West Africa. Adult lactase is much less common in southern European populations and in most other African black populations, as well as in all populations of east Asians, aboriginal Australians, and American Indians.

Once again races defined by body chemistry don't match races defined by skin color. Swedes belong with Fulani in the "lactase-positive race," while most African "blacks," Japanese, and American Indians belong in the "lactase-negative race."

Not all the effects of natural selection are as invisible as lactase and sickle cells. Environmental pressures have also produced more noticeable differences among peoples, particularly in body shapes. Among the tallest and most long-limbed peoples in the world are the Nilotic peoples, such as the Dinkas, who live in the hot, dry areas of East Africa. At the opposite extreme in body shape are the Inuit, or Eskimo, who have compact bodies and relatively short arms and legs. The reasons have to do with heat loss. The greater the surface area of a warm body, the more body heat that's lost, since heat loss is directly proportional to surface area. For people of a given weight, a long-limbed, tall shape maximizes surface area, while a compact, short-limbed shape minimizes it. Dinkas and Inuit have opposite problems of heat balance: the former usually need desperately to get rid of body heat, while the latter need desperately to conserve it. Thus natural selection molded their body shapes oppositely, based on their contrasting climates.

(In modern times, such considerations of body shape have become important to athletic performance as well as to heat loss. Tall basketball players, for example, have an obvious advantage over short ones, and slender, long-limbed tall players have an advantage over stout, short-limbed tall players. In the United States, it's a familiar observation that African Americans are disproportionately represented among professional basketball players. Of course, a contributing reason has to do with their lack of socioeconomic opportunities. But part of the reason probably has to do with the prevalent body shapes of some black African groups as well. However, this example also illustrates the dangers in facile racial stereotyping. One can't make the sweeping generalization that "whites can't jump," or that "blacks' anatomy makes them better basketball players." Only certain African peoples are notably tall and long-limbed; even those exceptional peoples are tall and long-limbed only on the average and vary individually.)

Other visible traits that vary geographically among humans evolved by means of sexual selection. We all know that we find some individuals of the opposite sex more attractive than other individuals. We also know that in sizing up sex appeal, we pay more attention to certain parts of a prospective sex partner's body than to other parts. Men tend to be inordinately interested in women's breasts and much less concerned with women's toenails. Women, in turn, tend to be turned on by the shape of a man's buttocks or the details of a man's beard and body hair, if any, but not by the size of his feet.

But all those determinants of sex appeal vary geographically. Khoisan and Andaman Island women tend to have much larger buttocks than most other women. Nipple color and breast shape and size also vary geographically among women. European men are rather hairy by world standards, while Southeast Asian men tend to have very sparse beards and body hair.

What's the function of these traits that differ so markedly between men and women? They certainly don't aid survival: it's not the case that orange nipples help Khoisan women escape lions, while darker nipples help European women survive cold winters. Instead, the varying traits play a crucial role in sexual selection. Women with very large buttocks are a turn-on, or at least acceptable, to Khoisan and Andaman but look freakish to many men from other parts of the world. Bearded and hairy men readily find mates in Europe but fare worse in Southeast Asia. The geographic variation of these traits, however, is as arbitrary as the geographic variation in the color of a lion's mane.

There is a third possible explanation for the function of geographically variable human traits, besides survival or sexual selection—namely, no function at all. A good example is provided by fingerprints, whose complex pattern of arches, loops, and whorls is determined genetically. Fingerprints also vary geographically: for example, Europeans' fingerprints tend to have many loops, while aboriginal Australians' fingerprints tend to have many whorls.

If we classify human populations by their fingerprints, most Europeans and black Africans would sort out together in one race, Jews and some Indonesians in another, and aboriginal Australians in still another. But those geographic variations in fingerprint patterns possess no known function whatsoever. They play no role in survival: whorls aren't especially suitable for grabbing kangaroos, nor do loops help mar mitzvah candidates hold on to the pointer for the Torah. They also play no role in sexual selection: while you've undoubtedly noticed whether your mate is bearded or has brown nipples, you surely haven't the faintest idea whether his or her fingerprints have more loops than whorls. Instead it's purely a matter of chance that whorls became common in aboriginal Australians, and loops among Jews. Our rhesus factor blood groups and numerous other human traits fall into the same category of genetic characteristics whose geographic variation serves no function.

You've probably been wondering when I was going to get back to skin color, eye color, and hair color and form. After all, those are the traits by which all of us members of the lay public, as well as traditional anthropologists, classify races. Does geographic variation in those traits function in survival, in sexual selection, or in nothing?

The usual view is that skin color varies geographically to enhance survival. Supposedly, people in sunny, tropical climates around the world have genetically dark skin, which is supposedly analogous to the temporary skin darkening of European whites in the summer. The supposed function of dark skin in sunny climates is for protection against skin cancer. Variations in eye color and hair form and color are also supposed to enhance survival under particular conditions, though no one has ever promised a plausible hypothesis for how those variations might actually enhance survival.

Alas, the evidence for natural selection of skin color dissolves under scrutiny. Among tropical peoples, anthropologists love to stress the dark skin of African blacks, people to the southern Indian peninsula, and New Guineans and love to forget the pale skins of Amazonian Indians and Southeast Asians living at the same latitudes. To wriggle out of those paradoxes, anthropologists then plead the excuse that Amazonian Indians and Southeast Asians may not have been living in their present locations long enough to evolve dark skins. However, the ancestors of fair-skinned

Swedes arrived even more recently in Scandinavia, and aboriginal Tasmanians were black-skinned despite their ancestors' having lived for at least the last 10,000 years at the latitude of Vladivostok.

Besides, when one takes into account cloud cover, peoples of equatorial West African and the New Guinea mountains actually receive no more ultraviolet radiation or hours of sunshine each year than do the Swiss. Compared with infectious diseases and other selective agents, skin cancer has been utterly trivial as a cause of death in human history, even for modern white settlers in the tropics. This objection is so obvious to believers in natural selection of skin color that they have proposed at least seven other supposed survival functions of skin color, without reaching agreement. Those other supposed functions include protection against rickets, frostbite, folic acid deficiency, beryllium poisoning, overheating, and overcooling. The diversity of these contradictory theories makes clear how far we are from understanding the survival value (if any) of skin color.

It wouldn't surprise me if dark skins do eventually prove to offer some advantage in tropical climates, but I expect the advantage to turn out to be a slight one that is easily overridden. But there's an overwhelming importance to skin, eye, and hair color that is obvious to all of us—sexual selection. Before we can reach a condition of intimacy permitting us to assess the beauty of a prospective sex partner's hidden physical attractions, we first have to pass muster for skin, eyes, and hair.

We all know how those highly visible "beauty traits" guide our choice of sex partners. Even the briefest personal ad in a newspaper mentions the advertiser's skin color, and the color of skin that he or she seeks in a partner. Skin color, of course, is also of overwhelming importance in our social prejudices. If you're a black African American trying to raise your children in white U.S. society, rickets and overheating are the least of the problems that might be solved by your skin color. Eye color and hair form and color, while not so overwhelmingly important as skin color, also play an obvious role in our sexual and social preferences. Just ask yourself why hair dyes, hair curlers, and hair straighteners enjoy such wide sales. You can bet that it's not to improve our chances of surviving grizzly bear attacks and other risks endemic to the North American continent.

Nearly 125 years ago Charles Darwin himself, the discoverer of natural selection, dismissed its role as an explanation of geographic variation in human beauty traits. Everything that we have learned since then only reinforces Darwin's view.

We can now return to our original questions: Are human racial classification that are based on different traits concordant with one another? What is the hierarchical relation among recognized races? What is the function of racially variable traits? What, really, are the traditional human races?

Regarding concordance, we *could* have classified races based on any number of geographically variable traits. The resulting classifications would not be at all concordant. Depending on whether we classified our-selves by antimalarial genes, lactase, fingerprints, or skin color, we could place Swedes in the same race as either Xhosas, Fulani, the Ainu of Japan or Italians.

Regarding hierarchy, traditional classifications that emphasize skin color face unresolvable ambiguities. Anthropology textbooks often recog-nize five major races: "whites," "African blacks," "Mongoloids," "aboriginal Australians," and "Khoisans," each in turn divided into various numbers of sub-races. But there is no agreement on the number and delineation of the sub-races, or even of the major races. Are all five of the major races equally distinctive? Are Nigerians really less different from Xhosas than aboriginal Australians are from both? Should we recognize three or 15 sub-races of Mongoloids? These questions have remained unresolved because skin color and other traditional racial criteria are difficult to formulate math-ematically.

A method that could in principle overcome these problems is to base racial classification on a combination of as many geographically variable genes as possible. Within the past decade, some biologists have shown renewed interest in developing a hierarchical classification of human popu-lations—hierarchical not in the sense that it identifies superior and inferior races but in the sense of grouping and separating populations based on mathematical measures of genetic distinctness. While the biologists still haven't reached agreement, some of their studies suggest that human genetic diversity may be greatest in Africa. If so, the primary races of humanity may consist of several African races, plus one race to encompass all peoples of all other continents. Swedes, New Guineans, Japanese, and Navajo would then belong to the same primary race; the Khoisans of southern Africa would constitute another primary race by themselves; and African "blacks" and Pygmies would be divided among several other pri-mary races.

As regards the function of all those traits that are useful for classifying human races, some serve to enhance survival, some to enhance sexual selection, while some serve no function at all. The traits we traditionally use are ones subject to sexual selection, which is not really surprising. These traits are not only visible at a distance but also highly variable; that's why they become the ones used throughout recorded history to make quick judgments about people. Racial classification didn't come from science but from the body's signals for differentiating attractive from unattractive sex partners, and for differentiating friend from foe.

Such snap judgments didn't threaten our existence back when people were armed only with spears and surrounded by others who looked mostly like themselves. In the modern world, though, we are armed with guns and plutonium, and we live our lives surrounded by people who are much more varied in appearance. The last thing we need now is to continue codifying all those different appearances into an arbitrary system of racial classification.